Ci, Gender and Social Change among the Asmat of Papua, Indonesia

Ci, Gender and Social Change among the Asmat of Papua, Indonesia

Onesius Otenieli Daeli

© 2020 Onesius Otenieli Daeli

Published by Sidestone Press, Leiden
www.sidestone.com

Imprint: Sidestone Press

Lay-out & cover design: Sidestone Press
Photograph cover: Bets river, Atsj - Asmat, 2008, by Fr. Eduar Daeli, OSC

ISBN 978-90-8890-929-0 (softcover)
ISBN 978-90-8890-930-6 (hardcover)
ISBN 978-90-8890-931-3 (PDF e-book)

Contents

Foreword by Nestor T. Castro, Ph.D — 9
Acknowledgements — 11
List of acronyms — 13
Introduction — 15

1 Asmat: An exotic and nostalgic world — 19
    1.1 The *ci*: an Asmat's *habitus* — 20
    1.2 Back to Asmat with new eyes — 20
    1.3 Learning to know, learning to preserve — 23
    1.4 Story from the field — 24
    1.5 Scope and limitations — 32
    1.6 Analytical framework used — 34

2 The *ci*: A significant key to understand Asmat — 37
    2.1 Select literature on the Asmat — 38
    2.2 The *ci*: the Asmat canoe — 41
    2.3 Gender power relations — 42

3 The Asmat: A never ending surprise — 47
    3.1 Asmat: a pregnant swamp of natural resources — 47
    3.2 Asmat in Papua Province of Indonesia — 50
    3.3 Asmat: a region that contains no stone — 52
    3.4 Asmat art: an *anamnesis* — 54
    3.5 Defining the Asmat people — 54
    3.6 Asmat: people of the tree — 57
    3.7 Warfare and headhunting practices — 58
    3.8 Some impressions about kinship — 61
    3.9 Mission "touch" — 64

4 Physical dimension of the *ci* — 69
    4.1 Material of the *ci* — 70
    4.2 Understanding the *ci* through its sections — 70
    4.3. Types of the *ci* — 72
        4.3.1 *Pakanam ci* — 72
        4.3.2 *Jicap ci* or *pakman ci* — 74
    4.4 Interpretations of the carvings in the *ci* — 74
        4.4.1 Decorative meaning — 74
        4.4.2 Identity of the owner — 75
        4.4.3 Symbol of responsibility — 75
        4.4.4 Representation of the dead spirit — 75
        4.4.5 Sign of intimacy — 76
    4.5 Bottomless *ci* — 76
    4.6 *Po*: The Asmat oar — 77

5 Social dimension of the *ci* — 79
    5.1 The sociality of the *ci* — 79
    5.2 *Cisi-ipits* – *ci* maker — 81
    5.3 The *ci* owned by the family — 85
    5.4 The *ci* triggers conflicts among the Asmat — 85
    5.5 The dynamics of *ci cimen* and *ci ep* — 88
    5.6 Rowing the *ci* — 95
    5.7 Social dimension of the *jicap ci* — 97
        5.7.1 *Jicap ci* is taken after a general meeting in a *jeu* — 97
        5.7.2 *Jicap ci* maker and carver — 97
        5.7.3 *Jicap ci* is involved in many rituals during its life span — 97
        5.7.4 *Jicap ci* owned by *ces omou* — 98
        5.7.5 *Jicap ci* is kept very safe — 98
    5.8 Social dimension of *wuramon* — 99
    5.9 *Ci* as an expression of art — 99
    5.10 The *ci*: symbol of masculinity — 100
    5.11 The *ci*: a dominant symbol of gender identity — 102

6 Supernatural dimension of the *ci* — 103
    6.1 The *ci*: symbol of power — 103
    6.2 Naming the *ci* — 104
    6.3 A distinct *ci*: *wuramon* — 107

7 Economic dimension of the *ci* — 113
    7.1 *Ci opak, jis opak* (no *ci*, no firewood) — 113
    7.2 *Ci* for men, *jouse* for women — 118

7.3 Power over *dusun*	122
7.4 Do not call him *bitni*	123
7.5 One family in one *ci*	124
7.6 The *Ci*: a key for Asmat economy and festive activity	125

8 Continuity and discontinuity in Asmat Society — 129

8.1 Social change	129
8.2 Water transportation is still needed	130
8.3 *Pes* (ironwood) and *ci nak* (*ci* tree) are in danger	131
8.4 The changed meaning and function of ritual	133
8.5 Carving: not because of inspiration, but because of order	135
8.6 Money-oriented mentality	136
8.7 *Asmat nak* – the real people	138
8.8 New style of hunting and gathering	139
8.9 The changed concept of gender	139
8.10 Urbanization: *dusun* and village unmaintained	141
8.11 Marginalization of the Asmat in many aspects	142

9 Reflection and conclusion — 143

9.1 Personal reflections as priest and as researcher in the field	143
9.1.1 Advantages	143
9.1.2 Disadvantages	145
9.2 Conclusion	146
9.3 For future research	149

Glossary of terms — 153

Bibliography — 157

Unpublished Articles/Papers	162
Websites	162

About the author — 163

Endorsement by Nick Stanley — 165

Foreword

By Nestor T. Castro
Professor of Anthropology
University of the Philippines

There have been many published ethnographies about the Papuans of New Guinea Island. Among the most known anthropological classics are Leopold Pospisil's study on Kapauku Papuan customary law (1958), Marshall Sahlin's study on the big man of Melanesia (1963), Roy Rappaport's study on pig feasts among the Tsembaga Maring (1963), and Karl Heider's study on the Grand Valley Dani and their warfare (1970). However, all of these studies focused on the highland peoples of Papua while we know very little about the culture of the Papuans in the coastal regions.

Onesius Otenieli Daeli fills in this gap by looking at the lifeways of the Asmat people of Papua Province of Indonesia. His study focuses on the centrality of the *ci* (pronounced 'chi'), the Asmat dugout canoe, in Asmat society and culture. He discusses not just the nature and function of the *ci* but also its symbolic meanings. I will not discuss here his findings since I will leave that to the author. I would like to stress, however, that this work on the Asmat of Papua broadens our understanding about Melanesian societies and cultures.

Although I have not personally been with Onesius during his fieldwork among the Asmat, I have personally worked with him in doing an earlier field research among highland Papuan communities in Tembagapura and Timika, Indonesia. It was during that engagement that I realized how serious Onesius is in doing anthropological research. He was patient in listening to the stories of ordinary people. He meticulously recorded his observations in his field notes and validated his findings with his informants. He asked questions when he needed clarification but also kept some time by himself to reflect on his data. I must say that these are characteristics of a true anthropologist.

And so, when he asked me to be his Adviser for his Ph.D dissertation on the Asmat, I did not hesitate to accept his offer because I believed that he would be a good advisee. Honestly, I could not boast of influencing him on his dissertation research because he already knew what to do. I just acted as a sounding board when he would ask questions to me to help him understand what he already knew.

Upon finishing his degree of PhD Anthropology at the University of the Philippines, I would have wanted to invite Onesius to teach at our Department of Anthropology, of which I was the Chair at that time. I wanted him to handle our course on Peoples of Southeast Asia and Oceania, because of his vast exposure to Philippine, Indonesian, and Melanesian cultures. However, Onesius decided to go back to Indonesia and continue to serve his flock in that area this time not just as a priest but also as an applied anthropologist.

I am sure that the readers, whether academics or laymen, will enjoy and learn from Onesius' study on the Asmat of Papua.

Acknowledgements

I was surprised when I heard from my Superior in 2007 that I was assigned to study Anthropology in the Philippines. At that time I was still the parish priest of two parishes – St. Paul of Atsj and St. Anna Yaosakor of the Agats Diocese in Asmat. Frankly, it was because of my Superior's initiative and motivation that I came to the Philippines to study Anthropology. So, first, I would like to express my deepest gratitude to Fr. Agus Rachmat Widiyanto OSC (alm.), the former provincial (2007-2010) and Fr. Antonius Subianto B., OSC his successor (2010-2014; and now bishop of the Bandung Diocese) and all the board member of Sang Kristus Province of Indonesia of the Order of the Holy Cross (OSC). They have supported me in many ways to complete my studies successfully. I was able to do fieldwork in Asmat, Papua Indonesia because of their agreement and great support. I would also like to thank my confreres, the Crosiers, in Indonesia, especially those who are now working in Asmat. Indeed, they facilitated and assisted me very well in doing my fieldwork, both in Agats city and in the Atsj district.

I owe the dissertation committee for their great contribution and guidance to my work, especially Dr. Nestor T. Castro (adviser), Dr. Soledad Natalia M. Dalisay (reader/critic), Dr. Maria F. Mangahas (panel member), Dr. Michael L. Tan (panel member), and Dr. Carolyn I. Sobritchea (panel member). They encouraged me to work on this topic, despite my weaknesses and limitations. They were the light to my path to walk in the darkness of thinking and to work in the jungle of ideas. Indeed, through their guidance, I met my goal.

I would also like to thank Dr. Michael Tan, the dean of CSSP of UP Diliman when I did my fieldwork, and all the university staff who assisted me in their own ways, especially those who working in the administrative section. My special thanks to Josefina Sebastian and Melanie Taganayon (Graduate Office), Anna Belle (Anthropology Dept. Office), Ester Mendoza (Office of Student Activities), and all staff in the OUR (Office of the University Registrar) of UP Diliman.

My fieldwork in Asmat was greatly facilitated by the pastoral ministers of the diocese of Agats, both in the center of the diocese and in the parishes. Therefore, I owe a great deal to many people, especially Mgr. Aloysius Murwito, OFM, the Bishop of Agats Diocese, Fr. Vince Cole, MM (vice bishop and parish priest of Sawa-Erma), Fr. Virgil Petermeier, OSC, Fr. Umar Sumardi, OSC, Fr. Charles Loyak, OSC, and all my confreres in Agats, Atsj, and Ewer. Aside from their hospitality and generosity, they enlightened me to sharpen my research questions in order to get more valuable data. My special thanks also goes to Mr. Erick Sarkol (Curator of Agats Museum) and John Ohoiwirin (Agats Museum staff) for their hospitality and good company whenever I needed their assistance. Furthermore, I would like to thank a number of friends, both in Agats and in Atsj, including those friends who shared and allowed me to use their photograph collections. Some of them became my field assistants, contact persons, or meeting organizers. I thank them all even without mentioning their names because I am afraid I might miss some of them.

Above all, I would address my deep gratitude to the Asmat people, especially my honorable informants, including Amatus Ndatipits, Bartol Bokoropces, David Jimanipits, Donatus Tamot, Karola Biakai, Florentina Bifae, Elisa Kambu, Paskalis Osakat, Pius Woyakai, and Primus Ostji. They were all my field teachers. I was able to do my fieldwork because of their cooperation and sharing. I am very happy because of the opportunity I had to meet and to talk with them all. From their stories, experiences and sharing, I gained a lot of knowledge and values about the Asmat people and their culture.

I am also very grateful to all the CMM brothers of the Manila community as well as my confreres who stayed with me in Manila for their inspiration and backing of my studies. Their fraternal support strengthened me to do my best and to overcome my weaknesses. I also want to extend my gratitude to all friends around P. Burgos St., Project 4, Quezon City, Philippines, especially the CB Sisters for their encouragement and endless support. Thank you very much to all CB Sisters in the Regional House Community who allowed me to use their house in the middle of a beautiful garden, so I could write my dissertation in a very comfortable place. It was a very valuable gift to me.

Furthermore, I would like to thank Fr. Tejo Bawono OSC, Laurentia and her daughter Priska, Julia Halim and her husband Ferry Tjandra. They helped me a lot in translating some fieldwork data from bahasa Indonesia into English. For all friends and relatives, thank you very much for your support and prayers. My special thank goes to Dr. Perlita G. Manalili, Marcelina A. Pedraza, Sr. Nance O'Neil RSCJ, and Fr. Remacle OSC who spent their time to read the draft of this book and did some corrections to make the English text better. Then, with a deepest feeling of gratitude, I want to say thank you so much to my friend Sandra S. Hariadi who worked hard but happily to collate a wonderful layout for the previous draft of this book.

Finally, thank you for a great support from Parahyangan Catholic University in Bandung and for for all sponsors who were helping me in doing this project, especially the Crosier International Trust. This publishing project is funded through a grant from the Crosier International Trust. Contributions to the Trust are made from donors to the Conventual Priory of the Holy Cross in the United States. God bless us all to promote peace and love for all generations.

List of acronyms

BPS	Badan Pusat Statistic – Central Statistics Bureau (CSB)
DPR	Dewan Perwakilan Rakyat – The Indonesian Parliament)
DPRD	Dewan Perwakilan Rakyat Daerah – The Provincial Parliament
FAR	Forum Antar Rumpun – Sub-tribes Forum
LMAA	Lembaga Musyawarah Adat Asmat – Asmat Tribal Council
MSC	Societas Missionariorum Sacratissima Cordis Jesu – Sacred Heart of Jesus
OFM	Ordo Fratrum Minorum – The Franciscan
OPM	Organisasi Papua Merdeka – The Free Papua Movement
OSC	Ordo Sanctae Crucis – The Order of the Holy Cross
Pemda	Pemerintah Daerah – Local government
SD	Sekolah Dasar – Elementary School
WKRI	Wanita Katolik Republik Indonesia – Catholic Women of Republic of Indonesia
YPPK	Yayasan Pendidikan dan Persekolahan Katolik – Catholic Education Foundation

Introduction

This book is basically grounded on my doctoral dissertation with some revisions and adaptations. The fieldwork was done in 2012, therefore, probably some statistical data are irrelevant today.

Actually, many friends were encouraging me to publish this account during the years before, however I did not pay much attention. I was waiting for many years to find out 'an excellent time' to work on it. In fact, the 'expected time' did not come. Perhaps, it will never come because 'the expected time' was waiting for me to take my first step. That is why, now I am motivated to take action to publish this book.

Ci is the Asmat word for a dugout canoe. The *ci* is an integral part of the everyday life of the Asmat people because their region is located geographically in the lowlands and in the middle of a huge tidal swampy area. Asmat is an Indonesian ethnic group residing in the Papua province, the easternmost part of Indonesia, and formerly called Irian Jaya. The Asmat area is surrounded by countless large and small rivers and jungles.

Owning a *ci* is part of the Asmat's habitus because the *ci* is a guarantee of mobility, both individually and collectively. An informant of this study said, "The *ci* and *po* (oar) are cores of the Asmat life. The *ci* is a bridge to reach livelihood; it is a primary instrument to fulfill the needs of a family. It is a guarantee for mobility and for continuing the ancestors' lives. The *ci* is a basic tool for life" (Primus Ostji). From this background, I do believe that the *ci* can become a significant key to understand the Asmat and their culture. It is a good vehicle to explore many things about the everyday lives of the Asmat community.

The general objective of this study is to investigate the relationship between the *ci* and gender among the Asmat of Papua. Indeed, I found out that the *ci* is a significant key to understand gender among the Asmat. The *ci* shows the distinction of roles between men and women. For example, the *ci* makers are men and never done by women. Moreover, positioning in a *ci*, both symbolically and practically, between man and woman is different - - a man stands upright at *ci cimen* while a woman sits down at *ci ep*.

In fact, the *ci* is essential for the everyday lives of the Asmat. However, the existence of the *ci* is now critical and there is a possibility that it may be replaced by mechanical boats. Internal and external factors cause its gradual extinction. The internal factors mainly come from the acculturation and assimilation of the Asmat with other cultures and the weaknesses of tribal leaders. The tribal leaders are not able to maintain their local values nor to adapt or to control a new way of life that overwhelms them. The tribal leaders themselves enjoy modern life style. I found that modern tools are more interesting and promising to the Asmat, while the traditional way of life is less interesting and out of date. Meanwhile, the external factor is the influx of people from everywhere to Asmat. The non-Asmat come to Asmat with their own cultures and backgrounds. Moreover, the advent of modern water transportation such as speedboats, longboats, and ships makes the existence of the *ci* worse. As a consequence, changes in the *ci* bring about changes in society, including the concept of gender. For example, the younger generation realizes that the decision makers are not always men and the elderly because in some cases youngsters and women are more powerful.

I used the *ci* as a focal point to understand gender power relations among the Asmat, particularly through social, economic, and supernatural dimensions. However, interpretations and attitudes towards the *ci* change through time. Changes in the *ci* will influence many other things including social, economic, supernatural, and gender power relations.

Socially, the *ci* shows the relationship between people in a community. Both symbolically and practically, the *ci* presents role divisions between men and women which cannot be exchanged easily because it is considered as sacred and secret. Economically, the *ci* helps people to meet their needs and to sustain their lives as illustrated through the saying, "*Ci opak, jis opak*" (No *ci*, no firewood) and "*Ci opak, jouse opak*" (No *ci*, no hearth). This means, a family will eat nothing without a *ci* because even a very simple thing such as firewood cannot be provided without a *ci*. In the Asmat context, if a household does not have firewoods, they cannot cook. Therefore, the *ci* is highly valuable to fulfill daily needs. Spiritually, the *ci* relates the visible and the invisible worlds – the world of the living and the world of the spirit. The *ci* represents the ancestral spirit. Thus, along with the *ci*'s extinction, perhaps the relationship with the ancestral spirit will be disconnected or at least will not be the focus of attention anymore. Consequently, many traditional rituals will not be celebrated.

Furthermore, the *ci* is a symbol of power and status as shown in the saying, "*Ci opak, cemen opak*" (No *ci*, no penis). It means, a man who does not own a *ci* is considered impotent

Figure 1. Aerial photograph of the Asmat area; huge jungles and numerous rivers can be seen.

or has no penis. An impotent man has no power to penetrate the woman's vagina, just like a man who does not own a *ci*. Without a *ci*, a man has no ability to cross the river and infiltrate the jungle. As a result, his status as *Asmat nak* (the real man) is nil. Of course, an Asmat man is not willing to be called *cemen opak* (no penis) or *bitni* (knows nothing) because it is very humiliating. In order not to be called *cemen opak* or *bitni*, an Asmat man must own a *ci* as a proof that he is an *Asmat nak*, a real man who knows how to work.

Above all, the *ci* brings hope, life, and happiness to the Asmat community, just like a penis which brings about fertility and new life to a family. A pregnant swamp of natural resources will sustain them if the Asmats preserve their *ci*. The *ci* makes the Asmat a happy society, an independent community, and a powerful people.

Culturally, the Asmat comprises twelve different sub-ethnic groups called *rumpun*, and these are: Emari Ducur, Bismam, Simai, Becmbub, Unir Sirao (Kenok), Unir Epmak (Tomor), Joerat, Safan, Kenekap (Kaimo), Aramatak (Yamugau), Yupmakcain (Citak), and Bras (Brazza).The sub-ethnic groups with whom I spent most of my time are Bismam and Becmbub. Every *rumpun* has its own language, or even within a *rumpun* there are some different languages or dialects. Therefore, the terminology or the name of material culture in this book may be articulated differently. For instance, Becmbub calls the traditional house of Asmat as '*jeu*', meanwhile another *rumpun* calls it *jae, je*, or *yeu*. Another example, the word "no" in English can be articulated as '*opak*' in a *rumpun* and in another would call it '*opok*' or '*apuk*'.

1

Asmat

An exotic and nostalgic world

When people go to Asmat, they may step ankle deep in mud or turbid water may sprinkle their beautiful outfit. However, they must not be afraid because from the muddy water, they may find a tremendous experience by catching numerous fish, shrimps, and other water creatures. In Asmat, one must be ready for surprises.

I believe that there are many ways to describe a selected group of people in order to understand them better. For example, the Asmat people know many ways of catching fish from a river: using fish nets, or fish-hooks, or simply by going down to the river and catching the fish with their bare hands.

This book will inform the readers how gender representation and social change are manifested through the *ci* of the Asmat of Papua, Indonesia. I hope, this book introduces

Figure 2. The Asmat on their *ci*s. (Photograph courtesy of Fr. Umar Sumardi, OSC).

Asmat and its valuable culture to other parts of the world and to the readers. Note: all figures in this book are the author's collection, except the figures with names are used with permission of their owners.

1.1 The *ci*: an Asmat's *habitus*

Ci is the Asmat word for dugout canoe[1]. The *ci* is an integral part of Asmat life. I conducted my fieldwork is the Asmat region and the people from the area are called Asmat. Geographically, the Asmat area is surrounded by the sea and countless rivers (see fig.1 and fig.2). It is located in the middle of a huge tidal swampy land.

Because of the area's geographical location, it is imperative for the Asmat to have a *ci*. Having a *ci* is an integral part of the Asmat's *habitus*. In other words, people in Asmat are people with the *ci*.

Unfortunately, nowadays the Asmat tend to abandon the *ci* and try to replace this with modern means of transportation. In the light of such observations, what are the implications of not owning a *ci* for the Asmat? How are gender representation and social change manifested in the *ci*?

1.2 Back to Asmat with new eyes

My relationship with the Asmat started in 2002 when my Superior in Indonesia assigned me to Asmat as a domestic missionary to do pastoral ministry in the diocese of Agats. I am an ordained Roman Catholic priest and a member of the Order of the Holy Cross (OSC). The members of the Order of the Holy Cross are called Crosiers (Hontheim 2010:131). As a Crosier, I was sent to Asmat.

The pastoral ministry has given me opportunities to know Asmat and its people. It has also given me a chance to be close to the Asmat people as well as their culture. Since then, I felt very happy to be there and I wanted fervently to know more about Asmat because it has a lot of remarkable things that cannot be found in other societies in the world. My experiences in Asmat as well as with the Asmat people reminded me of Boas' historical/cultural particularism. The Asmat culture has its own unique values and characteristics which cannot be compared with any culture in the world.

Even if I was not in Asmat as an ethnographer during that time, my initial experiences in Asmat enriched my cultural knowledge and enhanced my psychological connection with Asmat and its people. I felt very close to Asmat, more than what I feel toward my own hometown in Nias-Sumatera. I believe that I share the same feeling with Schneebaum (1988:32) who said, "Such were my introductions to Asmat. Everything intrigued me. In fact, I was so overcome by the carvings and the people that I decided to find a way to return." This connectivity motivated me to study the Asmat more through academic research.

I assumed the Asmat people would die without the *ci* because without the *ci*, they would not be able to meet their needs. This assumption is strengthened by 'The Social Analysis" conducted by the pastoral team of the Diocese of Agats in 2006-2007. This social analysis was a preparation for the Pastoral Council of the Diocese of Agats held on September 25-30, 2007 in Agats (*Hasil Musyawarah*, p.1). I was part of the pastoral team which collected data about the current situation of local churches in the Diocese of Agats, particularly in Atsj

---

1   In this study, I use "*ci*" (the Asmat word) instead of "canoe" in order to stress that the focus of discussion is the Asmat canoe. The *ci* specifically refers to the Asmat canoe. The 'c' is pronounced like 'ch' in 'chew'.

and Yaosakor parishes. Surprisingly, the local people themselves found that one cause of problems in Asmat is the *ci*. The *ci* is one reason why the Asmat people frequently fight with each other. For example, if a man uses another person's *ci* without permission, the *ci*'s owner gets angry. In some villages, stealing *ci* is frequent. That is one basic question which this study tried to determine – why does the *ci* trigger conflicts in Asmat society?

During the time when the Social Analysis was conducted, I agreed with the local people who believed that the *ci* is a trigger point of many problems in Asmat. However, I do not want to simply agree with them. I want to probe deeper into my assumption, thus, I chose the *ci* as the focal point of my study.

Aside from the Social Analysis conducted at the Diocese of Agats in 2007, the local government of Asmat also has a very beautiful motto: *"Ja Asamanam Apcamar"* (Asmat), *"Berjalan dalam keseimbangan"* (Indonesia). This means "Walk in a perfect balance." This motto is supported by a vision: *"Membangun Asmat di atas pilar budaya Asmat"* (To build Asmat on the pillar of the Asmat culture). Now, the question is: Do the motto and the vision of the local government work effectively in everyday practice in the lives of the Asmat? I hope this study yields significant results on the question about the motto and the vision. Another question that may be asked is: Does the local government of Asmat have programs to preserve the Asmat traditions, including the *ci*, in the Asmat heritage?

The *ci* is the only traditional means of transportation in Asmat because geographically, the Asmat region is surrounded by rivers and sea. It is located in the middle of a huge swampy land. Owning a *ci* is the Asmat's *habitus* in Bourdieu's terminology. This means, the native people in Asmat are people with *ci*s (see fig.3). The *ci* is an important element in the Asmat lives. It is a guarantee for mobility in everyday life of the Asmat, both individually and collectively.

Figure 3. Asmat children are playing with the *ci*s in the river. (Photograph courtesy of Fr. Innocentius Retobjaan).

Figure 4. Paskalis Osakat is drawing a *ci* in the author's fieldnote: illustrated and explained the sections of a *ci*.

Ironically, the *ci* is not only found in Asmat. However, in this study I tried to investigate the uniqueness of the Asmat canoe – the *ci*. Why is the *ci* so special? Can it serve as an identity tool for the Asmat? Or can the Asmat be identified thru the *ci*? This is the locus or specific aspect of this study. I am not referring to any other canoe in this research work, only the *ci*. I did not try to compare the *ci* with any other canoe. I believe the *ci* not only has functional, but also social, economic, and supernatural meanings.

Furthermore, studying the *ci* can be a significant key in understanding gender in the Asmat society. Based on my past experiences and observations, the *ci* has become an indicator of gender division in Asmat. For example, a *ci* maker is a man, while the woman is responsible in filling it up with sago, fish, and other family needs. This is why it is common to see Asmat women working hard at home and in the field – a part of labor division between men and women. The women engage in activities in the forests and in rivers in order to provide for the needs of the family. The gender division of labor in Asmat is very interesting to analyze to understand the reasons behind the tangible reality of the Asmats.

Other aspects that can be observed as kind of gender division are the position and the gestures of the man and woman in the *ci*. Schneebaum (1985:160) described that women paddle the *ci* sitting down, thus their paddles are shorter than those of the men. The men stand in the *ci* with one foot forward, bending the knees at the stroke of the paddle. The woman sometimes stands, with legs almost straight, bending at the waist. Normally, while paddling the *ci*, the man stands upright in the front section of the *ci* while the woman sits at the back. The way of holding the paddle also varies between man and woman. Thus, practically and symbolically, the *ci* itself shows differences in

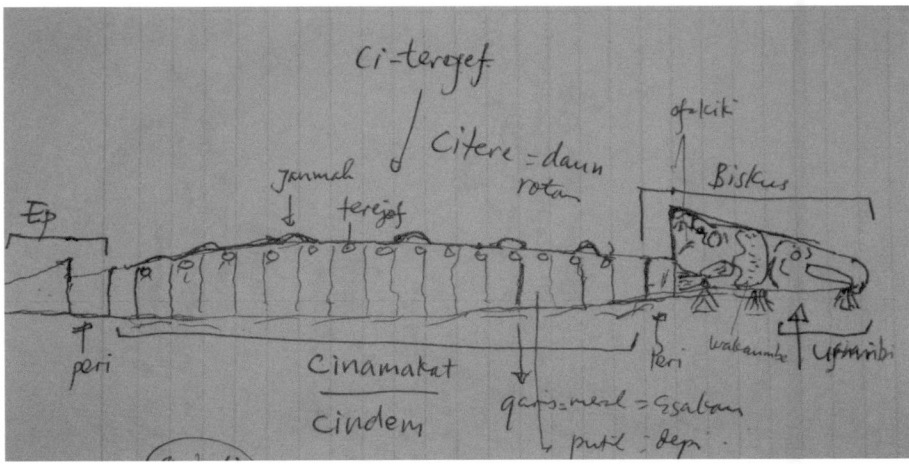

Figure 5. The *ci* – drawing of Paskalis Osakat.

gender roles among the Asmat. The *ci* can be a good locus for interpretive and symbolic anthropology (Geertz in McGee and Warms 2000).

Additionally, the *ci* is an excellent instrument to understand rituals, myths, and other traditional events in Asmat. As far as I know, the *ci* cannot be separated from many Asmat rituals and feasts. The primary reason for this is that the *ci* facilitates the completion or fulfillment of any activity that they have planned. Rituals and other traditional celebrations in Asmat are mostly related to the forest, river, spirit, or food. Therefore, the *ci* is sine qua non because geographically the Asmat area is surrounded by rivers. The Asmat are not able to reach forests, cross rivers, or get as many materials they use for rituals without the *ci*. In other words, the *ci* is a necessity in any Asmat ritual or feast celebration. The decision to hold a traditional feast or ritual is always based on the availability of the *ci*.

However, at present Asmat is experiencing changes, including the Asmat's perspective about the *ci*. It is good to question: Is the perception about gender among the Asmat changing because of the change in perception of the *ci*? The Pastoral Council of the Diocese of Agats in 2007 figured it out in a simple formulation, "*Jatidiri masyarakat setempat terancam*", the native's identity is threatened (Hasil Musyawarah 2007:2) because of the many problems brought about by both internal and external factors.

1.3 Learning to know, learning to preserve

I realize that I am not a pioneer in ethnographic work in Asmat. There were a number of previous ethnographers in Asmat such as Gerald A. Zegwaard (1959), Tobias Schneebaum (1985, 1988), Alphonse Sowada (2002), and Jan Pouwer (2010). In some aspects, my study is an expansion of previous works.

However, the previous studies did not focus on the *ci* as a key point in understanding gender in Asmat, which is the thrust of my research. This study uncovers the uninvestigated and undocumented topic about the everyday life of the Asmat. This topic therefore becomes a new contribution to the anthropological knowledge about the *ci* in particular and about world academic achievements, in general.

Figure 6. KII with David Jimanipits (in black T-shirt).

This study is not only useful for the Asmat to deepen their knowledge about their values and inheritance, but also for non-Asmat who wish to learn about the Asmat culture and for those who want to work in Asmat. The study can motivate the Asmat people to be aware of their own culture and then start to preserve it. For non-Asmat, it can pave the way to know the Asmat and their culture to understand the everyday life of the Asmat. As far as I have observed, many non-Asmat look down on Asmat, in particular and on Papuans, in general. We often hear observations that the Asmat are primitive, undeveloped, uneducated, lazy, and immature. The "Otherness" perspective as in classic anthropological theory is still very strong among outsiders in Asmat.

Furthermore, this study is valuable to the local Catholic Church which anchors herself to the local wisdom (see *Musyawarah Pastoral II* 2001: 17-18; *Musyawarah Pastoral III* 2007:3). For example, the Church can use the study as a reference to introduce the Asmat to new pastoral ministers. In the Agats diocese, as far as I have experienced, there is an orientation program for the new pastoral ministers to familiarize them with Asmat culture and to the pastoral ministries of the diocese. The pastoral ministers of the local Catholic Church can also use this study to emphasize the centrality of the *ci* in the everyday life of Asmat. Thus, the people hopefully will preserve it. Moreover, this study can be a model for local church's ministers to study the richness of the Asmat nature and culture. Lastly, this study can enrich the Agats Museum collections.

1.4 Story from the field

For the purpose of this study, I went back to Asmat and lived there from January to May 2012. My stay was shorter than my pervious one which lasted from December 2002 to January 2008. However, during my previous stay in Asmat, I was not yet an anthropology

Figure 7. FGD at the High School female dormitory in Agats. A girl is showing the women's style while paddling.

student, merely a domestic missionary of the Order of the Holy Cross. Going back to Asmat as an anthropology student gave me a new perspective to see it from a different angle. Nevertheless, my previous experience and knowledge about Asmat helped me so much and became a good background in my fieldwork. Thus, in a sense, I could say that this fieldwork was to deepen and to sharpen my knowledge about Asmat and to enrich my emotional entanglement with the people.

Aside from KIIs, I was also able to hold 13 Focus Group Discussions or FGDs (see fig.7) among different groups. At that time, I thought it is important to do FGDs to validate and to enhance the data which I gathered through KIIs.

During my fieldwork, I was able to interview at least 34 Key Informants (KIIs): 18 in Agats, 12 in Atsj, 3 in Sawa, and 1 in Yamas. They were from different backgrounds such as tribal leaders, local government officers, religious leaders, missionaries, teachers, *cisi-ipits* (*ci* makers), *wow-ipits* (sculptors), Asmat scholars, local women's organization leaders, and selected *ci* users (see fig.4, fig.6. fig. 8a and 8b). I used KII as a technique because I believed that not everyone among the Asmat are knowledgeable about all aspects of their culture. So, it was important to select those informants whom I believed to have a good knowledge about Asmat culture, especially concerning the *ci*. Likewise, seniority and hierarchical status among the Asmat are very strong. Some missionaries and villagers were the ones who recommended to interview selected informants. It is necessary to mention that elders and leaders in Asmat are always the first to speak and to give information about something. Sharing knowledge and information is something that is limited to the elders and leaders only because they are more confident about themselves and their culture and they are not afraid of any risk including a death. Moreover, my informants were mostly tribal or group leaders.

The FGD group could either affirm or negate the data that came from other informants. Therefore, I arranged some FGDs with my contact persons.

The number of participants for one FGD varied. The largest is the Catholic Youth of St. Paulus Atsj (66 individuals) which was conducted during a celebration on Valentine's Day. it was impossible to do an FGD for a group that big. So, instead I held a public consultation with them. However, I categorized it as FGD since it was done in a group. I asked the coordinators of the party if I could do a consultation with the participants. Fortunately, they gave me one session to do the consultation. I was assisted by two friends: one seminarian

Figure 8a. FGD with *cisi-ipits* (*ci* makers).

Figure 8b. FGD with the counsel of the Catholic Women Organization of Atsj.

and the other a high school teacher. We divided the participants into three groups to get more adequate data and to be closer to them. Because the number of informants was big, I addressed three basic questions to be answered in groups and later on the responses to be presented to the whole. The questions were: (1) Do the families in your villages (Atsj

Figure 9. Women dance (*cepes di em*) inside the new *jeu* in Atsj.

and Yasiw) still have *ci*? (2) How do you feel if your own family has no *ci*? (3) Why does the *ci* trigger conflicts in society? It was a surprise that the answers of the three groups were basically similar. To answer question #1 they said, most of the families in their villages do not own a *ci*. To meet their needs, they just borrow a *ci* from their relatives or join other families when they go hunting or fishing. To answer question #2 they said, "*Kalau tidak ada perahu: sedih, kecewa, gelisah, hidup jadi susah, dan rumah kosong.*" – (If there is no *ci*, we are very sad, disappointed, worried, find it difficult to live, and empty house). "Empty house" means, they have nothing, particularly nothing to eat.

Another big FGD is the one conducted at the High School Female Dormitory where the informants were members of Agats diocese (23 individuals). I asked the director of the dormitory to select some of the members prior to the FGD schedule. However, she did not select because she and the girls wanted to know what would happen in the FGD, so they just gathered together. There were 27 women in that dormitory, but four (4) of them were not able to attend the FGD because of personal business. The girls were all students in the junior and senior high schools in Agats. They came from different areas in Asmat. I was happy to do FGD with them because they provided me with the latest information about the *ci* existence in their own villages which are scattered around Asmat. Although I was not able to reach every single village in Asmat, the participants convinced me that the existence of the *ci* all around Asmat is almost the same, that is, many families do not own a *ci*.

I was also able to do Participant Observation in at least 11 documented situations, both in Agats city proper and in Atsj. The Participant Observation was important because I saw with my very eyes and I have experienced the behavior, attitude, movement, and

Figure 10. The Atsj men on their longboats and *ci*s after they distributed the nypa sprouts (*akam*) to their wives or sisters. They are about to go home. See the difference between the longboat and the *ci*.

Figure 11. Going to *dusun* by the *ci*.

many other activities of the Asmat to fulfil their daily needs, to celebrate their rituals, and to sustain their lives. Through Participant Observation, I obtained not only verbal information but also practical or tangible experiences (*i.e.* first-hand data).

In Participant Observation, I witnessed how the *cisi-ipits* (*ci* makers) construct the *ci*, including the material and the tools they used. In this part of the study, I tried to emphasize two Participant Observations conducted among others. First, the new *jeu* feast in Atsj village. It was the last ritual process of the new *jeu*, which is called cepes di em (women's feast). It is a very special occasion for women to enter and dance in a *jeu* because they are not allowed to enter it any other time. *Cepes di em* literally means, women dance with drum (see fig.9). At that time, very early in the morning, all the men went to a certain *dusun* (forest that is occupied by clans or families) to gather as many nypa (type of palm) sprouts (called *akam*). They gathered and brought these nypa sprouts to the new *jeu*. In the afternoon when they returned from the *dusun*, they handed the sprouts over to their wives or sisters who shared these with their relatives or close friends. It was highly valuable to participate in that ritual feast.

However, the most interesting thing to me was that the men used 13 longboats, among the 19 *ci*s available. In one *ci*, there were 5 to 9 men and no less than 15 men in one longboat (see fig.10). This means, the Asmat are allowed to use not only traditional transportation, but also modern vehicles to celebrate their traditional ritual feast which had never been permitted before. It mirrors the new way of life of the Asmat who prefer to use mechanical boats rather than the traditional *ci*. It also proves that the *ci* is now being replaced by modern equipment.

Next, I went with some Asmat to a *dusun* (forest) to observe closely the kind of *ci* trees and the initial process of making a *ci*. I joined them in their *ci*, paddled with them (see fig.11), and ate what they had prepared for a meal in the jungle. At that time, one of the Asmat showed me a *ci* tree. He cut down a *ci* tree with a steel axe, not only to show me how the initial process of making *ci* is done, but also because he himself needed a new *ci*. That occasion was also a good opportunity for him to start working on his *ci*. At that time, while he was cutting down the *ci* tree which had a diameter of about 90 to 100 cm, I could not imagine how many hours in the past the Asmat spent cutting down a *ci* tree using a stone axe. Even with a sharp steel axe, they spent almost an hour to fell the tree. We were all tired waiting for the *ci* tree to fall down, especially the cutters. So, after it fell, we took a rest on the fallen *ci* tree (see fig.12).

I was so lucky because just by chance, I found many *ci* trees were being cut in the middle of that *dusun* to make new *ci*s. However, I found out that there was only one of the *ci* makers who was constructing his *ci*. I observed closely how he made the *ci* using a very simple tool, a steel axe. He told me nobody helped him since he started working on that *ci*. According to him, it would take him at least one month to finish working on that *ci*. After roughly digging the log in the *dusun*, he will make a path to haul it out to the river and then finish it by the riverbank of that *dusun* or near his house in his village. Needless to say, it is very difficult to make a *ci* even with the use of a sharp steel axe. Nonetheless, the Asmat do it because it is their way of life.

Staying with the local people of Asmat helped me to collect as much data I needed through interviews and participant observations. I visited and interviewed the informants in different venues such as in their houses, *jeu*s, huts, and even in the forests. These visitations and interviews, helped me to be closer to the people, and to observe closely

Figure 12. Take a rest for a while on the *ci* tree that just fell down.

their daily activities and behaviors. I also visited schools, churches, libraries, carving halls, and local government offices to get more data about the Asmat and the *ci*.

For the interviews, I used semi-structured interview guides. This means, prior to the actual interviews I made some preparations - - how the interviews were to be conducted, including the formulation of the guide questions. The interviews were very flexible. In other words, I had already the structure of the interview in my mind, but I made some adjustments, taking into considerate the present situation. Most of my interviews were recorded thru an audio recorder and some of the participant observations were recorded using a video camera.

Many friends in Asmat assisted in my fieldwork. These friends were local people and from the pastoral ministries of the Diocese of Agats. Their support was useful and unforgettable. They helped me by being mediators, contact persons, field assistants, and people I could talk to. Above all, some parish priests helped me, not only by providing me a room to stay but also by arranging an interview schedule with the key informants. Some of my trips were arranged based on the parish priests' schedule in order to minimize my expenses in visiting a village for my fieldwork.

Most of all, I was delighted Bishop Aloysius Murwito, OFM, of the Diocese of Agats, answered my request. A feedback seminar about the Asmat culture was held (see fig.13). I requested this event to collect and to verify my data. The feedback seminar provided more data from informants having different backgrounds and information from areas which I could not see alone.

Bishop Aloysius Murwito was very enthusiastic about this feedback seminar because most of the pastoral ministers of Agats diocese were new. So, the seminar, according to him, could introduce Asmat culture for new pastoral ministers and provide a refresher

Figure 13. Feedback seminar on Asmat culture. The participants were pastoral ministers of the diocese of Agats.

course for those who had been there many years. It was a good feedback, not only for me as a researcher, but also for the pastoral ministers of Agats diocese. That is why he invited all pastoral ministers of the diocese of Agats and some special guests to participate. Some of the participants were Asmat. On this occasion, I shared my experiences in Asmat, especially on how to conduct fieldwork. I talked to the participants, especially regarding my topic, the ci's importance for the Asmat. However, the ci is being replaced by modern tools. Without the ci, many of the Asmat values would be extinct. From the discussions during the feedback seminar, I got a lot of ideas such as follow-up questions to be addressed, suggestions in order to get more input, and verification of my data. I considered the feedback seminar as part of my research method, to get more data from the different participants because I was the one who initiated in holding it through the support of the bishop. The participants added more data to my study and sharpened my analysis of the data. Most of my data were basically firsthand.

After the first month of my fieldwork, I realized that KII is more adequate and preferable than FGD. I found that in the FGD in Asmat, informants were not free to answer and to express their ideas about something. Usually, they looked at each other first before saying something or they asked permission from other informants before answering a question. Based on my observation, the informants seemed not to have confidence to talk about their ideas. They were not really sure what they were talking about. Actually, FGD is very useful to validate data among informants. Unfortunately, this was not the case with the FGD in Asmat. The Asmat would not disagree with each other in public. Another reason why FGD is not recommended in doing fieldwork in Asmat is that a person was selected from the informants to become the speaker on behalf of them all. Moreover, if there is a special case to talk about such as a story, they would not tell me or the other informants directly and freely because a story in Asmat has many versions. And so, there would be doubts about their own story. Therefore, I recommend for other social researchers to use KII rather than FGD in the Asmat region. It will help them save time and go directly to the focus of the discussion.

1.5 Scope and limitations

The Asmat area is quite big: 10 districts with 175 villages (see Senokos: 2011). Moreover, the transportation intra and inter-districts and villages is difficult and expensive. Because of this, I focused my fieldwork on two districts only – - Agats city proper and the Atsj district (see fig.14, 15). Culturally, Agats belongs to the *rumpun* (sub-ethnic group) of *Bismam*, while Atsj belongs to *Becmbub*. In my opinion, both Agats city and Atsj district are representations of the everyday life of Asmat in general, despite the uniqueness of each place.

I chose Agats city because it is a symbol and the center of Asmat development. Agats is the capital of Asmat where the regent (*bupati*) and other local government officers stay and have office. Aside from being the center of the local government, Agats is also the center of the Catholic Church mission where the bishop resides. The majority of the Asmat population is Catholic (60%), and the rest are Protestants and Muslims. Agats is a center for both civil and religious activities. Right now, people are constructing houses, local government buildings, bridges, schools, and even churches in the Agats area. In Agats, people can easily notice modern influences of development. In addition, Agats has become a center for urbanization. People from everywhere, both from the local Asmat and from outside (non-Asmat and non-Papuan) come to Agats. Therefore, Agats is a proper place to see the real dynamics of acculturation in Asmat.

Figure 14. Agats city.

Aside from Agats city, I also chose Atsj district. Firstly, I am more familiar with Atsj because I stayed there for five years. This background was valuable for me in collecting my data because I know the place and the communities as well. Secondly, Atsj is a picture of changing Asmat. Although, Atsj has not changed as rapidly as Agats, it is useful to understand the connectivity between the traditional and the modern ways of living.

It is noteworthy that there are many individuals and families in Atsj who do not own a *ci* for various reasons. The Asmat are highly dependent on others without the *ci*. Thus, they prefer to buy sago from fellow Asmat rather than travel to the *dusun* to get it. Furthermore, migration from Atsj to Agats is significant. The Atsj people migrate to Agats to look for jobs or to study. However, other people go to Agats and stay with their relatives and are content just being parasites. Hence, this reality can be a link to investigate the traces of the Asmat tradition through the *ci*. For example, if the Asmat people migrate to other places within Asmat, let us say from Atsj to Agats, do they bring their *ci*? If Agats is the center of urbanization, does it become a place for traditional rituals as well? In other words, do they bring and hold their traditional rituals in Agats, since Agats still belongs to the Asmat region? What is the impact of urbanization on the original village as well as to the destination places?

The focus and scope of my fieldwork is limited to the two areas: Agats city proper and Atsj. However, I also did fieldwork in other villages, i.e., Sawa-Er, Yamas, Ewer, Biwar Laut, and Amanamkai. Amanamkai and Biwar Laut are still part of Atsj district, while Sawa-Er and Yamas are part of Sawa-Erma district. Ewer belongs to Agats district. From Atsj to Amanamkai takes about 20 minutes by speedboat and Atsj to Biwar Laut about 60 minutes. I went to these villages to get more input and to validate my data about the *ci*. I found more families in these villagees who do not own a *ci* as compared to those in

Figure 15. Catholic Church in Atsj.

Atsj, except in Ewer. I did fieldwork in Yamas of Sawa-Erma because the *Wuramon* (canoe spirit) is only found in that area.

Above all, my topic focuses on the *ci*, the Asmat canoe. The canoe in general or the canoes found in other places were not discussed. I did not compare the *ci* and canoes in other places.

In everyday conversation, the Asmat usually use their native language. However, when they speak to non-Asmat they use bahasa Indonesia. So, I used bahasa Indonesia to communicate with my informants, since I am not an Asmat and I do not speak their language, I realized that knowing the local language is better than using only bahasa Indonesia. Sometimes, especially during FGDs, they speak the local language among themselves. Therefore, I realized the possibility that some information was lost because of language. Perhaps, some Asmat words have no equivalent translation in the Indonesian language or vice versa. To overcome this limitation, I did further interviews to cross-check or to verify information.

One of the limitations worth mentioning here is that the Asmat keep some stories or information to themselves. For example, when I asked this question, "Do you know a story or myth about the *ci*?" Some informants said, "No, I don't know." Others said, "Yes, we know, but we cannot share it. We can only listen to it." As far as I know, the Asmat believe that their stories are spirits that live. If they have no more stories for themselves, this means the end of their lives because they have no more secrets. Only the elders do not worry about dying and they are the ones who can freely share their stories or the myths of their communities. Therefore, it is understandable that many Asmat keep some stories for themselves or for their community because they do not want to die soon. I also kept some data for my personal knowledge only because I do not want to write or publish something that my informants shared secretly.

1.6 Analytical framework used

I used 'symbolic and interpretive anthropology' as theoretical framework for my discussion. According to Jon McGee, symbolic anthropologists believe that culture does not exist apart from individuals but rather lies in their interpretations of events and the things around them (2000: 467). Similarly, the *ci* as the central argument in this study does not exist apart from the Asmat, but it is rather an important element of their life.

I examined the *ci* as Geertz analyzed the Balinese cockfight. Geertz said, "Cockfights, being a part of 'The Balinese Way of Life'" (Geertz 1973), is Balinese culture. The Cockfight issue is applicable to many aspects of Balinese life such as court trials, wars, political contests, inheritance disputes, and street arguments. In a similar perspective, I wanted to say that the *ci* cannot be separated from the Asmat way of life. Despite cockfights being the object of his discussion, Geertz did not look at the cockfight per se. He developed his observations around the cockfight arena. I tried to interpret and apply his framework in looking at the *ci*.

Furthermore, Turner's idea in The Forest of Symbol (1967), particularly regarding the levels of the meaning of the symbol, guided me to explore the Asmat symbols. According to Turner, there are three levels of meaning of a symbol: (1) the level of indigenous interpretation; (2) the operational meaning; and (3) the positional meaning (1967:50). Moreover, I also anchored my study in Hoskins' Biographical Objects (1998) in analyzing the betel bag of Kodi society in Sumba Indonesia. The betel bag can be interpreted as perhaps the pre-eminent "biographical object" in Kodi society because it represents the identity of its owner in both private context and in a ritual stage. A man is not himself

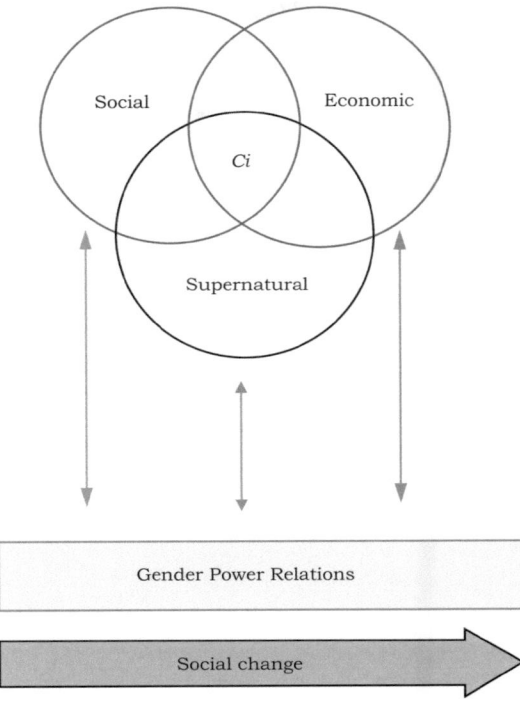

Figure 16. Conceptual framework.

without his betel bag; he loses his identity if it is lost. In a similar way, I wanted to investigate how the *ci* speaks about gender among the Asmat, as betel bag tells about the Kodi's society. The *ci* itself is a symbol of men and at the same time, it becomes a symbol of power. Without possessing a *ci*, a man can be considered as impotent; the Asmat call it, "*Ci opak, cemen opak*" – (no *ci*, no penis).

In this study, the *ci* becomes the focal point to understand gender power relations among the Asmat, particularly through social, economic, and spiritual dimensions. Socially, the *ci* regulates the roles of men and women in society. The *ci* shows the role divisions between men and women that cannot be easily exchanged. For example, men paddle while standing upright at *ci cimen*, while women paddle sitting down at *ci ep*. The *ci* is a symbol of power and status. That is why there is a saying, "*Ci opak, cemen opak*" (No *ci*, no penis). Economically, we can see that without a *ci*, the Asmat people will find difficulties in meeting their needs. This is expressed in these sayings, "*Ci opak, jis opak*" (No *ci*, no firewood) and "*Ci opak, jouse opak*" (No *ci*, no hearth). Providing *jis* and food is the women's responsibility. However, the women need the *ci* that is made by men to gather the food. Spiritually, the *ci* relates the living people to their ancestral spirit or to the transcendental world. In terms of gender relations, there are many prohibitions for women because they have menstrual blood that can bring about danger and misfortune to the society. For example, women are not allowed to use a new *ci* because they believe the *ci* will be heavier, will easily be broken, and it could lose in a race. Moreover, if women use a new *ci* especially the *jicap ci* (feast *ci*), most probably the spirit of the *ci* will go away. Consequently, the *ci* loses its power. With these, the *ci* is a proof and focal point to understand gender power relations through the three dimensions of Asmat lives as shown by the conceptual framework (see fig.16).

The interpretation and attitude toward the *ci* change through time. That is why, at the base of fig.16, there is an arrow to show the movement and change through time. Changes in the *ci* will influence other things around, including social, economic, supernatural, and gender power relations.

2

The *ci*
A significant key to understand Asmat

Choosing an object or an event to focus a study is one possible approach to examine the way of life of a selected group. Examples of this are the *kula* in Trobriand Islands (Malinowski 1922), cattle in the Nuer life (Evans-Pritchard 1968[1940]), headhunting practices of the Asmat (Zegwaard 1959), circumcision in Ndembu society (Turner 1967), Balinese cockfight (Geertz 1973), and betel bag in Sumba (Hoskins 1998). From a very specific topic, a researcher is able to unearth the values of a selected group because social realities are lived in a *web of significance* (Weber). A selected object can be a significant key to investigate the way of life of a certain community.

Geertz (1973) saw that cockfights are a part of the Balinese way of life. Cockfight is an important element to understand the everyday life of the Balinese. It is an arena to express Balinese feelings, emotions, desires, and even its kinship system. Indeed, a man will never bet against a cock owned by a member of his own kingroup (p.437). It means even in playing, one must take a position to support the cock from his kingroup. Thus, cockfight can be an indicator to see the social structure of Bali, including gender relations because the cockfight is entirely of, by, and for men (p.418). Moreover, Geertz urged, "In the cockfight, man and beast, good and evil, ego and id, the creative power of aroused masculinity and the destructive power of loosened animality fuse in a bloody drama of hatred, cruelty, violence, and death" (p.20-21).

In Kodi society of Sumba Indonesia, Hoskins (1998) used their betel bag as an entrance to discover their culture. She said, "The betel bag can be interpreted as perhaps the pre-eminent 'biographical object' in Kodi society because it represents the identity of its owner, both in a private context and on a ritual stage" (p. 56). Moreover, the betel bag is a kind of alter ego, a metaphor of someone's self. That is why to refuse betel is to refuse all social courtesy, to retreat into a world of the self alone. To give it, is to open and give oneself, to share knowledge and goodwill. In other words, the betel bag can be an instrument to understand someone's personality. Hoskins emphasized that in Kodi society, a man is not himself without his betel bag. He loses his identity if the betel bag is lost. And if his kin chooses to bury the betel bag that bears his name, he will also feel buried. So, betel bag for Kodi society is a personal object that bears social meaning. This notion can be compared to Strathern (1993) who said, "What people wear, and what they do with and to their bodies in general, forms an important part of the flow of information – establishing, modifying, and commenting on major social categories, such as age, sex, and status, which are also defined in speech and in actions."

In the light of the observations of previous researchers especially Geerzt and Hoskins, I chose the *ci* to examine the Asmat culture, particularly the gender power relations among them. The *ci* becomes a significant key to uncover the uninvestigated and undocumented aspects of Asmat life because the *ci* is very vital to them, just like the betel bag for the Kodi society, Kula for Trobriand islanders, and the cockfight for the Balinese. In a similar manner, the *ci* makes us understand the gender power relations among the Asmat because the *ci* is not only a personal object, but social equipment as well. According to Hilary M. Lips, gender refers to non-physiological aspects of being female or male – the cultural expectations for femininity and masculinity (2005:5; see Bartfield 1997:217).

2.1 Select literature on the Asmat

Basic and early information about Asmat comes from Fr. Gerard A. Zegwaard's (1953, 1959) account. Zegwaard, a Dutch missionary of the Sacred Heard (MSC), founded the first permanent settlement in Asmat in 1953 when he said, "I was the first white man to take up residence among them and there was no representative of the Dutch Colonial Administration to enforce the ordinances against headhunting that were carried out elsewhere" (1959:1020).

In his article *Headhunting Practices of the Asmat of Netherlands New Guine*, Zegwaard (1959) provided valuable background on the 'archic' society (see Mauss 1967) of Asmat. According to him, cannibalism is not the objective of the headhunting, but only a subsidiary part. Actually, the motivation for headhunting (see Trenkenshuh 1970, 1978) is complex and rather confusing. Zegwaard emphasized at least four factors of headhunting practices: (1) the cosmology of the Asmat; (2) the economic demand, sago-gathering and its cult; (3) fear of the spirits, expressed in the ritual of expelling the spirits as a characteristic feature of both large and small festivities; and (4) the need for prestige on the part of the male population, the desire for fame and the urge to impress the women of the village. Regarding prestige, Zegwaard said, "In Asmat society all prestige, and therefore all authority, is ultimately derived from achievements in war. It is impossible to be a man of social standing without having captured a few heads. A bunch of skulls at the door post is a measure of status" (1959:1040). In other words, headhunting is part of how to be a "real" man in Asmat, aside from retaliation for the murder of a relative.

Tobias Schneebaum provided more information about the everyday life of Asmat especially related to their arts and rituals. According to him, most of the Asmat arts and rituals are connected to their ancestors. For example, woodcarvings and headhunting activities are part of the Asmat ceremonial life to honor the dead. Specifically he said, "Carvings connect the life of this world with the world of the spirits. They are the medium through which the Asmat remain in contact with their ancestors. Since death, except in the cases of the death of small babies and old people, comes about only through magic or through the direct intervention of an enemy with physical weapons, all death must be avenged" (1985:40, see Fleischhacker 1991:4). The spirit of the dead will not rest in peace until vengeance has taken place. That is why warfare and headhunting are the ways to satisfy and to honor the spirit of the dead.

Although Schneebaum did not speak much about the *ci* directly, he explained how the *ci* and its paddle cannot be excluded from the Asmat life, especially from festive activities. In a way, people can categorize the *ci* and paddles as objects of Asmat art like shields and spears. Those objects relate the Asmat people to their ancestors; they are media to pay their respects to the spirits by carving objects. In other words, the *ci* mobilizes the Asmat to fulfill their responsibilities, both for the living and for the dead, including headhunting practices. According to Schneebaum, the prowheads of war *cis* are carved in great detail with ancestor figures and headhunting symbols that give the *ci* and the men in it the protection and prowess of those represented.

Specifically, in his book *Where the Spirits Dwell: An Odyssey in the New Guinea Jungle* (1988), Schneebaum shared his engagement and direct experiences with the Asmat. He provides a lot of information about Asmat in the 1970s. He seemed very innocent and honest in narrating evidence and events. For example, he wrote in the very first paragraph, "They had been so silent in their approach that we had not heard their footsteps. They looked wild and barbaric with their crocheted hair standing out in all directions, the black orbs of their eyes intense, fierce, full of bewilderment and wonder" (1988:1). Another example, he wrote, "It was only after the ceremony that I learned that being adopted meant giving gifts to my family" (1988:29). Schneebaum provided his readers the original feelings he had experienced among the Asmat. Therefore, his account is very valuable, not only in terms of feelings about the Asmat decades ago, but also to learn from him how to be an ethnographer.

Furthermore, Schneebaum in this book provided a brief experience with the missionaries in the field and also the explanation about homosexuality among the Asmat. In conjunction with homosexuality he said, "It was in Asmat, however, that I felt for the first time part of a universal clan, for Asmat culture in some regions not only allowed for sexual relationship between men but demanded that no male be without his male companion, no matter how many wives he had or how many women he might be sleeping with" (1988:43). Above all, related to gender, Schneebaum noted, "Of course, the girls almost never come to school. They have responsibilities to do fishing, chopping firewood, pounding sago, and helping with the youngest members of the family" (1988:65; see Tsing 1993:184).

To go deeper, the book of co-editors: Ursula Konrad, Alphonse Sowada, and Gunter Konrad's (2002; see also 1981, 1996) *Asmat: Perceiving Life in Art* is a model of understanding Asmat and its development through art, particularly woodcarvings. This book brings readers, not only to imagine the past, but also to experience the present and to anticipate the future of Asmat life. Through art, writers show that Asmat is now experiencing changes in many aspects. For instance, they show readers the development of woodcarving designs from the very simple to the very complex, from natural images such as animal motives to modern creations such as plates and chalices. This book is like a life story and life history of the Asmat through art. According to Gunter Konrad, through art, the Asmat people contribute to understanding the mystery of human existence that seems without end. The Asmat preserve their identity through art. It also means, the Asmat people articulate their identity through art (carvings). Therefore, woodcarving is a proper clue to understand the Asmat.

Additionally, Konrad et al. described the story and history of the Asmat art in this book not only in words, but also in many valuable and beautiful images. This book helps me to see Asmat through the *ci*. The *ci* is a center of discussion to understand the Asmat, just like Asmat art, especially woodcarving. Honestly, this book motivated me to pursue the *ci* as focus of my study because it proves that an angle of human life can be used to identify the whole thing. Identity of the Asmat can be seen through their carvings. In the same way, the Asmat identity can be unpacked also through the *ci*.

Asmat development cannot be separated from the "mission touch" (*Asmat Drums* 1980, 1981, 1982, 1983, 1984, 1985). That is why, the Hontheim's (2010) article *"Healing Despite*

Christianity; Struggles Between Missionary and Traditional Conceptions of Medicine" is very useful. Through this article, Hontheim showed that religion is an agent of change in Asmat. She investigated the different approaches between the Catholic and the Protestant missionaries to 'Christianize' the Asmat.

After providing the historical overview about the two religions, Hontheim looked at their methodology. Catholics use the word 'inculturation' to inseminate the Gospel. According to her, in order to 'inculturate' the Asmat society, the Crosier (a common name to designate the Order of the Holy Cross) added some elements of Asmat culture to Christian worship, with the long term intention of founding the "Asmat Church" complete with decorated churches and Christian ceremonies using adornments from Asmat everyday life (2010:134). Meanwhile, the Protestants also developed a similar concept with inculturation, named 'contextualization.' The aim of contextualization is to encourage target populations to adopt Christianity. The protestant missionaries criticize inculturation because it leads to syncretism. For Protestants, promoting syncretism is a form of heresy because its presence in Asmat society shows that satan is still operating within it.

Above all, Hontheim said, "Protestant missionaries dedicate themselves to medicine and Catholic to census, baptism and schools, which the Protestants view as less significant." As conclusion, though the Catholics and the Protestants use different in methods to 'Christianize' the Asmat, they are both agents of change in Asmat society.

The Asmat economy has been shifting from barter (local economy) to market based economy (see Daeli 2011:3; Muller 2009:126). According to Patrick Heady (2005:262), "Barter typically denotes the direct exchange of goods or services for each other without the medium of money." Like many other societies in the world, the present Asmat use money to exchange goods or services. In other words, instead of using the substantivism meaning of economics, they now use formalism, that is, market-based economy. According to Karl Polanyi, "The substantive meaning of economics was derived from man's dependence for his living upon nature and his fellows. It refers to the interchange with his natural and social environment, in so far as this results in supplying him with the means of material want satisfaction" (see Isaac 2005:15; see also Elardo 2010:417). Meanwhile, the formal meaning is derived from logic, the substantive meaning from fact. The formal meaning implies a set of rules referring to choice between the alternative uses of insufficient means (see Isaac 2005:15). Actually, the substantive meaning of economics truly happens in Asmat because their daily economy depends on gathering, hunting, and fishing that nature has abundantly provided. However, the market system and modernity that center on money have changed Asmat in many aspects.

Compared to Mahatao community as reported by Maria F. Mangahas (2001), the Asmat tend to abandon their substantive meaning of economic derives from man's dependence for his living upon nature, whereas the Mahatao community shares willingly their production to prolong their lives. According to Mangahas,

> "When there was a food crisis in Batanes because the NFA (National Food Authority) did not have enough supplies (of rice) we were not affected here in Mahatao because many had planted sweet potato, uvi, and rice. Those from other municipalities were coming to Mahatao to ask for food. And we didn't sell food to them but only give it away. So we never experienced hunger in Mahatao" (p.54).

The Mahatao community has a strategy to prolong their lives when there is a food crisis in their region. The Asmat should learn from them how to preserve their natural and cultural properties.

2.2 The *ci*: the Asmat canoe

One of the specific objectives of this study is to investigate the social life of the *ci*, particularly in the context of gender among the Asmat. That is why the *ci* is the focus of discussion for this study. The *ci* as material culture relates people in a community culturally as well as connects places socially. According to Arnold Ap and Johsz Mansoben in their article *Building of An Asmat Perahu* (in Walker 1974), the Asmat people could not live without the *ci*. During its life span, a *ci* relates and unites many people involved in many aspects of the *ci*, since it was a *ci* tree until it decayed. The *ci* has the capacity to relate and to transport commodities to be exchanged within and between communities. Moreover, the *ci* itself can be used as a commodity that can be exchanged with other commodities.

Arjun Appadurai (1986) in *The Social Life of Things: Commodities in Cultural Perspective*, proposed a new perspective on the circulation of commodities in society Just like persons, commodities have social lives. Commodities have their own values. Value is embodied in commodities that are exchanged. However, value is never an inherent property of objects, but it is a judgment made about them by subjects. That is why the value of commodities always relates to the desire and demand as well as to the knowledge of subjects who use or exchange them. Similarly, the *ci* is never separated from the people who produce, ritualize, and use it as a valuable object.

In Asmat, the *ci* is owned by a family or a clan. Unlike in Trobriand Islands, as explained by Malinowski (1922) in his book *Argonauts of the Western Pacific*, the owner of the canoe is the chief or the headman of a village or a smaller sub-division (Mead 1969). However, the canoe can be, and often is, hired out from a headman (p.119). It means, canoe ownership in Trobriand Islands is very limited.

The Trobriand Islanders have three types of canoe: (1) *kewo'u* – requires small, light, and handy canoes for coastal transportation; (2) *kalipoulo* – bigger and more seaworthy canoes for fishing; and (3) *masawa* – for deep sea sailing, the biggest type is needed, with a considerable carrying capacity, greater displacement, and stronger construction (p.112).

It is very interesting that the Trobriand's canoes create the sociological differentiation of functions among the members of society- the owner of the canoes, the expert, and the workers. This helps us to understand the social life of the canoe. Moreover, the canoe in Trobriand Islands is never separated from magic and ritual. Magic puts order and sequence into various activities. Magic and related ceremonials are instrumental in securing the co-operation of the community and the organization of communal labor. The *ci* of the Asmat is always related to such rituals also. The *ci* is a representation of the ancestral spirit (Fleischhacker 1991). The spirits are not angry spirits, but beneficent deities of a beneficent natural world (see Lunskow 2008:248).

The *ci* for the Asmat is a dominant symbol (Turner 1967) for gender power relations. The *ci* shows many distinctions between men and women, both symbolically and practically. According to Turner, symbol means "the smallest unit of ritual which still retains the specific properties of ritual behavior; it is the ultimate unit of specific structure in a ritual context" (p.19). Symbol is not merely a sign but a blaze or a landmark, something that connects the unknown with the known. It can be objects, activities, events, gestures, and spatial units. An example of this is 'the milk tree' in Ndembu society. It has different symbolisms. First, it is the 'senior' tree of ritual. Second, it stands for human breast milk and also the breasts that supply it. Third, the women describe it as 'the tree of a mother and her child' (p.20-21). Additionally, the milk tree represents harmonious, benevolent aspects of domestic and tribal life (p.22).

Social structures, rules, and other systems are very important in any community. Every social group or every community has its own way to maintain its social life. In the Ndembu society, an uncircumcised person remains a child and eats alone with women. No women would have sexual relations with him (p.152). So, to be an adult man of Ndembu, a boy must follow the traditional law, especially the liminal period in which the novices are reborn as men after a symbolic death. During this period the novices are secluded and finally emerge with new adult names. A circumcised man is "white" or "pure." What was hidden (and unclean) is now visible (p.154). That's why circumcision is a *sine qua non* to be a good man in Ndembu society. In addition, an uncircumcised man is permanently polluting just like a menstruating woman. However, a woman "pollutes" only during her period (p.154). This notion tells us about the power of community over an individual. Therefore, "a normal man acts abnormally because he is obedient to tribal tradition, not of disobedience to it. He does not evade but fulfills his duties as a citizen" (p.100). So, the voice of a community determines the status of an individual. A man cannot declare himself as a good or "real" man without community endorsement. He is a good man or a good member of the community if he follows the traditional laws.

Turner proposed three levels of meaning of what he called a symbol: (1) the level of indigenous interpretation or the exegetical meaning; (2) the operational meaning; (3) the positional meaning (p.50). The exegetical meaning is obtained from questioning indigenous informants about observed ritual behavior. The operational meaning comes from observing what the people do with the symbol, and not only what they say about it. The positional meaning of a symbol is derived from its relationship to other symbols in a totality.

Just like the Ndembu society, the Asmat also have a lot of symbols. In this study, the *ci* is the dominant symbol of the Asmat society. The three levels of meaning of the symbol as Turner described can be a good approach to identify such symbols in the everyday life of the Asmat, especially pertaining to the *ci*.

2.3 Gender power relations

Through his book, *The making of Great Man: Male Domination and Power among the New Guinea Baruya*, Godelier (1992) showed the inequality in Baruya society. He said that there are two types of inequalities in the social life of Baruya: a) the inequalities between men and women, and b) inequalities among men themselves. Sexuality plays a strong role among Baruya men both in their thoughts and theories. It is the foundation for women's subordinate position and even for the oppression of women (see p. xi). They interpret the anatomical and physiological differences between men and women as justification for inequalities. According to Godelier, women's tasks: (a) require less physical strength, (b) involve fewer risks of accidents, and (c) require less mutual help or cooperation among individuals (p.14). By defining women's tasks, the author highlighted that men's tasks require more physical strength and capability. In other words, men are stronger than women. The men are really powerful in the Baruya society. Women are excluded from land ownership, the manufacture and control of tools, or the material means of production. Baruya women are materially, politically, and symbolically subordinate to men. The only sphere in which superiority might have been possible is shamanism, in which the two sexes cooperate and compete in a common activity that is useful to society as a whole.

The situation in the Asmat society is quite similar to Baruya. In some respects, they share the same interpretations as Baruya's men about the anatomical and physiological differences between men and women (see Fleischhacker 1991:9). They use this to justify their power over women. I see the link between Baruya and Asmat society for they are all Melanesians.

According to Lutkehaus and Roscoe (1995) in *Gender Rituals: Female Initiation in Melanesia*, in many societies, especially in Melanesia, physiological maturity is not enough to state that a person is mature, but he/she needs to undergo a ritual in order to be a "real" man or woman. That is why the initiation ritual (see Gennep, 1960; Turner, 1969; Pandian 1991; Child and Child 1993) is relevant. The initiation ritual is a mark of an individual's transition from adolescence to adulthood. The purpose of the female ritual is to formally acknowledge that the initiates have come into a completely new social stage. Moreover, the essays in this volume suggest that there is a further dimension on the emphasis of the body in initiation ceremonies, one that is related more specifically to cultural notions of sexuality, beauty, and power that many Papua New Guinea cultures associate with male and female initiation (p.18). This book contributes information about female initiation rituals in Papua New Guinea to balance male initiation rituals elsewhere. I did not find any female initiation ritual among the Asmat. The female initiation ritual contains meanings and messages: such as the girl is taught not to be ashamed of her body and its incipient sexuality, but to value it and the power it affords her (p.13). The initiation ritual highlights the power of the community over the individual.

Furthermore, sexuality is an integral part of human lives. Based on this notion, Thomas Gregor (1985) in *Anxious Pleasure: The Sexual Lives of an Amazonian People* stressed that sexuality is very vital in human lives and can be an instrument to identify the personality of people in a particular community. In this book, the author introduced the Mehinaku society through their sexuality.

Gregor said that for Mehinaku, sex is an organizing metaphor for the villagers that structures their understanding of the cosmos and the world of men and spirits. A description of Mehinaku sexuality is also an account of their culture. One of the purposes of this book, according to its author is, to explain who the Mehinaku are by examining their sexual nature.

According to Mehinaku men, sex in their society determines the use of public space, the organization of religion, and the politics of village life. The system is maintained by the threat of phallic aggression. Sex is an overwhelming basis for relationships that permeates and deflects virtually every other social bond. Living in this "genderized" society, the Mehinaku villagers are conscious of sex as a fascinating human activity. Mehinaku culture, in many ways like our own, is an eroticized culture. One of the interesting sayings is "Good fish gets dull but sex is always fun."

It is very interesting to me that the author said that within the community, affairs may consolidate relationships between persons of different kindreds. Not only must a man find most of his mistresses among distantly related kinswomen, but he may be obligated to recognize children born of the relationships as his own. Additionally he says, the culture of sexual liaisons makes the village an exciting and interesting place. Mehinaku men and women enjoy an organic and complex relationship. For Mehinaku, sex is cohesion in community.

The perspective of the Mehinaku about sex is very different with my experience in Asmat Papua, Indonesia. As far as I have observed, most of the daily conflicts in Asmat community are caused by sexual behavior. Conflicts in Asmat, either in family or in society, mostly come from husbands' and wives' jealousies. In addition, an affair of husband or wife triggers raises conflicts among the Asmat. Therefore, instead of enhancing community stability, sex becomes a conflictual issue to the Asmat community. That is why, I was so surprised when I read that affairs may consolidate relationships between persons in different kindreds in Mehinaku. I did not find this in the Asmat society.

According to the author, the Mehinaku believe that sexual wishes and contacts with women may lead to failure in work, weakness, stunted growth, sickness, and death (p.202). I think that the Mehinaku men could easily have more than one sex partner and could easily have other sexual relationships. In fact, it is not easy for Mehinaku men to express their sexual desires because of their belief system, even though they are practically capable to do so. The point here is that the belief system or the moral system in the community has such a great impact on the activities of its members, including sexual behavior. Simply put, the Mehinaku sexuality is an "energy" or spirit to maintain their lives in the community. However, according to Gregor, becoming a Mehinaku man is a painful process fraught with tension and insecurity. On the one hand, sexuality makes them more alive; on the other hand, it makes them anxious and insecure.

Thomas Gregor spoke about the Mehinaku based on their sexuality. He introduced this community by investigating their perspectives and their experiences about sex. In another part of the world, Janet Hoskins (1998) through her *Biographical Objects: How Things Tell the Stories of People's Life* introduces the Kodi society of Sumba by examining their betel bag. According to her, betel bag represents the identity of its owner from both a private context and on a ritual stage.

Hoskins emphasized how the objects tell about people because she believed that people and the things they value are so complicatedly intertwined that they cannot be disentangled (p.2). Aside from this, Hoskins also pointed out about gender and duality. According to her, gender dualism is not necessarily a vision of gender equality, but it does highlight interdependence, complementarity, and what can be called an image of sexual union – the bringing together of male and female in an act of pleasure, release and potential production. For Kodi, objects are not just simple icons of maleness or femaleness but as representations of an urge to bring the two together. For example, the splinter or the drum is an idealized companion of the opposite sex; the betel bag and the snake skin shroud are both containers of an ancestral heritage that are crafted by women but serve as vehicles for male identity. Therefore, the idea of androgyny here is very important. Both men and women in Kodi society believe that their lives are incomplete without a counterpart. Double genderedness is not "made incomplete" but instead, made powerful by their union.

Although Kodi society believes in double gender, however, it is interesting to see more closely Hoskins' reflection when she said, "The identification of women and domestic animals in Ra Mete's story shows that women also feel they have "lost their voices" and been relegated to an inferior status" (p.81). She added, "... In telling me these stories, these women showed me their identification with possessions and used it to subvert masculinist privilege and express a dissenting viewpoint."

Jan Pouwer (2010), the author of *Gender, Ritual and Social Formation in West Papua* led us to see the lowland tribes of Papua and their cultures (see Muller 2011, Muller and

Omabak 2008)[2]. Particularly, Power compares the Kamoro and the Asmat tribes based on gender, ritual, and social formation as stated in the title of his book. In his conclusion, Pouwer said, "Similar yet different is a current phrase in my comparison of Kamoro and Asmat" (p.231). According to him, the Kamoro and the Asmat share as their habitat a vast, marshy coastal plain that widens, going from a small coastal zone and hinterland in the far northwest to a broad zone several hundred kilometers wide in the far southeast. Moreover, he emphasized that the same ecological situation, which crosscuts ethnic boundaries, may be considered common to the Kamoro and Asmat social formations. As a consequence, competition for sago and fishing areas has resulted in more conflicts and warfare than in the smaller settlements in inland and coastal areas.

The similarity of Kamoro and Asmat can be seen not only through environmental and ecological dimensions, but also through rituals. Kamoro and Asmat cosmology is by and large similar. For them, human lives in a world in-between the upper and the lower worlds; good and bad, are complementary. The example of Kamoro and Asmat similarity in rituals is *Ema Kame* in Kamoro and *Emak Cem* in Asmat. Based on this book, *Ema Kame/Emak Cem* celebrates and promotes fertility and growth, and is therefore classified as female, and as the source of physical reproduction. Both the Kamoro and the Asmat have spirit poles varying in size, to keep up with the relative importance of the honored persons; *Mbitoro* in Kamoro and *Mbis* in Asmat.

However, though Kamoro and Asmat are similar in some respects in many rituals, yet the rituals differ in orientation. For instance, Kamoro *Ema Kame* expresses a female-centered and matri-centered orientation. Meanwhile, the center of the Asmat *Emak Cem* is the spirit canoe. For the Asmat, canoes together with war shields are important components of their cultural complex of warfare, their male-centered orientation. That is why the *Mbis* ritual in Asmat is considered as the "male" coastal counterpart of "female" inland *Emak Cem*. Both rituals are commemoration of the dead which reflects ancestry. As a comparison to the Kamoro, the author said,

> "The 'female' side of the Kamoro initiation of young males as performed in *Ema Kame* is similar to the Asmat one, but more elaborate. It marks their passage to the social life of adults in terms of kinship, marriage and (matri)filiation in the same way. However, the 'male' aspect of initiation as apparent in nose piercing during *Mirimu Kame* differs from the Asmat one. It is connected not with warfare but rather with fertility and growth, with cosmology and its manipulation" (p.239).

Most of all, though Kamoro and Asmat are similar in some respects in many rituals, in Kamoro, headhunting has no place which is strongly practiced in Asmat. In Asmat headhunting is part of their rituals.

Another example of the differences between the Kamoro and the Asmat ritual, is the Asmat ritual of initiation of a new men's house (*jeu*) which is the promotion of communal strength and solidarity, explicitly including the relations between the sexes. *Jeu* is similar to *aa* (longhouse) of Kaluli society (Schieffelin, 1976) of Papua New Guinea. Kaware in Kamoro marks not the solidarity but the opposition between the sexes. Kamoro women have a higher status and a more powerful position than their Asmat counterparts.

---

[2]   It can be compared to the highlands of Papua (see Muller and Yunus Omabak 2008 and Muller 2009).

Asmat has *papis* (Konrad, 1975) – ritual-ceremonial wife-swapping in situations of socio-political or cosmological danger. This is not practiced by the Kamoro. *Papis* is not only for counteracting cosmological danger, but it is also used as a strategy for enlisting the support of or remunerating allies (p.234).

Lastly, Sherry B. Ortner (1996) argued that gender (see Eva 1985, Todd and Fisher 1988; Elliot 1996, Nicholson, 1998; Sorensen, 2000; Lips, 2005; Eller, 2009;) is a social construction which is always entangled with power and agency. To describe her view, she proposed a model of practice that embodies agency called "serious game." Clearly she said,

> "The idea of the 'game' is meant to capture simultaneously the following dimension: that social life is culturally organized and constructed, in terms of defining categories of actors, rules and goals of the games, and so forth; that the social life is precisely social, consisting of webs of relationship and interaction between multiple, shiftingly interrelated subject positions, none of which can be extracted as autonomous 'agents'; and yet at the same time there is 'agency,' that is, actors play with skill, intention, wit, knowledge, intelligence. The idea that the game is 'serious' is meant to add into the equation the idea that power and equality pervade the games of life in multiple ways, and that, while there may be playfulness and pleasure in the process, the stakes of these games are often very high" (p.12).

In short, gender as well as other aspects of social life is always culturally and politically constructed, which largely embodies a male point of view. So, according to Ortner, the problem in viewing gender is a tendency to see women identified with male games, or as pawns in male games, or as otherwise not autonomous (p.16). The concept of gender in the everyday life of the Asmat is also based on male games because they are basically patriarchal (Eilberg-Schwartz 1996).

3

The Asmat
A never ending surprise

"So what could have been an Eden became a place of war – a place of fear. They were trapped by their own dependence on the system they knew as the only system. Their food and their prestige (for individual and for village) depended on headhunting. Even their 'religion' was preoccupied with it. Their unique and complex art was determined by themes dictated by headhunting. They were a tall and handsome people, but no one was ever far from fear or danger. They were not a happy people" (Frank Trenkenshuh, OSC, 1970:10).

To appreciate the ci, one should have an understanding of the environment and the setting in which the maker and the user of the ci lived. As a response to this issue, I briefly introduce Asmat based on my own data and documented literature. It is necessary to provide an overview about Asmat because I agree with Boas (1955:4) who said, "Each culture can be understood only as an historical growth determined by the social and geographical environment in which each people is placed and by the way in which it develops the cultural material that comes into its possession from the outside or through its own creativeness."

The word "Asmat" is quite strange and weird for many people whom I have met. Many friends were surprised when they knew that I was in Asmat and I still survive. I think the reason many people feel strange with the "Asmat" is the news that spread about the Asmat is about its notorious past, like headhunting practices, warfare, and cannibalism. I had the same impression before I stepped on Asmat ground and breathed with its air in 2002. In fact, the Asmat opened my eyes and my mind to honor their natural and cultural richness, as well as to enjoy their hospitality and friendship. It was a tremendous experience to be with them for a period of time (Daeli 2011:1). Perhaps, Schneebaum (1988:32) felt the same excitement that I had when he said, "Everything intrigued me. In fact, I was so overcome by the carvings and the people that I decided to find a way to return." His statement implies that people will not look for a way back to Asmat if they have a horrific experience during their stay. I hope, this brief description could provide a short introduction to the Asmat.

3.1 Asmat: a pregnant swamp of natural resources

Trenkenshuh (1970) described the Asmat region as an Eden where the Lord God made various trees grow that were delightful and good for food, with the tree of life in the middle of the garden and the tree of the knowledge of good and bad (see Gn. 2:8-9). It is

Figure 17. Asmat children catch fish and shrimp using the traditional fish net.

Figure 18. High tide in Agats city. (Photograph courtesy of Fr. Innocentius Rettobjaan).

true that food is always abundant in Asmat. The Asmat people will not get hungry because their area provides a rich store of foods if they want to gather them, from both rivers and forests. From rivers, they can get various kinds of seafood such as fish, shrimps, crabs, mussels, snails, and even crocodiles. From forests, they can get birds of countless varieties, lizards (*biawak*), cuscus, and wild boars, aside from sago their staple and its grubs collected from decaying stumps of sago palms (Schneebaum 1985:25). More detailed information about the richness of Asmat is provided by Klaus Helfrich,

"This swampy habitat flooded with brackish water is the home of an extraordinarily diverse fauna capable of serving human needs in a variety of ways. The abundance of crabs, shrimps, crustaceans, numerous species of fish, including swordfish, sharks, dolphins, catfish and many others, as well as crocodiles, water snakes, turtles and different types of birds provide a surplus of protein-rich foods and materials needed for the production of tools, household utensils and jewelry. . . . Of greater interest to the human population is the increasing variety of huntable game available. Crocodiles, lizards, snakes, freshwater turtles, wild boars, flying foxes, numerous marsupials, as well as cassowaries and many other kinds of birds, including swamp hens, pigeons, cockatoos, parrots and birds of paradise provide food and often supply materials eagerly sought for the manufacture of tools and jewelry. Of major significance with respect to the fulfillment of basic needs, and thus of essential importance to the Asmat, is the great abundance of sago palm within the otherwise highly diverse regional vegetation" (in Konrad (eds.) 1996:37).

Unlike other places in Indonesia, the Asmat need not grow food themselves nor plant sago before producing it for daily food. The same thing also applies to getting seafood from the water because the water already provides fish, shrimps, and crabs abundantly. They can get these by using fishing net, or fishing-hook, or simply by going down to the river and catching the fish with their hands (see fig.17). It is a simple way to make them rich of food materials. They are a society of hunters, gatherers, and fishers. However, nowadays non-Asmat teach them how to be an agricultural society.

The Asmat region is located in the middle of a huge tidal swampy land. It is surrounded by countless large and small rivers and jungles (cf. Kunst 1977:19). In his description, Pouwer (2010:103) wrote, "The Kamoro, Sempan, and Asmat share a vast, flat, marshy coastal plain and adjacent hinterland, densely covered with mangrove trees, tidal forests and rain forests, intersected by numerous rivers, creeks, and connecting shallow waterways." Clearly, Asmat is located at the lowland and coastal area, without hills, mountains, and stones. Wood, especially ironwood, is used in almost every kind of building, including bridges (*jembatan*) to connect one place to another; one building to another either in a another. However, for Trenkenshuh (1970:9) the rivers make transportation easier. The huge jungle is rich with different kinds of trees that can be used for many purposes, including *cis* for transport. Their houses are built on poles to keep them above the tidal flooding and to provide natural air conditioning, both *jeu* (the traditional and communal house for men) and the domestic houses (see Trenkenshuh 1970:10). The interval between high tide and low tide can reach five meters (Smidt 1999:15; see fig.18)[3]. Therefore, to make any building safe from tidal flooding, it must be built on poles at least five meters above sea level.

The Asmat have a great indigenous knowledge so that they can interpret natural phenomena, including the dynamics of high and low tides. For example, by observing the surface (the top part) of the water the Asmat can predict the water levels for next two weeks or even a month. However, it is very difficult for non-Asmat and missionaries to predict water levels. That is why it is necessary for non-Asmat to get both a date calendar and a water calendar to plan for activities in the future. The water calendar (see fig.19) which is made by the Indonesian navy helps them to identify the water level on the date

---

3   Tides, according to Fr. Virgil Petermeier, OSC, an American missionary in Asmat for 36 years, can reach up to 6 meters in height.

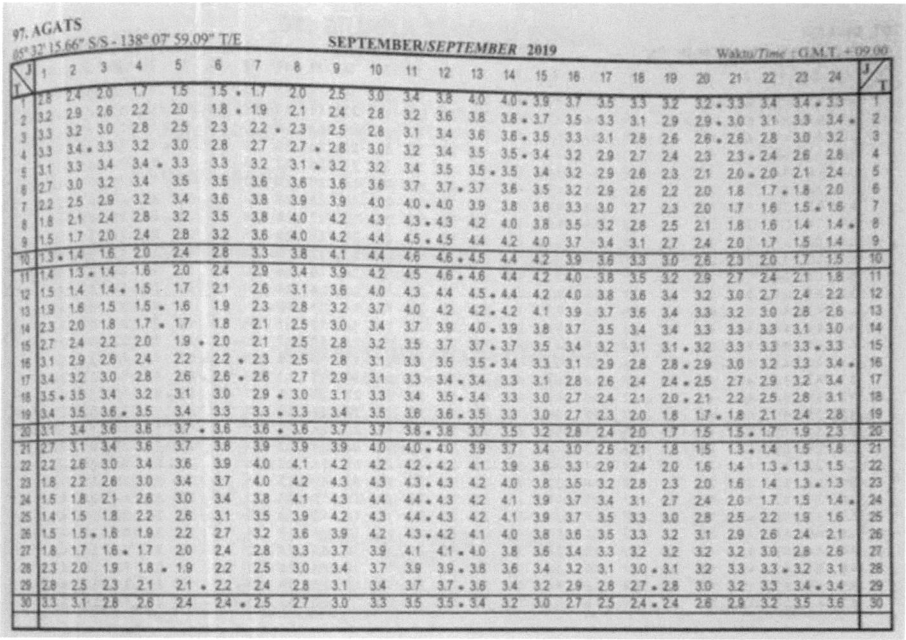
97. AGATS
05° 32' 15.66" S/S - 138° 07' 59.09" T/E
SEPTEMBER/*SEPTEMBER* 2019
Waktu/*Time* : G.M.T. +09.00

T \ J	1	2	3	4	5	6	7	8	9	10	11	12	13	14	15	16	17	18	19	20	21	22	23	24	J / T
1	2.8	2.4	2.0	1.7	1.5	1.5 •	1.7	2.0	2.5	3.0	3.4	3.8	4.0	4.0 •	3.9	3.7	3.5	3.3	3.2	3.2 •	3.3	3.4	3.4 •	3.3	1
2	3.2	2.9	2.6	2.2	2.0	1.8 •	1.9	2.1	2.4	2.8	3.2	3.6	3.8	3.8 •	3.7	3.5	3.3	3.1	2.9	2.9 •	3.0	3.1	3.3	3.4 •	2
3	3.3	3.2	3.0	2.8	2.5	2.3	2.2 •	2.3	2.5	2.8	3.1	3.4	3.6	3.6 •	3.5	3.3	3.1	2.8	2.6	2.6 •	2.6	2.8	3.0	3.2	3
4	3.3	3.4 •	3.3	3.2	3.0	2.8	2.7	2.7 •	2.8	3.0	3.2	3.4	3.5	3.5 •	3.4	3.2	2.9	2.7	2.4	2.3	2.3 •	2.4	2.6	2.8	4
5	3.1	3.3	3.4	3.4 •	3.3	3.3	3.2	3.1 •	3.2	3.2	3.4	3.5	3.5 •	3.5	3.4	3.2	2.9	2.6	2.3	2.1	2.0 •	2.0	2.1	2.4	5
6	2.7	3.0	3.2	3.4	3.5	3.5	3.6	3.6	3.6	3.6	3.7	3.7 •	3.7	3.6	3.5	3.2	2.9	2.6	2.2	2.0	1.8	1.7 •	1.8	2.0	6
7	2.2	2.5	2.9	3.2	3.4	3.6	3.8	3.9	3.9	4.0	4.0 •	4.0	3.9	3.8	3.6	3.3	3.0	2.7	2.3	2.0	1.7	1.6	1.5 •	1.6	7
8	1.8	2.1	2.4	2.8	3.2	3.5	3.8	4.0	4.2	4.3	4.3 •	4.3	4.2	4.0	3.8	3.5	3.2	2.8	2.5	2.1	1.8	1.6	1.4	1.4 •	8
9	1.5	1.7	2.0	2.4	2.8	3.2	3.6	4.0	4.2	4.4	4.5 •	4.5	4.4	4.2	4.0	3.7	3.4	3.1	2.7	2.4	2.0	1.7	1.5	1.4	9
10	1.3 •	1.4	1.6	2.0	2.4	2.8	3.3	3.8	4.1	4.4	4.6	4.6 •	4.5	4.4	4.2	3.9	3.6	3.3	3.0	2.6	2.3	2.0	1.7	1.5	10
11	1.4	1.3 •	1.4	1.6	2.0	2.4	2.9	3.4	3.9	4.2	4.5	4.6 •	4.6	4.4	4.2	4.0	3.8	3.5	3.2	2.9	2.7	2.4	2.1	1.8	11
12	1.5	1.4	1.4 •	1.5	1.7	2.1	2.6	3.1	3.6	4.0	4.3	4.4	4.5 •	4.4	4.2	4.0	3.8	3.6	3.4	3.2	3.0	2.7	2.4	2.2	12
13	1.9	1.6	1.5	1.5 •	1.6	1.9	2.3	2.8	3.2	3.7	4.0	4.2	4.2 •	4.2	4.1	3.9	3.7	3.6	3.4	3.3	3.2	3.0	2.8	2.6	13
14	2.3	2.0	1.8	1.7 •	1.7	1.8	2.1	2.5	3.0	3.4	3.7	3.9	4.0 •	3.9	3.8	3.7	3.5	3.4	3.4	3.3	3.3	3.3	3.1	3.0	14
15	2.7	2.4	2.2	2.0	1.9 •	2.0	2.1	2.5	2.8	3.2	3.5	3.7	3.7 •	3.7	3.5	3.4	3.2	3.1	3.1 •	3.2	3.3	3.3	3.3 •	3.3	15
16	3.1	2.9	2.6	2.4	2.2	2.2 •	2.3	2.5	2.8	3.1	3.3	3.5	3.5 •	3.4	3.3	3.1	2.9	2.8	2.8 •	2.9	3.0	3.2	3.3	3.4 •	16
17	3.4	3.2	3.0	2.8	2.6	2.6 •	2.6	2.7	2.9	3.1	3.3	3.4 •	3.4	3.3	3.1	2.8	2.6	2.4	2.4 •	2.5	2.7	2.9	3.2	3.4	17
18	3.5 •	3.5	3.4	3.2	3.1	3.0	2.9 •	3.0	3.1	3.3	3.4	3.5 •	3.4	3.3	3.0	2.7	2.4	2.1	2.0 •	2.1	2.2	2.5	2.8	3.1	18
19	3.4	3.5	3.6 •	3.5	3.4	3.3	3.3 •	3.3	3.4	3.5	3.6	3.6 •	3.5	3.3	3.0	2.7	2.3	2.0	1.8	1.7 •	1.8	2.1	2.4	2.8	19
20	3.1	3.4	3.6	3.6	3.7 •	3.6	3.6 •	3.6	3.7	3.7	3.8 •	3.8	3.7	3.5	3.2	2.8	2.4	2.0	1.7	1.5	1.5 •	1.7	1.9	2.3	20
21	2.7	3.1	3.4	3.6	3.7	3.8	3.9	3.9	3.9	4.0	4.0 •	4.0	3.9	3.7	3.4	3.0	2.6	2.1	1.8	1.5	1.3 •	1.4	1.5	1.8	21
22	2.2	2.6	3.0	3.4	3.6	3.9	4.0	4.1	4.2	4.2	4.2 •	4.2	4.1	3.9	3.6	3.3	2.9	2.4	2.0	1.6	1.4	1.3 •	1.3	1.5	22
23	1.8	2.2	2.6	3.0	3.4	3.7	4.0	4.2	4.3	4.3	4.3 •	4.3	4.2	4.0	3.8	3.5	3.2	2.8	2.3	2.0	1.6	1.4	1.3 •	1.3	23
24	1.5	1.8	2.1	2.6	3.0	3.4	3.8	4.1	4.3	4.4	4.4 •	4.3	4.2	4.1	3.9	3.7	3.4	3.1	2.7	2.4	2.0	1.7	1.5	1.4 •	24
25	1.4	1.5	1.8	2.2	2.6	3.1	3.5	3.9	4.2	4.3	4.4 •	4.3	4.2	4.1	3.9	3.7	3.5	3.3	3.0	2.8	2.5	2.2	1.9	1.6	25
26	1.5	1.5 •	1.6	1.9	2.2	2.7	3.2	3.6	3.9	4.2	4.3 •	4.2	4.1	4.0	3.8	3.6	3.5	3.3	3.2	3.1	2.9	2.6	2.4	2.1	26
27	1.8	1.7	1.6 •	1.7	2.0	2.4	2.8	3.3	3.7	3.9	4.1	4.1 •	4.0	3.8	3.6	3.4	3.3	3.2	3.2	3.2	3.2	3.0	2.8	2.6	27
28	2.3	2.0	1.9	1.8 •	1.9	2.2	2.5	3.0	3.4	3.7	3.9	3.9 •	3.8	3.6	3.4	3.2	3.1	3.0 •	3.1	3.2	3.3	3.3 •	3.2	3.1	28
29	2.8	2.5	2.3	2.1	2.1 •	2.2	2.4	2.8	3.1	3.4	3.7	3.7 •	3.6	3.4	3.2	2.9	2.8	2.7 •	2.8	3.0	3.2	3.3	3.4 •	3.4	29
30	3.3	3.1	2.8	2.6	2.4	2.4 •	2.5	2.7	3.0	3.3	3.5	3.5 •	3.4	3.2	3.0	2.7	2.5	2.4 •	2.4	2.8	2.9	3.2	3.5	3.6	30

Figure 19. Water Calendar made by the Indonesian Navy.

they schedule such activities. The water calendar shows the date, hour, and tide level. People have to adjust their plans and schedules to the water calendar so that everybody will come by their *ci* or speedboat. If it is low tide, probably most people can not travel by *ci* or speedboat, thus, the activity will not succeed because nobody would show up.

3.2 Asmat in Papua Province of Indonesia

Before going further into Asmat issues, it is better to understand where Asmat is located. According to the Central Statistics Bureau (CSB) of Asmat, the Asmat regency is located below the equator between 4 – 7 degrees South Latitude and 137 – 140 degrees East Longitude. Politically, Asmat is one of the regencies (kabupaten) of Papua province of Indonesia, formerly called Irian Jaya.

The Asmat region is bordered by Nduga and Yahukimo regencies on the north, by Arafura sea and Mappy regency on the south, by Mimika regency and Arafura sea on the west, and Boven Digoel and Mappy regencies on the east (CSB 2011:7) (see fig.20).

Culturally, Asmat comprises twelve different sub-ethnic groups called *rumpun*[4], and these are: Emari Ducur, Bismam, Simai, Becmbub, Unir Sirao (Kenok), Unir Epmak (Tomor), Joerat, Safan, Kenekap (Kaimo), Aramatak (Yamugau), Yupmakcain (Citak), and Bras (Brazza). The sub-ethnic groups with whom I spent most of my time are Bismam and Becmbub.

The Asmat regency is composed of 10 districts: Agats, Akat, Atsj, Fayit, Pantai Kasuari, Sawa Erma, Unir Sirauw, Suator, Suru-suru, Kolf Braza (see fig.21). Every district is lead by

4 *Rumpun* in this context can be translated as a sub-ethnic group. It is based on my understanding that Asmat is an ethnic group of Papua Indonesia. *Rumpun* is a smaller part of an ethnic group, therefore I perceive it as a sub-ethnic group. Thus, *rumpun* is comprised of clans.

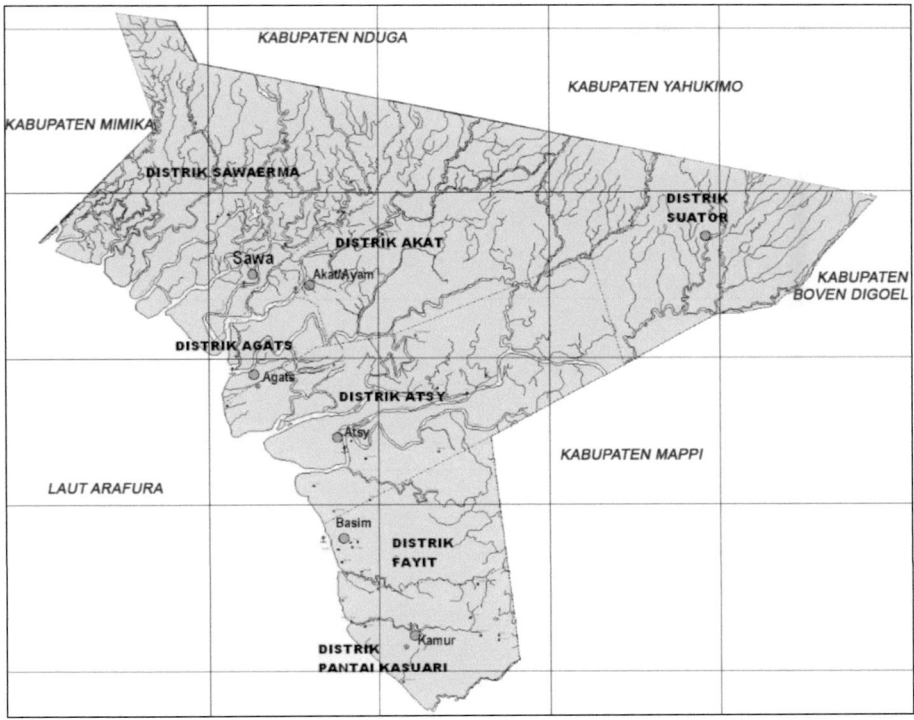

Figure 20. Map of Asmat. Source: Central Statistics Bureau of Asmat.

a district head called *Camat*. Based on the *Pemerintah Kabupaten Asmat* (Asmat Regency Government) of the Empowerment Village Society Office's data, there are 175 villages in the 8 districts as of 2010, excluding Suru-suru and Kolf Braza districts. The last two districts were not counted because the expansion of the district occured in 2012 after the official recapitulation of the villages.

According to *Pemerintah Kabupaten Asmat – Dinas Kependudukan dan Pencatatan Sipil* 2010, The population of Asmat is approximately 91,971 individuals as of 2009 (p.20), scattered in a territory of roughly 23,746 square kilometers (CSB *Kabupaten Asmat* 2011:3). Compared to Zegwaard (1978:17), the estimate of the total population of Asmat in 1953 is approximately 40,000 people, when the population was biologically homogenous Asmat. Today, the population of Asmat is relatively heterogenous, especially in central districts like Agats proper city, Atsj, and Sawa Erma.

Asmat is located in the Papua Province of Indonesia (see fig.19). Papua[5] province is the easternmost part of Indonesia, located on the island of New Guinea, the second largest island in the world after Greenland (Suter 1982:10). It is rich in natural and cultural treasures. Trees of many varieties have existed abundantly as well as other natural resources. Moreover, according to Ahmad Yunus (2011:129), the Europeans' ambitious expeditions have partly proved that Papua is an island of gold and copper. This statement

---

5   'Papua' in this book, means the easternmost part of Indonesia and it politically belongs to Indonesia; It is not Papua New Guinea.

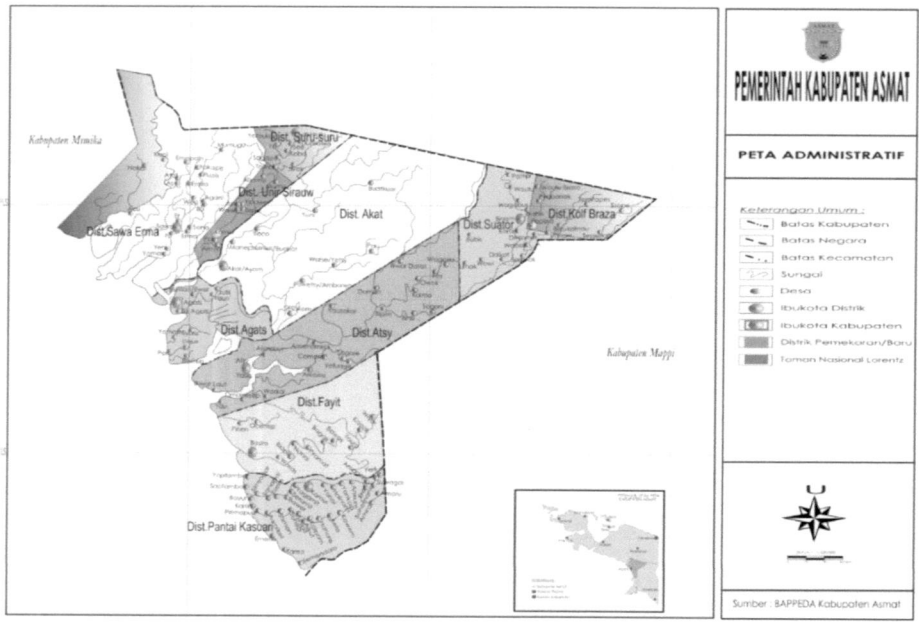

Figure 21. Administrative map of Asmat. Source: Local Government of Asmat.

has been proven there by PT Freeport's mining activities in this region since 1967 until today. PT Freeport Indonesia is one of the world's leading producers of copper and gold (PT Freeport Indonesia 2008:2). PT Freeport Indonesia is a subsidiary of Freeport McMoRan Copper and Gold, a U.S.-based mining company (Cook 2008:1). Paul M. Tylor provides information about the richness of Papua,

> "Within the range of habitants, from coastal swamps to snow-capped equatorial peaks, from 0 to almost 5000 m elevation, lives Indonesia's richest concentration of plant life. Mainland New Guinea holds an estimated 16,000 species of plants, as well as more than 200 species of land animals, over 700 species of birds, perhaps 6000-7000 species of fish, and perhaps 80,000-100,000 insect species." Again, according to Tylor, Papua is formed entirely from the western side, 47% of the great continental island of New Guinea and its nearby offshore islands, covering an area of 421,841 square kilometers (162,873 square miles). It is bordered by the Moluccan Sea on the West, by Micronesia and the Pacific Ocean on the North, and by Australia across the Arafura Sea on the South. It shares a land boundary on the east with the Republic of Papua New Guinea, which occupies the remaining 53% of the island of New Guinea (Tylor, in Konrad 1996:33).

3.3 Asmat: a region that contains no stone

The Asmat region is not only muddy, but it also contains no stone. Despite this, traditional culture in the lowland flood plains of Asmat is based upon the diversified use of Stone-Age tools (Konrad 1996:45). According to Smidt, although the Asmat used stone tools for so long, these were acquired from the foothills and highlands through trade networks (1999:15,

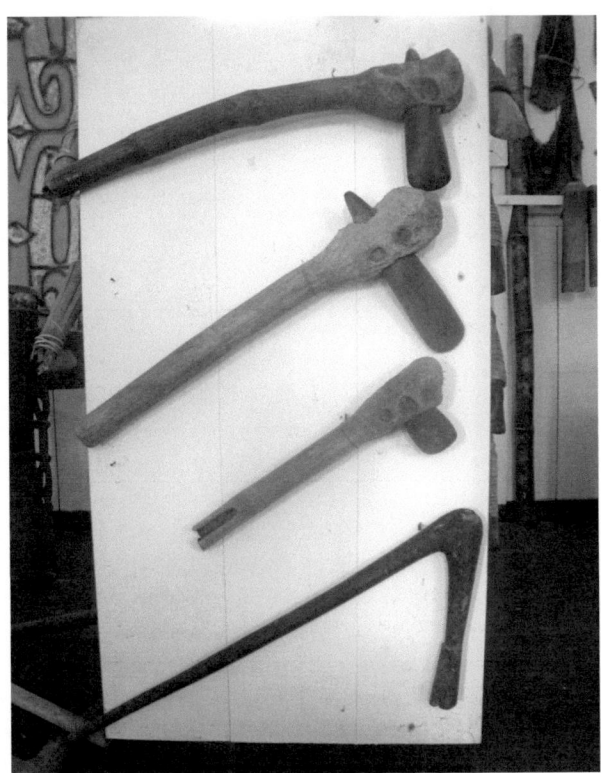

Figure 22. Stone axes. Photo taken at Agats Museum.

see *Tapol Bulletin* 1983:46, Fleischhacker 1991:2). Consequently, stone tools for them were very valuable for ritual feasts, marriage plans, adoptions, peace treaties, and other transactions (Konrad 1996:54). The stone axe is one of the goods that can be exchanged or bartered (see fig.22). Konrad said, "Today, wealth, values, and even the preservation of human life are still closely linked to the possession of hand-processed stone" (1996:45). Surprisingly, even from the very simple tools, the remarkable Asmat art emerges from the creativity of the gifted artists in using stone tools and other natural tools such as bones, shells, and animal teeth. Most of these traditional tools have been replaced by metal tools because metal and modern tools provide many benefits for the everyday life of the Asmat (Daeli 2011:7). However, possession of stone tools still remains significant in ritual feasts and in the Asmat heritage, these were rarely offered for sale (Konrad 1996:45). Again, according to Konrad (1996:60),

> "The stones symbolize the unshakeable continuity of family life and take on a similar meaning with respect to the village community at large. Marriage without the exchange of stone blades is still inconceivable in our day. The groom's gift to the bride must be honored in return by the presentation of a gift of equivalent value by the bride's parents in the form of a number of stone blades of corresponding quality. This ritualized exchange documents the social equality of the families involved."

So, it is tremendous to imagine the past life of the Asmat people prior to the advent of the first missionaries in the 1950s (Trenkenschuh 1978:14). It is also noteworthy to compare it with other parts of the world which introduced them to new things, including metal tools and tobacco to which many Asmat are now addicted.

Food has to be roasted over an open fire because they have neither cooking pots nor stones (Gerbrands:11). According to Gerbrands, river water used for drinking is usually fetched at low tide when the water is least salty (p.12). Another way to get drinking water based on my experience in Asmat is simply by saving rain in water containers. But when there is no rain for a long time, it is imperative to go to the middle of the jungle, dig a hole between the roots of the sago trees and wait for a while to get less salty water that can be used for drinking.

3.4 Asmat art: an *anamnesis*

Art is an essential part of the Asmat life. It connects them to the realm of their ancestors. Carvings and other kinds of Asmat arts are always related with rituals. According to Schneebaum (1985:40), arts, especially carvings, are the medium through which the Asmat remain in contact with their ancestors. Another writer said, "Carvings are embodiments of the ancestral spirit which control the universe. To keep the cosmos in order, the Asmat placated their ancestors through carvings, ritual feasts, warfare, the taking of heads and cannibalism" (Fleischhacker 1991:4). Furthermore, Sowada said that through woodcarvings, the Asmat artists make the invisible world and its magical power visible. Visible representations of the spirits are an element of the Asmat belief that the world of the living and the world of the dead coexist harmoniously (Sowada in Konrad 2002:48).

In my opinion, Asmat art is a kind of *anamnesis*[6]. In the Catholic liturgical context, anamnesis is understood as memorial sacrifice. Actually, it is not only a memorial of a past event, but also a celebration of present reality that may happen in future time. Apparently, *anamnesis* in the Catholic liturgical context says: "Christ has died, Christ is risen, Christ will come again" (The Roman Missal 1985:550). It has three dimensions of time: past, present, and future, but the subject is not changed – Christ. This means Christ is alpha and omega, the beginning and the end. The world and time might change, but Christ is still the same. I use this perspective because I find that the Asmat art unites the dimensions of time. The ancestor's life in the past becomes present here and now through art in order to sustain the life of the living in the future. The *ci* as part of Asmat art is also an anamnesis of a past event that is useful for the present in order to sustain life in the future.

3.5 Defining the Asmat people

Even if everybody has his or her own experience and impression about the Asmat, I found that the first written impression about the Asmat comes from Fr. G. Zegwaard's account. He wrote,

"They are a good looking and a very healthy and strong people. Physically they make a far better impression than the Auju peoples from the Mappi area to the east of Asmat. Their powerful physique makes a deep impression on anyone who encounters them. Actually this impression is intensified because the Asmatter is a very sly and

---

6 *Anamnesis* comes from the Attic Greek word ἀνάμνησις meaning reminiscence and/or memorial sacrifice. This word is used in Catholic liturgical statements in which the Church refers to the memorial character of the Eucharist and/or to the Passion, Resurrection and Ascension of Christ. It is also used in psychology – a recalling to memory, as well as in medicine – to complete history recalled and recounted by a patient (see Webster's Third New International Dictionary 1976:77).

cunning person – and he seems to be a born comedian. Although intrigue is a way of life and their battles are bloody, all of this is considered, by the Asmatters, to be a virtue. I estimate that they are a very intelligent people – sometimes they demonstrate superior intelligence" (Zegwaard 1953:17).

Additionally, in 1970 as I quote at the beginning of this chapter, Trenkenshuh (1970:10) wrote about the Asmat, "They were a tall and handsome people, but no one was ever far from fear or danger. They were not a happy people." Moreover, according to Jan Pouwer (2010:11), "They are more powerful; in pre-colonial times the Kamoro feared attacks by them and cannibalism, which was not practiced by the Kamoro." The Kamoro is the western neighbor of the Asmat.

The descriptions of Zegwaard, Trenkenshuh, and Pouwer are considered as *etic* perspectives or the outsider's opinions about the Asmat. But, how about the *emic* or the native Asmat's perspectives about themselves? Yuvensius Biakai, an educated Asmat, expressed his feeling about his society in a seminar regarding *inculturation* in 1995 in Agats (*Notulen Lokakarya* 1995:8). To open his presentation in that seminar, Biakai raised a fundamental question, *"Siapa manusia Asmat?"* – (Who is the Asmat?). Then he continued with his own answer. The following is a summary of his presentation:

> *Tidak gampang untuk mengatakan siapa manusia Asmat itu. Ia sungguh sangat rumit dan misteri atau unik. Orang Asmat sendiri sulit untuk memahami dirinya, apalagi orang luar.* (It is not easy to define who the Asmat is. He is very complicated, mysterious, and unique. An outsider would find it very difficult to understand who the Asmat is because even the native Asmat himself is not able to define who he is).

> *Orang Asmat percaya bahwa setiap benda mempunyai roh, bahkan setiap bagian anggota tubuh punya roh. Roh yang memberi daya, yang membakar semangat orang atau manusia Asmat.* (The Asmat believes that everything has a spirit, moreover every part of the body has a spirit. The spirit empowers and enlightens the Asmat).

> *Orang Asmat punya rasa bersaing dan kebanggaan diri yang tinggi. Masing-masing orang atau kelompok etnis akan menunjukkan diri bahwa mereka lebih hebat dari yang lain. Manusia Asmat ingin meraih kebanggaan dalam segala hal.* (The Asmat bear a competitive trait and high self-esteem. Every individual or ethnic group would claim that he is the best. The Asmat dreams to be the best in everything).

> *Manusia Asmat punya filsafat "Sinak" – masuk menghilang di sini, tapi akan muncul di sebelah sana. Hari ini kalah, besok menang. Hari ini kamu berhasil, besok kami berhasil. Maka, bila ia diam bukan karena ia merasa minder, tapi sabar karena dia yakin bahwa dia akan menang pada waktunya.* (The Asmat philosophy is *"Sinak"* [a kind of shrimp that lives in the mud] – The *sinak* goes invisible here, but it appears beyond. Today we are lost, tomorrow we will win. Your turn to be the winner today, but tomorrow will be ours. Therefore, if an Asmat is speechless, it does not mean that he feels inferior, instead, he is waiting for his winning time).

Comparing the *etic* and *emic* perspectives as stated above, we can see that the non-Asmat and the native Asmat observe the same thing from a different angle. On the one hand, the non-Asmat tends to observe the external or physical appearance of the Asmat. The non-Asmat are interested in shape, form, and physical performance. For example, the people of Asmat are healthy, tall, and handsome. They examine the surface or outer experience and judge based on the capacity of the eyes to see. On the other hand, the native Asmat goes beyond the physical appearance. His interpretation does not deal with the external expression, but goes deeper to character, personality, philosophy, and strategy. For example, the '*sinak*' philosophy: It states that the Asmat goes invisible over here, but appears beyond. Today he might lose, but tomorrow he will win. Your turn to be the winner is today, but tomorrow will be mine. The *sinak* philosophy is applicable to the political strategy of the present time. For instance, many political parties campaign aggressively at the beginning of the campaign period. However, one party is waiting for the best time, as if it has nothing to show, but actually its supporters are working on a great strategy to suddenly appear at the end and become the winner. I think, the *sinak* philosophy and strategy was used by Biakai himself to attain his position as the Asmat regent (*Bupati*) since 2004 and stay as such until the end of his regency.

I do agree with Biakai's statement, "It is not easy to define who the Asmat is." It is very difficult for both Asmat and non-Asmat to define people as *bla, bla, bla* because we are dealing here with living people who have personal character and other capabilities. Biakai's statement was highlighted by Nicolaus Ndepi in his article, "Asmat Bukan Patung Kayu melainkan Pengukir Terbaik" – (The Asmat are not woodcarving objects but are talented sculptors – see fig.23).

"Apa yang menurut orang luar merupakan 'masalah' justru bagi orang Asmat merupakan 'solusi.' Orang Asmat bukanlah patung kayu yang bisa dibentuk-bentuk begitu saja oleh orang luar yang tidak tahu mengukir dan membuat patung kayu Asmat. Padahal orang Asmat adalah Asmat nak – manusia sejati – yang mempunyai masa lalu dan masa depan dan juga mempunyai mimpi-mimpi yang tidak sepenuhnya bisa dimengerti oleh orang luar" (2012). (A thing for outsiders being a 'trouble', on the contrary being a 'solution' for the Asmat. The Asmat are not woodcarving objects that can be shaped easily by outsiders who do not know how to carve the Asmat carvings. The Asmat people are *Asmat nak* – the real people – who have history in the past and dreams for the future that cannot be fully understood by outsiders).

Although one can get a glimpse of the data for this study, these are still limited because Biakai is observing living creatures which has the capacity and capability to change and to be changed. Everybody can describe his or her impressions about the Asmat people, but I believe that all descriptions are limited and partial because they come from personal interpretations. Father Pitka, an American missionary of the Order of the Holy Cross, wrote in his diary about the American missionary who just arrived in Asmat in 1958, "Even the imagery he has conceived from the books that he has read and from the accounts that he had heard does not, he finds, represent the reality as he now sees it" (*Asmat Drums* 1983:1). Nevertheless, we need to see and study even the partial impressions of selected communities to obtain a better understanding and hope for a more comprehensive description about a selected group. Therefore, both *etic* and *emic* perspectives as mentioned above are valuable perspectives to know the Asmat people.

Figure 23. A young sculptor is carving a pole for *jeu*.

3.6 Asmat: people of the tree

Social and spiritual relationships among the Asmat happen not only between the living and their neighbors, but also between the living and the dead. These relationships are expressed and connected by myths and rituals. In a sense, ritual is a representation of a myth. One of the myths pertaining to the origin of the Asmat is "Fumeripits", the Creation Myth. A brief summary of the creation myth is as follows:

> "The first men were created from wood by the creator whose name is Fumeripits. At that time there was nobody on the face of the earth. Fumeripits saw this and then gathered together his tools to carve wooden figures of humans for both male and female. He then placed these carvings in a *jeu* which he personally built. He then sat down again and carved an *em* (drum) which he began to beat as he danced to and fro in the men's house. At the beat of the drum, all his wooden carvings began to move and finally to follow the dance to the beat of Fumeripits' drum. As these carvings danced, they began to become flesh and blood, to become Asmat or human beings. These first humans became the original ancestors of the Asmat people. They moved to the sea and still live there in a place of happiness and continue to assist in the process of creation of new human life" (Kuruwaip 1974:32).

Based on the creation myth, the Asmat stick to the point of human existence. They are not concerned about how the universe came into existence because they believe that it has always existed as a cosmos in which they are participants integrated within a complex pattern of interrelationships comprising the totality of things within it (Sowada 1996:65).

Asmat means *The real People*, in contradiction with others (Fleischhacker 1991:3; Ndepi 2012; see also Schieffelin 1976:9). The Asmat call themselves the *Asmat-ow*, the people of the land or people of the tree (Schneebaum 1990:12) because their ancestors were created from a piece of a tree by the great creator Fumeripits. Moreover, to make the wooden figures alive, Fumeripits also used *em* which was made of wood. Thus, the Asmat frequently compare themselves to a tree: the feet are the roots, the torso is the trunk, the arms are the branches and the head is the fruit of the tree (Zegwaard 1959: 1039; Fleischhacker 1991:3).

The Asmat believe that all living things (humans, animals, and plants) possess *ndet* (soul) as Biakai stated in his explanation about who the Asmat is (see also Sowada 1996:68; Muller and Omabak 2008:27; Monagle 2012). This means, non-living things possess no *ndet*. However, in his accounts, Sowada wrote,

> "The Asmat also give *ndet* names to animate objects, such as the figures of the ancestor poles, statues, central ceremonial house poles, foundation poles of ordinary dwellings, shields and the prows head of dugouts. Once these objects have been named for ancestors, the ancestors imbue them with powers and thereby protect the bearer" (1996:68).

In this context, the *ndet* of a non-living object means supernatural power. Despite the fact that non-living things possess no *ndet*, the action of human beings as living creatures animates an object to be a sacred and powerful object. For example, the Asmat believe that the *ndet* of an ancestor dwells in a *ci* that is named after him. That is why the enemy can be frightened by a *ci* because of its *ndet* or the supernatural power in it. The human action of naming the objects after the ancestors becomes real in rituals. Rituals transform the ordinary object into an extraordinary and powerful object. Moreover, the performance of rituals, according to Rappaport (1968:2; see also Bowie 2006:138), suppresses anxiety, dispels fear, and provides a sense of security because rituals reveal values at their deepest level (Wilson 1954:241). Rituals invite, unite, validate, celebrate, and transform someone or something to a certain quality in a community. For example, the initiation ritual is a mark of an individual's transition from adolescence to adulthood (see Lutkehaus and Roscoe 1995:18).

3.7 Warfare and headhunting practices

It was not without reason Trenkenshuh said that the Asmat were not a happy people. They were a tall and handsome people, but no one was ever far from fear or danger because of warfare and headhunting practices in the past. This means, warfare and headhunting situated them into perpetual fear and unhappiness. For instance, Zegwaard documented 83 deaths from November 1952 to November 1953 by violence as part of the headhunting culture of the Asmat (1953:25). This evidence made them an unhappy community.

An indication of warfare and violence in Asmat, according to Zegwaard (1953), is the Asmat language that has many words related to warfare such as 'fight', 'argue', 'quarrel', 'murder', and 'headhunting'. Moreover, he said, "Any conflict between two persons will usually escalate into involvement of all members of their immediate families, then their clans and finally, it can involve the entire village" (1953:19). The most common causes of violence and warfare are adultery, rape, stealing sago grubs, stealing or breaking the *ci*, and trespassing other's *dusun* or sago boundaries. It was a surprise when Fr. Vince Cole,

Figure 24. Skulls – (hanging): The enemys' skulls (signed by a small hole at the parietal area to take the brain. (Below): polished and decorated – skulls of ancestors. Photo taken at Agats Museum.

an American priest who has lived in Asmat for more than 30 years, during an informal conversation told me, "Fighting or quarreling is a daily habit of the villagers. If there is no fighting in a day, the village will not be cheerful." I think, this statement highlights Zegwaard's remarks on violence as stated above. During my stay in Asmat, both during my last visit and especially during the first stay, I frequently witnessed people quarreling or fighting over a simple matter.

Nobody knows how headhunting began (Trenkenshuh 1970) and it is rather confusing (Zegwaard 1959:1037). Nevertheless, Zegwaard himself tried to discover the primary factors that led to the headhunting practices in Asmat. Below are Zegwaard's summaries of the reasons for headhunting.

"Among the important factors are (1) the cosmology of Asmat (or rather, the influence of cosmic events on their lives), but this has now lost much of its significance; (2) the economic demand, sago gathering and its cult; (3) fear of the spirits, expressed in the ritual of expelling the spirits as a characteristic feature of both large and small festivities; and (4) the need of prestige on the part of the male population, the desire for fame and the urge to impress the women of the village" (1959:1037).

Sowada (1996:79) confirmed these factors in his article as he wrote, "Headhunting and cannibalism gained acceptance within a homogenous Asmat culture as natural, integral parts of life, though they never become daily routine. …. It ensured the perpetuation of their existence and mirrored their world view." Thus, if it is natural to be happy when they win the war and are successful in headhunting. This is proven by the enemy's head as Jan van Baal said in the Marind-Anim of Papua context that headhunting is essentially a festive occasion (1966:717). In other words, at least for a moment, they are a very happy people because of their latest achievement, but not long after the celebration, they have to be ready for the enemy's attack or revenge. The picture in fig.24, especially the hanging skulls, is an evidence of headhunting and cannibalism in the past. The hanging skulls were the heads of the enemies (see Saulnier 1961:23).

Another writer, Smidt, pays attention to the initiation ritual. According to him, the importance of captured heads in traditional Asmat life is clearly demonstrated by the role they played in male initiation. It was impossible for boys to become men without taking a head (Schneebaum 1985:41; Smidt 1999:21; Zubrinich 1999). This notion can be compared with the circumcision rite in Ndembu Society as Victor Turner (1967:152) described, "For Ndembu society, an uncircumcised person remains a child and eats alone with women, since he cannot join grown and circumcised men in their meals. No women in the past would have sexual relations with him." So, taking a head is a condition to leave boyhood for adulthood. For other men it is a chance to increase their status and power. In this way, whether good or not, a man has to take a head to gain pride and maturity. Turner said, "A normal man acts abnormally because he is obedient to tribal traditions, but not disobedient to it. He does not evade but rather fulfills his duties as a citizen" (1967:100).

The motivation of headhunting in the Asmat is quite different with Marind-Anim Society in Merauke Papua. One of the headhunting motivations, according to van Baal is the Marind love to sally forth and see many places, always looking forward to a new journey, new adventures. That is why a headhunt is essentially a festive occasion. Another motivation for headhunting for the Marind is that a father looks for names for his children. A father takes pride in having "skull-names", because not every father is a successful headhunter and not everyone has a head-name to spare for a new-born child (Baal 1966:717).

Aside from the need for prestige, it is also important to emphasize that death among the Asmat is never "natural", but is always seen as the result of malevolent black magic or bloody violence. One Asmat belief is that the spirits of those killed in headhunting cannot go to *safan* (the spirit world), until an equal number of people who have been killed come from those who caused the imbalance (Schneebaum 1985:41; Fleischhacker 1991:5; Helfrich 1996:42). Therefore, headhunting and warfare are needed to please the spirits and to keep the cosmos balanced. However, in reality the victims of the fighting parties were always unbalanced, so this leads to a never-ending cycle of warfare and headhunting. Consequently, the communities are always in danger which engenders unhappy Asmat people.

Although nobody knows how headhunting and warfare began, it has become a historical and cultural background of the Asmat. According to Zegwaard (1959:1020), "Even when the Asmat people will no longer hunt head, they will have these ideologies." It had created a lot of great warriors as well as victimized plenty of souls in the past. On one hand, great warriors and their people were very happy because of their battle-achievements; on the contrary, the victims and their families were very sad. Headhunting and warfare make the Asmat men warriors, guardians, carvers, and performers of rituals. An Asmat father teaches his son to be a great warrior in order not to be an easy prey for their enemies, as Mbai recalled that his father told him repeatedly "You must be strong just like me" (Mraz 1976:84). This background strengthens the patriarchalism in Asmat society (Fleischhacker 1991:10).

3.8 Some impressions about kinship

To understand kinship in Asmat society, one should not forget to discuss *jeu* – the traditional house of Asmat or men's longhouse because it is very central in the Asmat society. There are two types of dwellings for the Asmat: first, the family house which is lived in only by married couples with their children, and second the *jeu* where young unmarried men and widowers usually live. (see Kuruwaip 1974:61). Helfrich reports that a family house is usually occupied by several closely related core families, brothers with their wives and children. However, within this communal dwelling, each family unit possesses its own fireplace, the actual center of family life and the focal symbol of emotional ties (in Konrad 1996:38).

Another type of communal dwelling in Asmat is the *jeu*. Usually, each village has one *jeu*, although some villages have more than one *jeu*, depending on the number of clans. A *jeu* is always surrounded by family houses. This fact symbolizes the centrality of a *jeu* in an Asmat village. It is the center of social, political, cultural, intellectual, and religious life in Asmat. A *Jeu* is constructed much like the family house but much larger (see fig.25). Helfrich wrote, "The men's houses contain long rows comprised of the cooking or fireplaces (see fig.26) of the clans represented there, each identified by its own large ancestor pole bearing carved figures" (in Konrad 1996:38).

In his article entitled "Rumah *Jeu* dan Fungsinya" (*Jeu* and Its Functions) Kuruwaip (1974) explained the functions of a *jeu*. According to him, the functions of *jeu* are (a) as a symbol of a clan's existence; (b) Moiety (*aipmu*) sign; (c) A place for ritual and traditional celebrations; (d) A place for social and political activities; (e) Storehouse for weapons; and (f) dwelling place. Through his explanations, Kuruwaip tried to emphasize the centrality of a *jeu* in Asmat society. The *jeu* is central for the Asmat village activities. Therefore, it is very helpful to understand the social life of the Asmat, especially the kinship system.

I want to highlight one of the functions of a *jeu*, as stated by Kuruwaip, that is, the moiety sign. Moiety or *aipmu* in the Asmat word of sub-ethnic Kenok, Helfrich (in Konrad 1996) described it clearly:

> "Roughly in the middle of the room a central[7], 'sacred' fire-place (see *wayir* on fig.27) not assigned to any specific clan divides the men's house into two halves: the 'upstream' and the 'downstream' sections. In accordance with this principle of duality the community occupying the men's house is divided into two groups based on the location of the fire-places" (p.38-39).

For example (see fig.27), the moiety of *jeu* in Atsj village is Firmenmakurupits (A-upstream) – Atcurupits (B-downstream) and in Yasiw village is Kamerpits (A-upstream) – Jasurupits (B-downstream). The people from upstream marry the downstream people or vice versa (see arrows on fig.22a). In other words, marriage in Asmat is normally *jeu-endogamous* which means that preference is for individuals to marry only within their particular kinship group (see Barfield 1997:150), that is, within the *jeu*. However, *jeu-exogamous* or *aipen-exogamous* is also possible when an individual marries someone from a different *jeu* or moiety (see Kuruwaip 1974:64-65). The Asmat follow the patrilocal or virilocal (see Eller 2009:190) system where the married couples settle in or near the residence of the man

---

[7] The main fireplace as central of a *jeu* is called *wayir* where the tribal leaders gather together to discuss something or where the drums are beaten.

Figure 25. A *Jeu*, an exterior view.

Figure 26. *Jeu* – Fireplaces inside the *jeu*.

and his family. Most marriages are monogamous, yet polygymy is accepted and esteemed, especially for those who are considered 'big men' (see Fleischhacker 1991:9).

Based on my observations during my first stay in Asmat (2002-2008) as well as from the accounts of Fr. Virgil Petermeir, an American Crosier, the initiative to begin a marriage usually comes from the girl's family. Fr. Virgil said that, "They may have picked their daughter's marriage partner as early as during school age, or later, upon spotting some young man, who appears promising, energic and preserving. Being handsome or not is not the issue" (*Asmat Drums* No.42 – Fall 1980:1). Some Asmat men told me separately that they were pulled out from the *jeu* by their brothers when they got married. This means, it was not the man's initiative to marry his wife, but the wife's family. Perhaps, it was not also the girl's choice to marry a man. However, she has no choice to say 'no' to her father or brother who provides her a husband. To have a bit of understanding about the traditional Asmat marriage ceremony, the following is the description of Fr. Virgil (*Asmat Drums* No.42 – Fall 1980:2-3).

"The afternoon seems to be a favorite time for the traditional marriage ceremony. The bride's parents or her older brothers and uncles decorate her with feathers, dogs-tooth necklaces, opossum fur cap and sometimes a stone ax over one shoulder. She

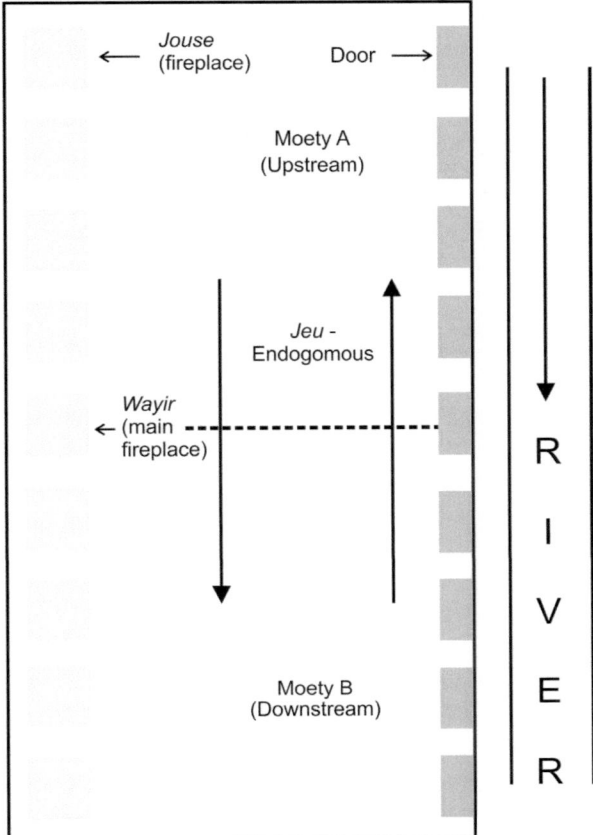

Figure 27. Floor plan of a *jeu*.

is then led or even carried to the house of the groom who is seated on a mat near the fireplace. She is placed sitting back-to-back (the position may vary from village to village) with her husband-to-be. She then prepares sago, baking it on the fire. Once the sago is ready, the husband turns about facing the bride who presents him the sago, while speaking out his name. He then rises to divide the sago bit by bit with her older brothers and uncles."

Once he has returned to the side of his new wife, the uncles and brothers of the girl come one-by-one and press down on the shoulders of both the bride and groom. They advise the two to never separate. The bride is not to return to her parents when there is trouble, but to remain in the house of her husband, permanently like bamboo which is well rooted in the soil. In some areas the new wife is even forbidden to visit or be visited by her family until she has given birth to her first child.

On the following morning, the young couple goes with both families to gather sago. Together they will demonstrate how well they can produce sago flour from the sago palm tree. Much of the produce is then given to their parents. Throughout their married life, they must not forget to give some of their produce to their parents."

This description underlines the patrilocality or virilocality and even patriarchy in Asmat society. This is proven by the marriage ceremony itself. For example, the bride's family leads the bride to the groom's house. It means the marriage ceremony will take place in the groom's house. Moreover, the advice saying that they should not separate and not return to the bride's parents when there is trouble, but to stay permanently in her husband's house like bamboo which is well rooted in the soil, is a great argument for the Asmat *patrilocal* or *virilocal* belief system.

Usually, the bride price is not paid immediately during the marriage ceremony. It can be paid later on when the husband and his family are physically ready to pay and are emotionally satisfied with the wife. Again, Fr. Virgil provided very valuable information about the bride price, as he said,

> "The next stage in the marriage process is the payment of the bride price. Sometimes a portion of it is paid immediately at the marriage ceremony. But most often it is paid one to three months after the marriage ceremony. In still other villages a portion of the bride price won't be paid until the first child is born. Seemingly, the groom's family demands some time to evaluate the solidity and quality of the marriage" (*ibid.*, p.3).

The common bride price in Asmat are stone axes, cassowary bone daggers, cassowary feathers, shells, and dog-teeth necklaces. Nowadays, money and modern tools such as steel axes can be considered as part of bride price. As far as I have observed, the bride price can trigger conflict in Asmat society if the husband and his family do not satisfy the wife's family with the payment of the bride price, even if the wife has given birth to her first child. The capability of giving birth is one of the woman's qualities to be a good Asmat wife. This is why many Asmat families pay the bride price only after the first child is born. As a former parish priest in Asmat, I have encountered some conflicts in the community triggered by the bride price. I even experienced that some wives' families asked me to mediate or at least to motivate the husband's family to pay the bride price.

3.9 Mission "touch"

In my opinion, it is not enough to discuss today's Asmat, without mentioning the missionaries and their mission. It is important to introduce the "missionary touch" or work because they are one of the most influenced agents of change for the Asmat, aside from the Indonesian government, and travelers. We can say that the Catholic missionaries as well as the Protestants are the pioneers of changing Asmat, although prior to the missionaries' settlement, the Dutch had been there for some expeditions and explorations. The local government of Indonesia follows the missionaries' steps and then implements its own programs.

A simple example of the mission touch is the Catholic mission which started the formal education system by opening schools in Asmat villages. One of the missionaries, Fr. Jan Smith OSC, was shot dead by a local government administrator in his attempt to raise the standards of Asmat education (Trenkenschuh – Tome II:165; see fig.28). Through this educational program, many Asmat can obtain good jobs and positions, both in the local government and in private services.

In this study, I highlight some significant evidence to emphasize the mission effects in Asmat. Fr. Gerard A. Zegwaard, a Dutch missionary of the Sacred Heart, built the first permanent settlement in Asmat in 1953 as he said, "I was the first white man to take up residence among them and there was no representative of the Dutch Colonial Administration to enforce the ordinances against headhunting that were carried out

Figure 28. Statue of Fr. Jan Smith, OSC. This statue was erected in Agats city by the local government of Asmat to honor his attempt to develop the Asmat through education.

elsewhere" (1959:1020). Soon after his arrival, Zegwaard began intensive research into the Asmat language, customs, and social structure. However, he was not the first missionary who arrived in the Asmat region because prior to his arrival between 1936-1943, the teachers from Key of Moluccas had been assigned in Syuru, Ewer, and Ayam by Fr. Herman Tillemans MSC after his visitation to that area in 1936 (Trenkenschuh – Tome II:153; Petermeier 2012). Later, the Protestants TEAM (The Evangelical Alliance Mireassion) started their work in Asmat in 1955 (Hontheim 2010:132).

According to Hontheim (2010), methodologically the Catholic and the Protestant missions were different. The Protestant missionaries dedicated themselves to medicine, while the Catholics to censuses, baptisms and schools, which the Protestants viewed as less significant. Moreover, the Catholics used the word '*inculturation*' to spread the Gospel, while the Protestants developed a similar concept with *inculturation*, and named it 'contextualization.' The aim of contextualization is to encourage the target population to adopt Christianity. The Protestant missionaries criticized *inculturation* because it led to syncretism. As a conclusion to this observation, although the Catholics and the Protestants used different in methods to 'Christianize' the Asmat, they were all agents of change in the Asmat society (p.134).

Another obvious example of the "mission touch" aside from the educational programs in schools is the extinction of headhunting and warfare. During earlier times of the mission in Asmat, headhunting and warfare were still being practiced. Fortunately, from time to time the Asmat themselves were aware that headhunting and warfare are not good if they want to live in harmony with their neighbors. The Asmat themselves long to live in harmony without violence as described by Trenkenschuh (1970):

"Of course they didn't know, nor they could be expected to understand, the gospel of Jesus Christ that these missionaries preached. They understood only that where these missionaries were there was no killing. They knew that their women could go to the jungle to gather food and return at night safe from sudden attacks. They longed for that safety. They also understood that the missionaries brought the treasures of the west-mysterious flashlights, cameras and pictures, tin cans and bottles. They also knew that the missionary would bring tobacco."[8]

Thus, the coming of missionaries brought about transformation in the Asmat way of life. They accepted the missionaries and Christianity, first because they longed for safety, which also fits their expectations. Under the influence of Roman Catholic and Protestant missionaries, the traditional animistic beliefs and rituals were gradually replaced by, merged with, or persisted alongside Christian views and practices (Corbey and Stanley in Hoogerbrugge 2011:8). In his account, Zegwaard (1953:25) said, "Although I am not overly optimistic, it seems clear that the presence of the mission has been improving this situation. I don't suppose this is because of a conversion but because the people may be afraid that the teachers and the pastors may send on the information to government agencies." Based on his personal knowledge, Zegwaard recorded that between November 1952-November 1953, 1% to 2% of the population died a violent death, as compared to the year before where death by violence was approximately 2% to 3% per year (1953:24-25).

On December 15, 1958, the first four Crosier missionaries arrived in Asmat. From this date, the Sacred Heart (MSC) gradually transfered the mission to The Order of the Holy Cross (OSC) (Trenkenschuh – Tome II – An Asmat Sketch Book vol. 2). Alphonse Sowada OSC, the first *Crosier* (the designated name for a member of the Order of the Holy Cross) to graduate in anthropology, was appointed the first bishop of the diocese of Agats-Asmat in 1969. One of his dreams was to preserve the Asmat culture. According to him, earlier missionaries did not understand the traditional ritual feasts, so they did not see the significance of the local culture as basis for development. Thus, the Crosiers started to collect objects of the Asmat art and built a museum in Agats which was officially opened in 1973 (Konrad 2002:56).

In a sense, we can say that the Catholic missionaries are "culture rescuers" (see Hontheim 2010:134) because Asmat arts and rituals were almost extinct, and the local government prohibited traditional activities such as building *jeu* (traditional house), holding rituals, and creating woodcarvings. The local government considered that the traditional Asmat rituals and their carvings were dangerous because these invite satan and tend to lead to free sex (see Rutherford 2006:240). Moreover, the rituals often led to headhunting and warfare. However, Bishop A. Sowada explained to the local government officers at that time the meanings of the rituals and convinced them that every society has the right to celebrate their lives based on their own culture (Konrad 2002:58). Recently, the Asmat became famous around the world because of their remarkable designs in woodcarving. To introduce their rich natural and cultural resources, the Diocese of Agats, supported by the local Asmat government, hold a yearly festival of Asmat culture, especially woodcarving, dance, and *ci* racing.

---

8   See also "No Tobacco, No Hallelujah": Missions and the Early History of Tobacco in Eastern Papua, written by Terence E. Hays in Pacific Studies, Vol. 14, No. 4 – December 1991.

Figure 29. Ewer Airport in Asmat.

Asmat became an autonomous regency (*kabupaten*) in 2002 separate from *kabupaten* Merauke. In my opinion, the development and the transformation of Asmat cannot be separated from the "missions touch", both in the past and in the present. For example: the Asmat airport located at Ewer (fig.29) is an initiative of the Catholic mission, as are hospitals and clinics in some places. Today, Ewer is an entrance to Asmat by airplane.

4

Physical dimension of the *ci*

Ci is a guarantee for mobility in everyday life of the Asmat, both individually and collectively. Although the canoe is not only found in Asmat; the Asmat canoe, called "*ci*", has its own uniqueness. In this chapter, I discuss the physical dimensions of the *ci* in order to understand better its uniqueness and the reasons for choosing it as the focus of my study. Fig.30 shows one function of the *ci*, that is, to transport people from one place to another.

There is a proverb in Indonesia, "*Dari mana datangnya lintah, dari sawah turun ke kali. Dari mana datangnya cinta, dari mata turun ke hati.*" It means the leech comes from the rice field then goes to the river. Love starts from the eyes. The first impression of a person towards someone or something usually comes from physical contact through the senses such as eye contact. The *ci* of the Asmat "touches" one's eyes once he looks at it. The *ci* persuades people to honor the Asmat' skill, not only their performance in using it, but also their ability to construct

Figure 30. The researcher with two Asmat friends paddling the *ci* and going to a forest.

Figure 31. Men (standing) and women (sitting) while paddling the *ci*. The man without paddle is elderly.

such a good product (see fig.31). The physical appearance of the *ci* charms someone's eyes looking at it, even if just only for a glimpse. A *ci* can measure 15 to 20 meters long, 60 to 70 centimeters width, and 50 to 60 deep (Arnold Ap and Mansoben 1974: 64).

4.1 Material of the *ci*

To produce a quality *ci*, one must look for the best material. The Asmat area is rich in good wood. However, only a few kinds of wood can be used as *ci* material. The Asmat people selectively take the *ci* material from the jungle because it is really vital in their lives. They choose high quality soft wood because it is easy to form. It is durable, light, and artistic. The types hat are good *ci* materials are the following: *ci* (kayu kuning/Nonau Cleaspp), *jewer* (gempol/Nauclea spp.), *jiran* (ketapang/Terminalia Canicu), *soaramak* (katakao), *juwur* (mersawa/anispotera spp.), *tow* (pala putih/Myristica argentea Warb.), and *tinaw* (pala merah) (cf. Ap and Mansoben 1974:62). According to my informants, especially the *ci* makers (*wow-ipits*), *ci* wood (Nonau Cleaspp; fig.32) is the best choice for making a *ci* because it is lighter but it is durable.

4.2 Understanding the *ci* through its sections

In order to easily understand the *ci*, I describe the *ci* based on its sections. Physically, the *ci* can be divided into three sections: (1) *Ci Cimen* (prowhead), (2) *Cindem/cinamakat* (keel or body of the *ci*), and (3) *Ci Ep* (*ci* tail). Although these sections form one whole (the *ci*), every part has its own characteristics; they cannot be separated from each other. Here are the *ci* sections with Asmat names.

a. *Ci Cimen* (prowhead) is comprised of *ufirmbi* (the head of a black king cockatoo), *wakanmbe* (special motif behind *ufirmbi*), *focep* (cuscus tail), *biskus* (man's head figure), *peri* (*ci*'s neck)

The *ci cimen* of *jicap ci* (feast *ci*) or *Jo ti* (clan's *ci*) is usually carved according to the owner's order or the personal expression of the carver (fig.33). However, every sub-ethnic group in Asmat has its own carving styles or characteristics. They do not use motifs that belong to another sub-ethnic group in their carvings. For example, the *ci cimen* of *Safan* area is different from *becmbub* or *bismam*. The *ci cimen*'s motive of *Safan* is not used by the Atsj carvers of *becmbub* nor vice versa. However, they could easily imitate the designs.

Figure 32. Small *ci* tree (Nonau Cleaspp).

Figure 33. *Ci Cimen* with its ornaments.

They have their own style and they keep it as part of their heritage and it is a means of characterizing them. They do not easily copy other's motifs or styles because they are proud of their own. Therefore, the *ci cimen* is a good identification material to distinguish the *cis* of other sub-ethnic groups in Asmat. Most of all, the *ci cimen* possesses its carver's motifs and is considered as the 'spirit' of the *ci* itself. The *ci cimen* can also be interpreted as manifestation of the ancestor's spirit or the power of the animal that is carved in it. A *ci cimen* without carving is called *bar*. *Ci ep* (*ci*'s tail) is the other pole of a *ci*, as contrasted to *ci cimen*. *Ci ep* is shorter than *ci cimen* and it is pointed (fig.34). Mostly, *ci ep* is not carved. If it is carved, it is always simpler than the *ci cimen*.

Figure 34. A woman's paddling style while sitting at *ci ep*.

b. *Cindem* or *cinamakat* (keel) is the middle and the dugout part of a *ci*

The *cindem* is the main container of a *ci* (fig.35). Everything can be placed in here, including people. People either stand or sit there while paddling. *Cinamakat* is comprised of various elements with its name: *cimen-afir* (first part of the *ci*'s curve), *ci aman* (*ci*'s curve – inner), *ci ak* (*ci*'s curve – outer), *ci wowuts* (middle of the *ci*'s curve), *ci pim* (edge that resembles a lip), *ep afir* (last part of the *ci*'s curve), *cimbak* (*ci*'s back), *cimbai* (*ci*'s legs), *ci yan* (*ci*'s ears), *ci tereyef / cipine* (*ci*'s ears hole), *citere* (decoration from rattan leaves), *pinwo* (carving around *cindem*). Additionally, *cindem* of the *jicap ci* is painted by two vertical colors: *esakam* (red) and *depi* (white) to make it beautiful and dignified.

4.3. Types of the *ci*

Based on my interviews and direct observations, the Asmat categorized the *ci* into two types: (1) *pakanam* or *pokomber* or *pomer ci* (ordinary *ci*) and (2) *jicap* or *pakman ci* (feast or ritual *ci*). The classification is not based on the seasons (weather) or on size, but on its traditional functions. If we look at the Trobriand Islanders, they have three types of canoe: (1) *kewo'u* – requires small, light, and handy canoes for coastal transportation; (2) *kalipoulo* – bigger and more seaworthy canoes for fishing; and (3) *masawa* – for deep sea sailing; the biggest type is needed, with a considerable carrying capacity, greater displacement, and stronger construction (Malinowski 1922:112). The Trobriand classification is based on size and function to transport people and goods.

Aside from *pakanam* and *jicap cis*, the Asmat also recognize an extraordinary type of *ci* which they call *wuramon*, the spirit canoe. This type of *ci* is only found in Joerat region, one of the sub-ethnic groups in Asmat. *Wuramon* is not developed or celebrated in other sub-ethnic groups of Asmat.

In this study, I provided a brief information about each kind of *cis*. However, I realized that my discussion on this part is quite limited. Nonetheless, I hope this part can be the start of a better understanding on how the Asmat categorize the *ci*.

4.3.1 *Pakanam ci*

Pakanam ci, also called *pokomber* or *pomer ti*, is used for daily activities (see fig.36). It is used to fulfill the everyday needs of a family or to transport people to meet their daily needs such

Figure 35. A man is standing at *Cindem* or *Cinamakat*. (Photograph courtesy of Fr. Vince Cole MM).

Figure 36. *Pakanam cis* for daily use.

as fishing, hunting, and gathering. The *pakanam ci* is often called the family's *ci* because everybody can use it. Basically, there is no special ritual or taboo related to the *pakanam ci*. The material used in making it can be taken anywhere and anytime. There is no need to wait for the collective decision of the family if they want to have a *pakanam ci*. It is a personal or family decision to own and to manufacture a *pakanam ci*. It is typically simple, smaller, and it is usually without decoration or carving. Everybody can use it anytime to go anywhere. However, as compared to *jicap ci* (the other type of the *ci*), the *pakanam ci* is physically simple and is not governed by many rules or taboos in making or using it.

Figure 37. *Jicap ci* – for ritual feast. (Photograph courtesy of Fr. Vince Cole).

4.3.2 *Jicap ci* or *pakman ci*

Jicap ci is exclusive to Asmat (see fig.37). It is also called *jia ci* or *pakman ci*, the feast *ci*, because it is used for special or festive occasions such as *bis pole ritual*. It was also used for warfare and headhunting in the past. In some sub-ethnic groups of Asmat such as Kenok, they call *jicap ci* as *jo-ti*, the clan's *ci*. "Jo" means clan, and "*ti*" means *ci* or canoe. So, *jo-ti* means, *ci* which is owned by a clan. Since it is owned by a clan, the *jo-ti* is not used for daily activities. Likewise, *jicap ci* is sometimes called *ces ci*, which means the war *ci* because it was used for warfare in the past.

Physically, *jicap ci* is bigger and longer than *pakanam ci*. It is also ornamented and carved with a certain figure particularly in its *ci cimen*. It is used only once in a while, when there is a special celebration such as holding a ritual or other festive occasion. When the *jicap ci* is not in use, it must be kept in a certain place, like a garage (see again fig.34). And so, the *jicap ci* is dry, light, durable, and ready to use when it is needed. A grounded *jicap ci* must face water and to be covered by sago leaves. If it is parked and tied in a riverbank, the prowhead must face the river so as it can easily be used anytime.

4.4 Interpretations of the carvings in the *ci*

The *ci*, particularly the *jicap ci*, is usually carved by *wow-ipits*. It is right to say that the carvings in the *ci* are remarkable art expressions. Next, the *jicap ci* is full of symbols and meanings. The carving in the *ci* is a form of communication, both for the living and for the spirits. The following are some interpretations of the *ci* carvings. I do not offer a detailed or technical view of a *ci* carving, rather, I tried to go beyond the technical aspect to get more insights.

4.4.1 Decorative meaning

Daniel Ayas (*Fieldnote*, 55), a *cisi-ipits* (*ci* maker) and also *wow-ipits* (sculptor) from Atsj said, "*Ukiran perahu dimaksudkan sebagai hiasan supaya perahu tersebut kelihatan bagus dan indah. Kalau polos saja kurang indah*" (The first purpose of the *ci* carving is to make the *ci* good looking and beautiful. It is not good to see an undecorated *ci*). Fig.38 shows the *ci* with its carvings and decorations. Whatever the motif of the *ci* carving, it is aimed to decorate or to make it more beautiful. In other words, a *ci* can be an object of art of a *wow-ipits*. The *ci* can be a medium to express art. Through the *ci*, an artist can communicate publicly his feelings or his talents.

Figure 38. A carved and decorated *ci*.

4.4.2 Identity of the owner

Ci Cimen is a symbol of the many characteristics of the different sub-ethnic groups in Asmat. As mentioned earlier, every sub-ethnic group has its own style of carving including the motif of the *ci cimen*. Therefore, the *ci cimen* carving first and foremost becomes an identity tool for a certain sub-ethnic group. Second, it becomes an identity for a clan. Every clan has also its own model which is passed on through generations. Thus, a clan will not easily imitate any other model of carving from another clan because if they imitate, this means abandoning their own custom. Lastly, the carving can become a personal identity of its owner. This means the owner has freedom to express his feeling, passion, sentiment, spirit, and creativity through his *ci*.

4.4.3 Symbol of responsibility

According to Abraham Kuruwaip, the *Bis* ancestral carving is a reminder of revenge-obligation. The Asmat society places great importance on the obligation to revenge any death especially the death of one killed in battle. Failure of this obligation involves rendering the spirit impotent in his obligation to the on-going renewal of life among the Asmat (Kuruwaip1974:32). In the same sense, the *ci* carving is also a symbol of responsibility to revenge the death of a relative. It is the appropriate sign to show to the relatives' spirit that his brothers love him by making a *ci* and carving and naming it after him. It is also a symbol of responsibility to the community - - that a family or clan wants to remember and even to revenge the death of their loved ones. Moreover, the carving is a symbol of responsibility and obedience of a *wow-ipits* to his community - - that he is not imitating other's carving, but continues his clan's style. Although a *wow-ipits* is able to carve any design on his work, it is considered a violation if he carves any motif in a *jicap ci*; and a violation will bring about misfortune. This is the reason I say that the *ci* carving is a symbol of *wow-ipits*' responsibility to his community.

4.4.4 Representation of the dead spirit

The worlds of the living and of the dead are quite inseparable in Asmat. Therefore, Fleischhacker (1991:4) said,

> "Carvings are embodiments of the ancestral spirits which control the universe. To keep the cosmos in order, the Asmat placated their ancestors through carvings, ritual feasts, warfare, the taking of heads and cannibalism. The carvings make evident the vital interdependence between tangible and the intangible."

Carvings, including the *ci* carving, are representation of spirits. Carvings show the relationship between the world of the living and the world of the spirit. Every time the

Asmat see the carving, it reminds them of someone whom they carved there, just like when a Christian sees Jesus whenever he looks closely at the cross. According to David Jimanipits, the main part of the *ci* carving exists in the *ci cimen*. However, the *wow-ipits* also carves all around the *ci* as a symbol of the spirit's protection for the *ci* entirely.

4.4.5 Sign of intimacy

Generally, the Asmat symbolic motifs of carvings are inspired by daily experiences with nature. The elements of nature such as plants, animals, or specific part of an animal become motifs of their carving. Choosing the carving's motif is not by chance because the motifs are well organized in a remarkable manner. The selected motif can be an expression of the carver's feelings, emotions, and hopes. He chooses a certain symbol because he likes and feels comfortable with it. In other words, he has a personal or intimate touch with the symbol. Thus, he recreates it to be a fixed reality, an anamnesis, just like a photograph. Taking something or someone's picture means perpetuating the present situation of an object to re-experience it. In this sense, taking a motif to carve means perpetuating the experience or the feeling with a certain object or symbol.

Through the following examples, we can see how the Asmat use the elements of nature in their carvings. These are the common symbols of the Asmat motifs: *amer* (snake), *asesinokos* (centipede), *bipane* (double-curved shell nose ornament), *eu djim* (crocodile ribs), *was* (cuscus tail), *facep* (cuscus tail ending), *fofoyir* (hornbill head), *woro* (frog), *tarep* (flying-fox foot), *cenepir* (pelican head), *wenet* (praying mantis), *mbianam* (stone axe) (see Huber 2009:36). All motifs symbolize the personal experience and intimacy of the Asmat with a special object. The symbols are very close to the everyday life of the Asmat. Moreover, the common symbols are mostly related to their basic needs.

In conjunction with intimacy, I remember an experience when an Asmat family came to the parish priest's house and asked him to be their adopted son. It was a surprise for the parish priest. Before answering, the parish priest asked this: "Sir and ma'am, why me? Why do you want me to be your adopted son?" The husband said, "Because we love you so much. We like your attitude, your homilies, your visitations, and your friendship with the people. We will be very happy to have you as member of our family. We do not want to be left behind. We do not want another family to take you ahead of us as their adopted son." This experience inspired me to bravely say that the Asmat put a specific motif in their carving because they like it and feel intimate with it, just like the family who loved the parish priest so much, such that they wanted him to be their adopted son in order to enjoy forever the intimate feeling with the priest.

4.5 Bottomless *ci*

Wuramon is a distinct *ci* in the Asmat community. It is made of *ci nak* (special *ci* tree) and used for the rite of passage from boyhood into manhood. It is carved from a single piece of wood, and shaped like a dugout *ci* (Fleischhacker and Schneebaum 1976:95). The basic shape of *wuramon* (see fig.39) is not very different from the ordinary *ci*. However, it has specific characteristics that make it distinctive. It is a bottomless *ci* (see fig.40) and several figures are carved in it as symbols of good and bad spirits. This figures represent both ancestor figures and environmental spirits (Schneebaum 1989:63).

In a *wuramon*, one can find different figures such as *eco* (the human figure), *dat* (satan), *amerak* (man's head bird), *mbu* (turtle), *okom* ("Z"-like figure), *jinicowut* (woman in sitting

Figure 39. *Wuramon*, hanging in the guestroom of Yamas parish Priest's house.

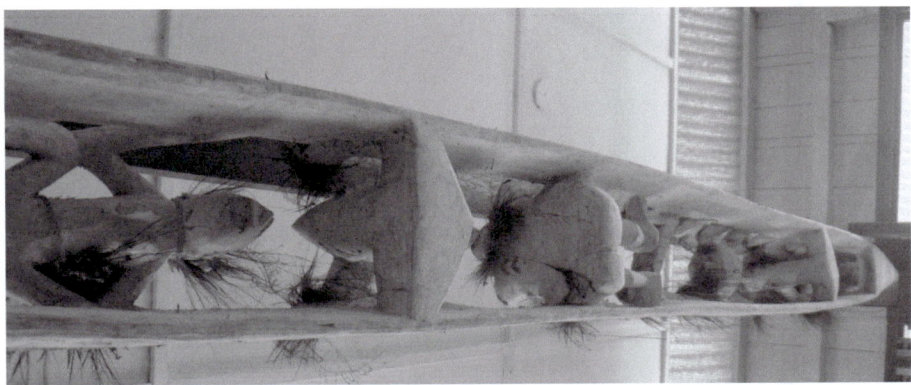

Figure 40. Bottomless *ci* (*wuramon*).

position), and *irimbi* (black king cockatoo beak). *Eco, dat, Amerak, jinicowut,* and *irimbi* are carved in pairs and placed symmetrically before and after the *okom* and *mbu*. Every figure has a meaning. This is more elaborated in Chapter 6 in relation to the supernatural dimension of the *ci*.

4.6 *Po*: The Asmat oar

The paddle is an integral part of the *ci*. The Asmat's name for oar (paddle) is *po*. The *ci* can be moved if there is an oar and oarsman, whereas an oar will be meaningful if there is a *ci*. Indeed, *ci* and *po* are complementary. These material cultures of the Asmat are very important for daily activities, aside from *dusun* and *jeu* (Bifae – *Fieldnote*, 4).

The Asmat oar is made of hard and strong wood. Sometimes it is used as a spear to kill either animals or enemies. That is why, some oars are pointed on the top. The following kinds of wood are possible materials for making an oar: *pes* (iron wood), *po nak* (oar wood), *betspo* (damar), and *jasinpo* (buah gayang). If the oar material is good and strong, it will be durable and can be passed on to the next generation as a valuable inheritance.

It is very interesting to note that the men's and women's oars of the Asmat are different, especially in terms of length and ornamentation (see fig.41 and 42). The men's oar is typically longer than the women's because the men paddle the *ci* standing upright, whereas women paddle while sitting down. So, the men need a longer oar to reach the water, while women need a shorter oar because they are closer to the water. This is the very basic reason the oar of men and women differ from each other.

Generally, aside from its length, the men's oar is usually carved and ornamented by bird feathers or young sago leaves to make it much more beautiful and powerful. The women's oar can be carved and ornamented with sago leaves only. However, the carving motifs of men and women's oar are also different to emphasize the difference between men and women. There are at least three kinds of oars based on ornaments: *Poyiwi* (oar ornamented by cassowary's feathers), *Pomat* (oar ornamented by cockatoo's feathers), and *Pocemakan* (oar ornamented by young sago leaves, usually used by women). According to my informants, women can use the men's oar if it has no ornaments.

Figure 41. Ornamented men's oars.

Figure 42. Holding with the right hand is the man's oar while the other is the woman's oar.

5

Social dimension of the *ci*

As I have said earlier, the *ci* is a guarantee for mobility in the everyday life of the Asmat. It facilitates the transport of people from one place to another. It connects two or more places such as one village to another, or a *dusun* to another, or a river to another. Basically, the *ci* is utilized to connect or to take someone to meet his needs.

5.1 The sociality of the *ci*

The *ci* relates people in many ways, both intra and inter-communities. The *ci* is not only used as a means of transportation, but it also builds good social relationships among the members of a community. The *ci* itself is a symbol of unity because it binds people in one space to reach the same direction. The following illustrates the Asmat values in creating life in harmony through the *ci*. These illustrations show the social life of the *ci* (see Appadurai 1986).

First, the Primus Ostji's (*Fieldnote*, 41) story. "There are three siblings – – two males and one female. Let's say, the oldest brother is named Jakawut and the youngest Cipicak, while the sister's name is Tewer. One day Cipicak goes to their *dusun* to cut down a tree and make a *ci* because he has no *ci*. Despite his efforts to create a new *ci*, Cipicak cannot possess it automatically. To validate his ownership over the *ci*, he has to follow the traditional norm. First, he needs to meet Jakawut, his elder brother, and give the new *ci* to him because traditionally, Jakawut is the first person who has right over the *ci*. Jakawut then would think deeply if he wants to own the *ci*. In fact, Jakawut knows that Cipicak has no *ci*. Therefore, he decides not to take the *ci*, but gives it back to Cipicak. From Jakawut, Cipicak with the new *ci* then goes to Tewer, his elder sister to do the same as he did to Jakawut. Finally, Tewer gives the *ci* back to Cipicak after thinking wisely, considering that Cipicak has no *ci*. From then on, the new *ci* officially belongs to Cipicak."

This story shows the intimate relationship between siblings in Asmat. They honor their brother and sister in such a good way. Through this way, they obtain their right with honor too, just as Cipicak who claims ownership of his *ci* with honor from his siblings. This is a very beautiful brotherhood relationship that I have found. Above all, from the story, we can see the level of ownership in Asmat society. That is why I worry that this value might become extinct through modernization, along with the *ci's* gradual extinction. Water transportation in Asmat may continuously exist using modern tools, but not with the *ci* and its uniqueness.

Second, the Amatus Ndatipits (*Fieldnote*, 22) story. "If a neighbor wants to borrow a *ci*, the owner of the *ci* would not say directly that it cannot be borrowed. Instead, the woman of the house would say, while attending to the fireplace: "Oh…, we do not have any firewood in the hearth. More so, last night the small child cried loudly because there was no fish in her sago.' These words will be understood by the neighbor that the *ci* cannot be borrowed. These words are signs of rejection. Therefore, the neighbor will go back to her house peacefully. She knows that the *ci* will be used by the owner, so it is understandable that it cannot be taken away. If the owner says directly that the *ci* cannot be borrowed, the borrower will probably become angry and might consider vengeance. Someday, she might find a good moment to express her anger to that family.

Third, anger expressed because of the *ci* (see *Fieldnote*, 77). Take for an example, Tewerauts has an elder brother Beworpits. One day, Tewerauts borrows Beworpits' *ci* to go to *dusun* to look for firewood. When she goes, Tewerauts asks Bis, her friend, to join her. Accidentally, the *ci* crashes a log in the middle of a big river. As a consequence, a small part of the *ci* is broken. When they come home, Beworpits gets angry because his *ci* was damaged. However, he does not address his anger directly to both Tewerauts and Bis. To express his anger, he takes his axe and beats the *ci*, so the damage became worse. Seemingly, Sarkap, Bis' husband, observed what Beworpits did to his own *ci*. Sarkap gets angry too because his wife, Bis, also used Beworpits' *ci* together with Tewerauts. Nevertheless, Sarkap did not challenge Beworpits to fight at that time. Instead, he goes to his *dusun* quietly and makes a new *ci*. Then, during a very special occasion, for instance, when there is a traditional celebration in their village, Sarkap shows intentionally his new *ci* before Beworpits. Through this action, Sarkap tried to say to Beworpits, "You are not the only man who can make a *ci*. I am also a man. I am able to make a new *ci*!" This action and message challenged Beworpits' anger. If Beworpits was not satisfied and could not accept Sarkap's action, he would do the same thing. He would go to *dusun* quietly and makes a new *ci* as well, and when the right time comes, he will show his new *ci* to Sarkap implying the same message.

These illustrations are evidence that the *ci* has power, not only to relate two or more separated places, but also to communicate with two or more people in a community. It relates the feelings and emotions of people in a community, whether positive or negative. The *ci* strengthens the relationship among family members, especially the extended family. It is only the family or clan members who can enter the same *ci*. The Asmat will not allow anybody to enter their *ci*, if they do not truly know who the person is. They assume that an outsider might do a bad thing to their *ci*, such as damage it or lose in a race or battle.

The relationship among the family members can be seen in the agents who are involved in making a *ci*: *tuan perahu* (owner), *cisi-ipits* (canoe maker), *wow-ipits* (carver), *ipar* (brother-in-law), and other relatives. The owner of the *ci* is responsible in providing food and some facilities for *cisi-ipits* and *wow-ipits* so that they will do their work fast and happily. Brothers-in-law and other relatives are responsible in helping the *cisi-ipits* and *wow-ipits* when needed. For example, their help is needed when the *ci* needs to be moved to a certain position. The presence of a brother-in-law is also a sign of his loyalty to his wife's brother, the owner of the *ci*.

Going back to the discussion above, I found that the Asmat have their own art of communicating. They use symbols to tell something else. Based on the example above, I found that the Asmat do not clearly and directly state what they are thinking or arguing with others. It is just like Sarkap making a new canoe quietly and then showing it before the very eyes of Beworpits to express his anger. Among the natives of Asmat, it is easy for them to understand the traditional way of expressing feelings and emotions. Unfortunately, it is not the same thing with non-Asmat. It is very difficult for non-Asmat to understand the Asmat way of life. Therefore, I do understand why the Asmat and the non-Asmat sometimes find difficulties in their relationships because they do not understand each other. The Asmat say something symbolically, while the non-Asmat do so practically. The non-Asmat do not understand the Asmat symbol, while the Asmat do not want to be told directly and practically what they have to hear. For instance, the Asmat do not like to be told, "No, I cannot lend you my *ci* because I will use it." Instead, they do like to listen to, 'Oh…, we do not have any firewood in the hearth. So, last night the small child cried loudly because there was no fish in her sago,' if somebody wants to borrow their *ci*. Consequently, there will be a perpetual conflict if each party does not understand the other; in this case, the Asmat and the non-Asmat. So, to be friendly with the Asmat in particular, one has to learn their way of life, especially their way of communication – - their way of expressing their emotions and feelings. In other words, what I wanted to say is "to use their door to enter their house."

5.2 *Cisi-ipits* – *ci* maker

One of the responsibilities of Asmat men is to make a *ci* (see fig.43). The initial stage in the process of making a *ci* is done in the middle of a jungle and is finished in front of a *jeu* (traditional house) in the village. All the stages in making a *ci* are men's responsibilities, except when they haul the timber out from the middle of a jungle to the river where women can be involved. According to Nico Ndepi, when the people haul timber from the middle of a jungle, usually they utter, "*Jumlah kami sedikit, sementara batang kayu ini begitu besar, tetapi kami akan mencoba!*" (We are few, while this timber is huge, but we will try!). By saying these words, they believe that the log is listening to them, just like a living person and then it will be easy to haul. If the timber is still heavy and difficult to haul, the men will ask a mother to help. There is a belief that the *ci* is a mother's son. So, when a mother or a woman is involved in hauling the timber of the *ci*, it will be light and easy to haul because "his mother" is there. This is somewhat similar to Amatus Ndatipits' (*Fieldnote*, 22) experience when he was a child. He shared his story with me,

> "*Kalau pada waktu perahu ditarik dari hutan terasa berat, maka ibu-ibu bisa dilibatkan untuk membantu. Saya sendiri sebagai contoh. Ketika pada masa kecil ada kayu besar ditarik dari hutan, sangat sulit, lalu saya dan ibu ikut naik di atas kayu perahu tersebut. Ketika ditarik, kayu perahu tersebut menjadi laju sekali.*" (Whenever the *ci* is heavy to haul, we need to ask women to be involved. I had an experience on this. When I was a child, many people were hauling a very big and heavy *ci* from the jungle. It was very difficult for the men. Then my mother and I rode in the *ci*. At once, the timber became lighter and easier to haul).

Pius Woyakai (*Fieldnote*, 49) added more information about how the *ci* tree obeys a mother's request when he said,

> "*Kalau perahu terasa berat ketika ditarik, biasanya kita minta ibu-ibu untuk memberi susu kepada kayu perahu tersebut seolah-seolah sedang menyusui anak sendiri. Setelah itu kayu pasti akan jadi ringan untuk ditarik ke kali.*" (When the timber is very heavy to haul, usually the men ask a mother to give her breast milk to the timber as if she is feeding her own child. After that, the timber will surely be lighter and easier to haul to the river).

From these experiences, we can note that despite the fact that the major work in the making of a *ci* is a man's responsibility, the woman's involvement cannot be excluded because in her own way, she supports his man to make the work a success. Therefore, mythological, a woman is the mother of the *ci*.

After hauling the timber from the jungle, the other steps will be completed by men. The women's jobs while the men are carving or digging out the *ci* are: preparing food for the *ci* maker(s); weaving a new mat (*tapin*), a traditional bag (*noken*), and a new *ci* wiper made of young sago leaves. These things will be given to the *ci* maker once the new *ci* is done. This is part of the payment for the *ci* maker, especially when the *ci* maker is not the woman's husband.

Thus, women are not involved in making the *ci* with their own hands, but they support the men to accomplish their work. Based on her observation, Sr. Korina Ngoe (*Fieldnote*, 20), the director of Yan Smith Foundation of Agats diocese said,

> "*Dalam membuat perahu, sangat terlihat bahwa perempuan Asmat seolah-olah hanya pemain di belakang layar. Namun, tanpa keterlibatan perempuan acara-acara adat yang umumnya dilakukan oleh laki-laki tidak akan terjadi dengan baik.*" (In the process of making *ci*, it is very apparent that the Asmat women are just like players behind the scene. Nonetheless, without women's involvement, many traditional rituals which are performed mostly by men will not be successful).

This observation underlines the fact that somehow women's involvement in rituals and other activities in Asmat is very important.

In spite of the indirect involvement of women in making a *ci*, the Asmat men realize that the women's support during the *ci* making process is very important. The Asmat men themselves do not claim that they are the only *ci* makers. The men realize that without food which is prepared by the women, they will not be able to make a good *ci*. The *ci* maker can focus on his work because of the women's support, particularly food availability while doing his job. The Asmat men admire the women's involvement in any activity or ritual celebration, including the making of a *ci*. In other words, women have a huge contribution in making of the *ci* successful, although they are not the ones who physically cut the *ci* tree, shape the log, or carve it until it becomes a useful *ci*. As an analogy, sometimes the Asmat consider that there is similarity between the making of a *ci* and going to war. While the men prepare themselves for warfare, the women provide food for them in order to gain physical strength and win the war. Without food, instead of bringing war's benefits, they may probably become prey to their enemies. This is why the women's support is very important, both in making a *ci* and in warfare. According to Karola Biakai, the Asmat women can be called *cem aman jur*. It means, a woman is like a dog who is always loyal to protect his lord. Moreso, women are men's shields in facing difficulties. Without women's contributions, men will not able to do their duties successfully. In short, men and women complement each other.

Figure 43. An Asmat man is making a *pakanam ci* behind his house.

The *ci* makers are talented men and this job is never done by women. The Asmat men will not allow their wives, sisters, or daughters to make a *ci*. It is taboo for an Asmat woman to cut a *ci* for herself or her family. The Asmat women themselves will not try to do so because it is taboo and dangerous for them and the community. The Asmat believe that the division of labor between men and women come from their ancestors. Hence, nobody objects or even questions anything that the ancestors have regulated. So, for the Asmat, it is useless to question why Asmat women are not allowed to make a *ci* because it is a given truth. That is why answering similar questions, most Asmat just say, "*Itu sudah. Sudah dari nenek moyang!*" ("Yes, it is. It was regulated by our ancestors!"). It means one needs not ask more because one will not get the answer.

According to Nico Ndepi (*Fieldnote*, 11), if an Asmat woman makes a *ci*, it means she is cursing men and puts them in danger. It is also a significant warning for the husband, son, or other men because they are not taking their responsibility as men. The community will be in danger if a woman makes a *ci* because, on the one hand, the man lets a woman fulfill the male's social responsibility, and on the other hand, the woman violates the customary law. Violation brings about misfortunes and death. Above all, spiritually and culturally there is one belief among the Asmat – - the *ci* is a son of a mother (Samson Pirap, in Notulensi Study Budaya 2012:4). So, logically a mother will not cut a *ci* tree because it is like ripping or killing her own son.

Therefore, in dealing with *ci* making, Tadeus (*Fieldnote*, 45) one of the tribal leaders of Yasiw says, "*Tidak pernah ada kasus bahwa perempuan membuat perahu. Itu karu. Perempuan sudah langsung tahu bahwa itu bukan bagian mereka.*" (It never happens that a woman makes a *ci*. It is taboo. Women themselves already knew that making *ci* is not their responsibility). Pius Woyakai (*Fieldnote*, 49) highlights Tadeus' words by saying,

> "*Perempuan tidak boleh membuat perahu. Seandainya ada yang nekad membuat perahu, maka laki-laki yang jadi korban, mati. Kalau sampai seorang perempuan membuat perahu sama artinya menyumpah suaminya. Bahkan ibu janda pun tidak boleh menebang perahu. Dia harus meminta bantu dari saudaranya laki-laki. Di dalam masyarakat Asmat, pembagian tugas antara laki-laki dan perempuan sangat jelas. Kerja perempuan tidak boleh dikerjakan oleh laki-laki, begitu pun sebaliknya.*" (Women are not allowed to make *ci*. If there is an obstinate woman who makes a *ci*, it means she puts the men to death. If a wife makes a *ci*, it means she curses her own husband. Even a widow is not allowed to cut down a tree to make a *ci*. She must ask her brother to make a *ci* for her. In the Asmat society, the division of labor between men and women is so obvious. Men's labor cannot be done by women or vice versa).

It is therefore apparent that the *ci* maker is always a man because it is part of his responsibility as a male.

I think, it is a little bit flexible for Asmat men to acknowledge women's job while they are working on the *ci*. It is quite different for men in Marquesas, one of the many islands of Polynesia, as reported by Mead (1969:41),

> "In the Marquesas, where all work was taboo, the chief prohibition was against all connected with women. All of those engaged in the operation were purified by bathing or charms before they began their labor; they lived in a sacred house; their food was taboo and they were denied all intercourse with women. Women were not allowed to enter a canoe or even to bathe in a lake in which a canoe floated. If a fishing canoe were profaned by the touch of a woman, human hair must be burnt on the bow to purify it."

Asmat men also construct the *jicap ci* (feast *ci*) in a particular place, usually in front of a *jeu*. However, their food will still be provided by women. They are not totally separated from women. The Asmat and the Marquesas share the same taboo in terms of not allowing women to enter a canoe; especially the *jicap ci* for the Asmat.

Even if Asmat men are responsible in making a *ci*, there is no guarantee that every Asmat man is able to make a *ci*. The *ci* maker is a talented man, as mentioned earlier. Consequently, those men who are not skillful in making *ci*, *sine qua non*, hire a talented *ci* maker, usually one from their own kin. For example, Daniel Ayas (*Fieldnote*, 55) said that he has made more than 50 *cis* already for his family and relatives during his life time because he is the most talented person in making *ci* among his kin.

There are some of the general divisions of labor in Asmat society, according to Hermina Ndatipits (*Fieldnote*, 27) and Seravia Tojamter (*Fieldnote*, 60; see also Fleischhacker 1991:9). Both men and women have their own specializations in laboring for their society. Woman's labors are included: Weaving mat (tapin) and bag (noken), making sago sieve (ov), fishing nets, ci cleaner (cocomit), nipper (jokomen), apron (awer), providing food for her family, pounding sago (with her husband), gathering firewood, fishing, cooking, providing food for traditional rituals, taking care of the house and the ci, as well as the children. Meanwhile man's labors are: making ci, house, paddle (po), drum (tifa), spear (oten), bow (amon) and arrow (firakom), shield (salawaku), daggers (pi pisuwe), sago pounder (amosus); woodcarving (wow-ipits) activity, making necklace and other feast accessories, hunting, going to war and headhunting, making a path in the jungle, protecting his village, creating strategy and plan for war and headhunting.

5.3 The *ci* owned by the family

The *ci* is owned by a family, especially the *pakanam ci*. The *pakanam ci* is not owned by either husband (man) or wife (woman), but by the family members. It is a shared ownership. However, in everyday life, the business pertaining to the *pakanam ci* after it is constructed is the wife's responsibility. Remember, the *ci* maker is a man. Therefore, it is reasonable that a person who wants to borrow the *ci* will deal with the wife and not with the husband of the *ci* owner. The wife will decide if the *ci* can be borrowed or not, even without consulting her husband because she is the one who knows the availability of all needs of her family such as sago, firewood, etc. A husband will not lend their *ci* without his wife's permission.

Ideally, a household owns at least one *ci*. Unfortunately, a *ci* is usually used by more than one family because typically the Asmat live together in one house. One house in Asmat is usually occupied by more than one household, although each family has its own hearth. So, it is not a guarantee that each family owns a *ci*. They can share the one and only *ci* as they do with a house. At present, there are many families in Asmat who do not own a *ci* (see Ndepi, Ostji, Woyakai, Ayas, and a Participant Observation in Atsj Elemetary School). Consequently, those who do not own a *ci* are highly dependent on other people's help, or remain parasites.

5.4 The *ci* triggers conflicts among the Asmat

According to my informants and also based on my own observations, the Asmat frequently quarrel or fight because of the *ci* (see Ayurkap, Woyakai, Bifae, Ndepi, Pasauran). The informants agreed that the *ci* indeed triggers conflicts among the Asmat. For example, a family wants to go fishing, but they cannot find their *ci* at the riverbank because somebody used it secretly. When eventually they found out that their *ci* is being used by someone else without permission, sooner or later a big quarrel will follow. The owner of the *ci* can express his anger by destroying the *ci*, which is a symbol of his fury to the person who used the *ci* without permission. According to Ap and Mansoben (1974:63), using other's *ci* without permission is similar to raping someone's wife that is why it possibly brings about fighting. A dispute regarding the *ci* can also take place when the borrower returns the *ci* without payment. For instance, the borrower uses the *ci* to go fishing, but when he comes back to return the *ci*, he does not share his gains.

The *ci* is a key, a guarantee for mobility, a symbol of life, a symbol of independence, a symbol of responsibility, and a representation of the ancestors' lives. Therefore, it is but justifiable that an individual or family would take care of it seriously. I do believe that people everywhere will seriously look after their valuable possessions, including relationship, religion, and other belief systems. The Asmat take care of the *ci* and if it cannot be avoided, they are ready to fight for it because it is the source of their lives. If a man destroys another man's *ci* intentionally, it can stimulate fighting from individual to group levels (Ap and Mansoben 1974:63). Everybody will fight for something or someone that is significant for them. Moreover, according to Ndepi, the *ci* can trigger conflicts among the Asmat because the *ci* is named after one's relative's who has been killed in a battle. Thus, the *ci* can arouse anger among the dead relatives whenever they see the *ci*.

Fr. Vince Cole, a Maryknoll priest from the United States who lived in Asmat for more than 30 years, collected a lot of Asmat myths, including myths about the *ci*. I want to share one such myths, with his permission, to emphasize how the *ci* can trigger conflict among the Asmat in their society (Cole (ed.):121-124).

Mbewirap leaves his wife stranded without a canoe

I am going to tell you the story about Mbewirap and why he left his wife stranded in the village without a canoe.

As long as Mbewirap and his wife had been living together she had never taken any responsibility to care for the canoe. Every time Mbewirap told her to clean it out or tie it up, etc., she always refused. "It's not mine," she would say.

This went on for a very long time. Mbewirap was forced to care for the canoe by himself.

Then one day there was an announcement that they were going to move the village to a new location. Everybody became very busy making the necessary preparations. They pulled their canoes up onto the riverbank and built fires under them. They prepared the food that they would need. Finally they put their belongings into the canoes and covered them with pandanas leaf mats to protect them from the weather.

Early the next morning everyone departed. They left behind only those things that were no longer useful. Everyone was excited anticipating their new move.

Mbewirap was the last to leave. After loading his canoe he waited until everyone else departed. Then he ran from one end of the village to the other. He completely destroyed all of the old but still serviceable canoes that had been left behind. He smashed them into such small pieces with his stone axe that they could never possibly be used again. Also whenever he spotted an old broken paddle lying about he threw it into the river to float away. After he had done all of this Mbewirap set off to follow the others. He left his wife and children (five boys and four girls) behind.

When Mbewirap's wife realized that she had been abandoned she said to her oldest son, "Go and see if you can find a canoe that we can use."

The boy searched the whole village. He couldn't find a serviceable canoe anywhere. Mbewirap had destroyed them all.

So rather than trying to follow the others Mbewirap's wife decided to set out on foot and start a village of her own. She and her children loaded all of their belongings onto their backs and set off walking into the forest. They walked until the mother could walk no further.

They stopped and made a small shelter while the oldest boy went hunting. He shot a large pig. That night they didn't go to sleep hungry. The next morning they continued their journey. They left the uneaten meat behind in the shelter. They walked all day. Toward evening they came to a small a sago grove. "We will stop here," said the mother. So everyone got busy and made a shelter.

When the shelter was finished their mother said, "I am about to give birth." She went into labor and that night gave birth to a boy.

The next morning the woman's eldest son asked, "Mother are you able to continue walking today? This is not a good place to establish our village. The sago trees are too few and too small."

So the woman forced herself to get up and walk.

They walked the whole day. Toward evening they arrived at an area that was full of sago trees. It was the perfect location to establish their village. They decided to stop and make their village there.

They immediately went to work building their houses. Each child had his/her own house. They also built a large bachelors' house. They spent the whole night drumming to celebrate the establishment of their new village.

In the morning the oldest boy called his brothers together. "We will make a pathway to the river," he said.

While he marked the trail the others began cutting a pathway through the dense forest. They went on and on until they finally came to the Sirets river.

Next they chopped down a huge tree intending to make a canoe. But when the tree hit the ground it threw itself into the water and started floating down river. The boys ran after it along the riverbank. They shot arrows into it as it floated away. The current carried the huge tree far down river until it came to the new village where Mbewirap was now living.

When the people there spotted the tree one of them paddled out to investigate. He saw that it was a fine tree for making a canoe. He tried to bring it to shore but he couldn't divert it from its course. He quickly returned to shore. "it is a perfect tree for making a canoe," he said.

Everyone rushed out. They tried pulling the tree toward shore. They pulled and pulled but could no divert it. So they left it to continue floating on its down river course.

Finally Mbewirap paddled out to the tree. He jumped from his canoe onto the floating tree. The tree immediately changed its course and started floating toward the edge of the river. Once there it leaped out of the water onto the shore. Everyone who saw this was dumbfounded. They couldn't understand why they couldn't divert the floating tree. All Mbewirap had to do was jump onto the tree and it settled itself onto the shore.

Back upriver the older brother said, "Little brothers go back home. I am going to stay here and keep watch. When that tree is discovered with arrows sticking out of it surely someone will come to investigate. Before long three canoes appeared in the distance. They headed directly for the pathway. The men disembarked. They searched the area. "This path must lead to a village," they said.

They went back to their village to inform the others. That night they would all return armed for battle.

The boy observed them from his hiding place. After they had left he ran back home and informed his brothers. They were delighted to hear this. They immediately began decorating themselves for battle. As they made the necessary preparations their excitement continued to grow. "My brothers let us beat our drums now," said the oldest boy.

It was already far into the night by the time Mbewirap and the others arrived. They surrounded the bachelors' house and waited for the first light of day.

Just as the boys were preparing their sago the men attacked. Great battle cries broke the silence. But the boys were ready. With the very first cry the oldest boy jumped up with his spear and shield in his hands. He ran toward the door screaming. His brothers followed closely behind. The enemy became afraid. They scattered and ran back down the pathway toward their canoes. They boys pursued killing large numbers of them. The whole length of the trail back to the Sirets River was strewn with the men's bodies.

When they reached the Sirets the young man and his brothers stood on the bank. They watched as Mbewirap and the other survivors paddled frantically away from shore. Once they were a safe distance away Mbewirap shouted, "Who are you?"

"I am Mbewirap," answered the boy.

It was then that the older Mbewirap realized that this must be his son. When he asked he was told that indeed they were all his children.

The boys captured Mbewirap and took him to back to his wife.

After butchering their victims they celebrated their victory and reunion with a feast of human flesh.

The story about Mbewirap only goes this far.

(Told by Mbas from the village of Sa. The Asmat title for the myth is *Mbewirap Armo Ti Owok Tiapmer*).

5.5 The dynamics of *ci cimen* and *ci ep*

The two poles of the *ci* are different. The prowhead is called *ci cimen*, while the end section is called *ci ep*. Both points not only differ in name, but also in shape. The *ci cimen* is usually carved beautifully and becomes a symbol of power of the *ci* and its owner, while the *ci ep* is mostly simple, pointed, and without carving. The differences between *ci cimen* and *ci ep* are not merely physical binary opposites such as beginning-end, front-back, complicated-simple, with-without carving, but they also influence gender relations in the Asmat society.

Figure 44. Positioning in a *ci*: husband is at the *ci cimen*, wife is at *ci ep*, and children at *cinamakat*.

The most obvious example is that men stand upright at *ci cimen*, while women sit down at *ci ep*. Fig.44 illustrates it clearly.

Positioning in a *ci* is not without meaning, but it can be seen as a representation of the everyday life of the Asmat, particularly regarding social status and gender roles (see Lips 2005:69). To make it clearer, let us take a household as an example. Normally, a household comprises a husband, wife, and children. If we put the household members in a *ci*, the arrangement will be like this: the husband is at *ci cimen* (prowhead), the wife at *ci ep* (rear), and the children at *cindem* (middle). In other words, the man at *ci cimen*, while the woman at *ci ep*. This kind of arrangement is indeed a fact. This tradition has been passed on from ancestors through generations until the present time. The positioning in the *ci* is considered sacred, so the Asmat observe it seriously in order not to experience disharmony in their community. However, there are some cases when the arrangement is not as usual.

Based on my firsthand data, I discovered that there are at least three reasons why the Asmat place men at *ci cimen* and women at *ci ep*. First, the physical difference between men and women is strongly underscored. They interpret the anatomical and physiological distinction between men and women as justification for inequalities (see Godelier 1992: xi). The Asmat men feel different and even stronger than women. Asmat men believe that physically they possess a better capability than women to anticipate and to overcome every probability that might hit them such as a wild animal or enemy attack (see Ostji, Ayurkap, Yuvensius and Nada – *Fieldnote*, 9, 39, 42). This notion can be analyzed from these expressions, "*Perempuan tidak sekuat laki-laki.*" (Women are not as strong as men).

Or other saying, "*Laki-laki di depan perahu sebagai penunjuk jalan, supaya tidak salah jalan; perempuan hanya ikut saja.*" (Men at *ci cimen* serve as as guides in order not to go astray; women just follow). Moreover, Nico Ndepi confidently states,

> "*Perempuan berbeda dengan laki-laki dalam mendayung perahu. Itu tergantung gaya: gaya laki-laki berbeda dengan gaya perempuan secara natural. Fisik laki-laki berbeda dengan perempuan. Perempuan tidak boleh disamakan dengan laki-laki. Laki-laki membawa keperkasaan. Wanita tetap sebagai wanita, seorang mama.*" (Women are different from men in paddling the *ci*. It depends on style: naturally, men and women's styles are different. Men and women's physiques are different. Women cannot be seen as equal to men. Man brings power. The woman remains a woman, just like a mother).

Thus, these expressions lead us to say that men always feel superior to women. Patriarchalism in Asmat society is strong. Whenever men speak, women should not interrupt. Therefore, to show their domination, men place themselves before others as pioneers, guides, leaders, and protectors. They are proud of being males in their society. This is symbolized by occupying the place at the *ci cimen* in order to protect those who are in the rear, who are considered weak and needing protection.

Second, this involves a local belief. One of the Asmat beliefs is that menstrual as well as natal bloods are very dangerous, particularly for men (see Tsing 1993:184). The menstrual blood is believed to be very dirty and brings about disease and misfortune. Therefore, Asmat men avoid the two kinds of dirty blood, just like vampires who avoid the sunlight in many horror movies. To relate a case, I recall my own experience in 2003 when an Asmat family came to me and earnestly requested me to pray for the husband who was about to be paralyzed. The wife explained that the illness came to her husband just after helping a mother who was giving birth, and perhaps the blood of the mother affected him. They thought that the illness came from the natal blood. They came to me to pray and to drive away the illness that might have come from the evil spirit through the natal blood.

This experience convinced me that Asmat men are really afraid of natal and menstrual blood. I then realized that it is very easy for a wicked woman to paralyze or to kill any man just by using her menstrual blood. This is similar to what Tsing (1993:184) said in the context of Meratus Dayak of Borneo Indonesia, "Not surprisingly, menstrual blood is a potent sorcery substance, used against men by women."

In my opinion, (grounded by the patriarchal society), the Asmat society forbids women to enter *jeu*, new *ci*, and partake directly in many traditional rituals because of the anxiety of men. The men are afraid of menstrual blood and are not able to identify who among the women present in the activity is menstruating. Therefore, to make it easy, they made a general rule not to allow all women to enter a *jeu*, new *ci*, nor participate in traditional rituals (see Strathern 1988:101). The men say that the *jeu* is a sacred place and cannot be polluted by the "dirty blood" of a woman. All men's instruments such as spears, shields, drums, bow and arrows are placed in a *jeu*. They believe that the power of these instruments will be lost if menstrual blood affects them.

Furthermore, in the context of the *ci*, the Asmat believe that if the menstrual blood trickles down to a *ci*, the *ci* will be heavier, can easily be damaged, will lose in racing, and the spirit of the *ci* will go away. Menstrual blood is not only considered as "dirt", but also bears negative power to bring about disease and death in a community, especially for men.

Therefore, dirt-avoidance through menstrual blood is a creative movement and a positive effort to organize the environment (see Douglas 1966:2). To have a better understanding of this notion, I quote the Amatus Ndatipits' (*Fieldnote*, 39) words when he said,

> "*Haid dan vagina terbuka juga berkaitan dengan posisi di dalam perahu. Oleh sebab itu, seorang perempuan harus di belakang supaya penyakit tidak mudah masuk dan dia juga tidak meneteskan atau mereciki laki-laki yang ada di belakang dengan darah haidnya. Orang Asmat meyakini bahwa darah haid bisa melemahkan dan melumpuhkan laki-laki. Wanita tidak boleh di depan perahu supaya angin tidak mudah masuk. Kalau perempuan di depan angin bisa masuk karena wanita punya vagina yang bisa menjadi pintu masuk angin dan penyakit. Hal ini bisa memperberat perahu dan melemahkan kekuatan laki-laki.*" (Menstruation and opened vagina is related to the arrangement in a *ci*. Therefore, a woman has to sit at *ci ep* at the back in order not to spread the menstrual blood to the man. There is a belief among the Asmat that menstrual blood can paralyze men. Women are not allowed to occupy the position at *ci cimen* so that the wind would not easily enter. If a woman sits at *ci cimen*, wind and disease can enter the *ci* through her vagina. These things can paralyze men and make the *ci* heavy).

In fact, the positioning in a *ci* is basically rooted by the male domination in the Asmat society. This is quite similar to Marilyn Strathern's (1988:99) analysis in the Papua New Guinea context about imposition upon reality. She said clearly, "The claims Highlands men make in context of their rituals have been interpreted as strenuous assertions by which they as one dominate women and mystify themselves." Basically, Asmat men want to show their physical strength and then hide their weaknesses and fears by placing themselves at the *ci cimen*. They believe that women have magical power that can be used to weaken or kill men. That is why it is very rational for a senior woman especially *tesetor* (the big men's wife) to be allowed to enter the *jicap ci* (war *ci*) because she possesses a tremendous killing power. Again, men are really afraid of the evil power of women that comes from menstrual blood, so they excluded women from many traditional rituals as well as from entering a *jeu* or a new *ci*. Psychologically, I would say that putting women at *ci ep* is one of the defense mechanisms of men.

Still in the realm of patriarchy, the social status of the Asmat men seems superior to women, at least from the men's perspective as Primus Ostji (*Fieldnote*, 41) said,

> "*Perempuan boleh di bagian depan perahu, dan bisa diterima secara publik, kalau ia mempunyai prestasi khusus. Kalau tidak, ia akan ditegur oleh tua-tua adat. Perempuan juga bisa di depan perahu kalau suaminya berprestasi tinggi, misalnya dia sebagai kepala perang atau sudah membunuh banyak musuh.*" (A woman can be seated at *ci cimen*, and be publicly accepted, if she has a special achievement. If she is only an ordinary woman, she might be warned by the tribal leaders. A woman can also be at *ci cimen* if her husband is a big man or a great warrior and has killed many enemies).

In fact, it is accepted in Asmat society for a *tesetor* (big man's wife) to stand at *ci cimen* because her husband is a big man and has achieved a lot of honors in battles. A big man has the privilege to put his wife anywhere in the *ci*. He is a great honorable man, so nobody will question or criticize him when his wife does not sit at *ci ep*, but at the *ci cimen*. It is a different case and is questionable if an ordinary man puts his wife at *ci cimen*. He can be misinterpreted as a suspicious husband (see Ndepi, *Fieldnote*, 11). It seems funny but it makes sense because a husband cannot control his wife along the way when she is at the rear of a *ci*. In other words, a wife at *ci ep* is uncontrollable by her husband, so she is free to *"main mata"* (literally would means "make a code with the eyes") with other men. When the husband is at the *ci ep*, he has the power to control not only the *ci*, but also his wife because he can observe her every action since she is in front of him.

At present, we can see the similar degree of the honorable status of women in an Asmat community such as being regent's wife, the local government officer's wife, the wife of a village chieftain, the principal's wife, and a party leader's wife. These wives of honorable husbands are accepted to publicly occupy the position at *ci cimen* because their husbands are considered as great men (see Ndatipits – Fieldnote, 39).

Another reason why a woman takes position at *ci cimen* aside from her husband's status is when she obtains a special job in society such as being a teacher, nurse, local government officer, or leader of an organization. These women who occupy good positions in any public service can be categorized as *cescu cepes* (great women). Therefore, they can stand upright at the *ci cimen*.

It is a different case if a family works in the middle of a *dusun*. Nobody will question if a wife takes position at *ci cimen* because there is nobody else with them. In addition, they are the masters of the *dusun*, and as masters, they obtain the privilege over it, including the *ci*. The explanation of Woyakai (*Fieldnote*, 49) described the custom of the Asmat, either at the middle of the forest or in a village. He said,

> *"Laki-laki biasanya di bagian depan perahu. Hanya saja, kalau sedang di sungai di dalam hutan, laki-laki boleh di belakang, tetapi kalau sudah di dekat kampung, perempuan tidak boleh di depan. Perempuan boleh di depan kalau seorang ibu sudah diberi kepala manusia oleh suaminya atau saudaranya."* (The man is usually at *ci cimen*. However, when they are in the river and at the middle of the jungle, the man's place can be at *ci ep*, but when they are about to reach the village, the woman cannot be at *ci cimen*. A woman can have the position at *ci cimen* if she has been given an enemy's head by her husband or her brother).

The social and traditional regulations of the Asmat are valid in the public sphere and not in the private arena. When they are staying in their own house or in a *dusun,* they are the king and queen; they are independent persons who have their own regulations.

In fact, some of the Asmat women are aware of this inequality in their society. For example, Karola Biakai (*Fieldnote*, 15), the wife of today's regent of Asmat said,

> *"Perempuan Asmat jadi kelas dua dan terjajah karena 'ego laki-laki.' Laki-laki Asmat melihat bahwa perempuan harus dinomorduakan dan tidak boleh lebih dari laki-laki."* (The Asmat women have socially become second class citizens by being colonized because of the men's ego. Asmat men put women at the second class level and can never be higher than men).

Moreover, Bifae (*Fieldnote*, 4) disagrees if men consider themselves as stronger than women because at present, women are actually working harder than men. According to her, men spend so much time doing nothing in the village. Bifae is an educated Asmat woman. She is now living in Agats city and working as a staff member of the Social Delagates unit of the Diocese of Agats. She does not want to go back and stay in her village because, according to her,

"Kembali ke kampung sama dengan kembali ke tabiat, hanya bisa mengikuti keputusan laki-laki. Adat tidak memberi kesempatan kepada perempuan untuk terlibat mengambil keputusan." (Back to the village means back to the natural habit of following men's decisions only. Our customary law gives no opportunity to the women to participate in decision making).

As I have said, an Asmat woman has the power and opportunity to express her ideas if she has a special achievement or occupies a good position in public service like Bifae and Karola Biakai. Karola Biakai has the power to articulate the voices of Asmat women because she is a senior elementary school teacher. Moreover, her husband Yuvensius Biakai is the regent of Asmat which is equivalent to the "big man" in the past. In this case, Karola Biakai can be considered as *tesetor* (the big man's wife). She is also the founder and leader of some women's organizations in Asmat like *Akat Cepes* (Great women organization). According to her, the Asmat men are probably threatened if women obtain a higher position than men. She hopes that men and women in Asmat will be equal and will have the same opportunity to look for jobs as in other places. More than this, Bifae wished that someday patriarchalism in Asmat will be replaced by matriarchalism.

As symbolized by the position at the *ci cimen*, Asmat men are aware that they are expected to be the protectors of their families, clans, and village. They are expected to defend their relatives not only from enemy attacks, but also from any harmful events such as disease and famine. The position at *ci cimen* means a man is always ready to be the first person to face any possibility that might disturb their existence, particularly in a *ci*. He must protect those who are in the rear of the *ci* as well as those in the village. He must help those who are weak and those who suffer. This responsibility cannot be separated from warfare and headhunting in the past. During that time, men must be strong in order to protect their lives, their families, and their village. This background situates the Asmat men always to be ready anytime and anywhere, either to defend or to attack. Consequently, the Asmat men spend a lot of their time in a *jeu* or in a village while their wives, sisters, or daughters work hard to provide food and take care of the children. This situation shows the mentality of many Asmat men; they pretend that they are defending their village from sudden attacks just like in the past when warfare and headhunting were still practiced.

According to David Jimanipits (*Fieldnote*, 35), positioning in a *ci* can also symbolize the availability of a man to have sex with his wife. In his own expression he said,

Di Joerat, kalau bawa istri di dalam perahu, laki-laki di belakang berarti tidak boleh melakukan hubungan sex. Tetapi, kalau laki-laki di depan boleh melakukan hubungan sex. Seandainya laki-laki di belakang, berarti dia memposisikan dirinya seperti perempuan sehingga tidak bisa melaksanakan tugasnya sebagai laki-laki. (In Joerat (one of the sub-ethnic groups) area, if a man brings his wife in a *ci* and then takes his position at the *ci ep*, it means he is not available to have sexual intercourse. But, if he stands at *ci cimen*, it means he is ready for sexual intercourse. If a man takes his position *at ci ep*, it means he puts himself in the female's position and like the female he cannot do his work as a male).

It is important to pay attention to this matter because in the past and even up to now, the Asmat couple engages in sexual intercourse in the middle of a *dusun*. Normally, aside from looking for firewood and other needs, the couple goes to the *dusun* to have sex. In order to go to the *dusun,* they need a *ci* to transport them. It is understandable if a husband or a wife makes a sign during the trip that one is not available to have sex.

Another notion of the positioning in the *ci* is that the elders must be placed neither at *ci cimen* nor at *ci ep*, but at *cindem* or *cinamakat* (middle of the *ci*). The elders must be protected by the young generation because they are physically getting weak and have poor eyesight. The elders still have the power and authority to lead the young men and to give orders. Usually, an elder holds the commander oar as a symbol of power and authority. Through his commander oar, he leads and gives orders to the group to move ahead or backward. According to Ndepi (*Fieldnote*, 11), the positioning in a *jicap ci* is a simple form of the positioning in a *jeu* in which the chief elders stay around *wayir* (the central of the *jeu*) when traditional rituals are held and when village issues are discussed.

It is very interesting to observe and to reflect that even if a woman is placed at *ci ep*, she is the one who controls the direction of the *ci*. This means she is the one who controls the movement and the direction of the *ci*. She can move it to the right, to the left, or straight. Of course, her steering control is still under the man's guidance or signal who is in the *ci cimen*. This fact tells us that men and women complement each other. Working together in the *ci* is a symbol of togetherness and it is complementary in family life. Although each member of a family has his or her own role and position, they all build a peaceful and harmonious family. It is just like when a man and a woman paddle together the *ci* to reach their destination. The man is standing, leading, and pioneering the *ci* trip, while the woman is controlling the *ci* direction. Their complementary work brings them to their destination. It mirrors the everyday life of the Asmat. They consider that men are physically stronger than women, but it does not mean that everything can be done by men themselves. The men must be strong to do their part of the labor, and the women must do the same. For example, despite being a *ci* maker, a man is not able to work on it without food that is provided by his wife. This is why the *ci* can be an excellent symbol of everyday life in the Asmat society.

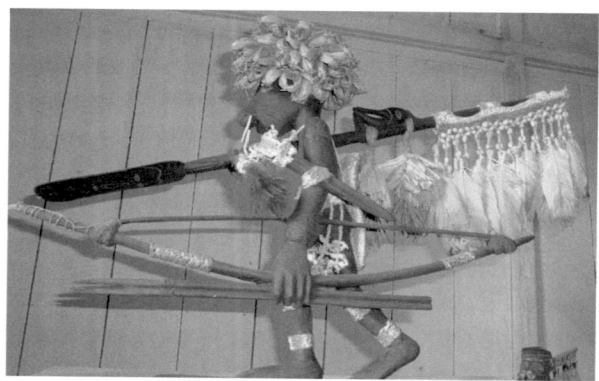

Figure 45. The carving of a typical *cesmaipits* as he carried his oar.

Again, positioning in a *ci* is a representation of the everyday lives of families in the Asmat society. The husband (man) as leader of the family has the responsibility to take care and protect his family, meanwhile his wife (woman) has the responsibility to maintain and provide everything in relation to the fireplace and the "kitchen." The kitchen in this context can be understood as maintaining all family needs so as not to go hungry or to suffer. An Asmat expression says that, *"Perempuan harus menjaga dan mengusahakan supaya tungku tetap menyala."* (Women must try to keep the fireplace always burning). It means do something or cook something in the fireplace; do not let the family get hungry. Because of this responsibility, the woman is always busy in providing food for her family and most of the time, she has no time to relax.

5.6 Rowing the *ci*

The oar and its ornaments can be used as tools for identification. The oar shows the identity of a man or a woman because their oars are different in terms of size, carving, and other ornamentation. An oar can be identified as belonging to a man or to a woman just based on its size and ornaments. Next, an oar is also helpful to identify and differentiate the social status of a person in his community, whether he is a big man, a tribal leader, or just an ordinary person. For example, an ordinary person will not put his oar on his shoulder because this is reserved for *ces-omou* (great men – see fig.45). An ornamented oar is only used by *ces-omou*, especially *cesmaipits* (big men), including *cesmacepes* (great women). Ordinary people usually use unornamented oars. Therefore, the social status of a person can be identified through his or her oar.

Figure 46. The oarswoman's style in holding the oar.

Figure 47. An oarsman's style in holding the oar.

The style of an Asmat man or woman in rowing the *ci* is different. A man and woman have their own styles in using the oar. People can identify even from a long distance whether it is a man or a woman who is rowing the *ci*, just by observing the way they hold the oars. For a better understanding of this matter, refer to fig.46 and fig.47 to see the different styles of women and men in holding the oars and in rowing the ci. The oarsman's position and style are: standing upright at ci cimen, the distance between the right and left hands of oarsman is quite long, around 90-110 cm. One hand of the oarsman (either right or left) holds the oar over his head, and the other one is on the same level as his belly, the four fingers of the hand of the oarsman which is holding the upper part of the oar must face the man's body. Meanwhile the oarswoman's position and style are: Sitting down at *ci ep*, the distance between the right and left hands of the oarswoman is shorter around 35-50 cm. One hand of the oarswoman holds the oar as high as her chest and the other one on the same level as her belly, the four fingers of the hand of the oarswoman must face the opposite direction of the woman's chest.

When I asked my informants why men and women differ in using the oars, their general and spontaneous answer is that, "*Laki-laki berbeda dengan perempuan!*" (Men and women are different!). Truly, men and women are physically different. However, the Asmat want to perpetuate the biological differences between men and women in gender power relations that are socially constructed. Nicolaus Ndepi (*Fieldnote*, 11) used the physical or biological differences between men and women as basic justification in rowing differentiation. According to him,

> "*Laki-laki berbeda dengan perempuan!" Jadi dayung dan cara dayung pun harus berbeda; tidak boleh sama. Itu sudah dari nenek moyang sehingga kita tidak boleh ganti-ganti. Fisik laki-laki berbeda dengan perempuan. Perempuan tidak boleh disamakan dengan laki-laki karena laki-laki membawa keperkasaan.*" (Men are different from women, so their oars and the way they paddle should also be different. This has existed since our ancestors, so we must not change it. Men and women are physically different. Women should not be equal to men because most men are brave).

Hence, the basic reason in oar differentiation between men and women among the Asmat is physical. However, in my opinion, the difference in the Asmat way of holding the oar is not merely the physical aspect, but it is also related to social status. In his book *Orientalism*, Edward W. Said (1978:3) wrote, "Orientalism as a Western style for dominating, restructuring, and having authority over the Orient." I think this perspective also fits the Asmat men in defining who they are. In the light of Said's statement, I want to emphasize that Asmat men try to define and place themselves as dominant, greater, better, and more powerful than women (see Said 1978:1-2). Asmat men feel more powerful than women both physically and emotionally. Moreover, they are not happy to be treated as equal with women, including the use of the oar.

The differences in using the oar has been taught and inculcated in the minds of Asmat men and women. Each one knows how to hold the oar. When a woman enters a *ci* and starts to paddle, she will automatically hold the oar using the women's style. I think the native Asmat will never ask themselves why men and women are different in using the oar, neither will an outsider ask. Perhaps this is because it is routinely practiced, hence they no longer see the difference how a man or a woman use the oar. Moreover, probably they perceive it as natural or sacred such that they do not dare to question or to debate it because it has been given by their ancestors.

It is quite new information for me that the mode of existence in a *ci* can be a strategy for warfare and hunting. Amatus Ndatipits (*Fieldnote*, 39) explained this matter by giving examples. He said, to manipulate their enemies, the men in a *ci* use women's ornaments and they paddle like women. When the enemies see the *ci*, they may think that the people inside the *ci* are all women, thus, they find no need to be afraid. But when the *ci* gets nearer to the enemy's position, they appear as men with great power and ready to attack. Another example, to frighten the enemy, the women in a *ci* paddle like men. The enemy may think that they are all men inside the *ci*, so they will be afraid and will run away. Because of this, all the women in the *ci* can go home safely. Therefore, holding and rowing the *ci* can be used for identification purposes. However, in very specific situations this it can be manipulated for certain purposes.

5.7 Social dimension of the *jicap ci*

In many aspects, the *Jicap ci* is quite different from the *pakanam ci* (family or ordinary *ci*). *Jicap ci* is much more specific and complicated. It is not for personal use but for communal use to celebrate a festive occasion. Therefore, it requires a collective decision to make and to use it. The following points are specific aspects related to the *jicap ci*.

5.7.1 *Jicap ci* is taken after a general meeting in a *jeu*

Before going to get the *jicap ci* material in a *dusun*, the tribal leaders hold a general meeting. For one night, the tribal leaders, together with the adult men of the village, gather in a *jeu* to decide when and where they have to go to take the *ci* trees. Taking the *ci* tree from a *dusun* is not a personal decision, but it is through collective agreement. Once an agreement has been reached, during a very early morning, all the adult men must go out in groups according to their clan, except the singers and the drummers, to take the *ci* trees from the chosen *dusun*. Thus, a man will not go alone, but will be with his fellow men from the same clan.

5.7.2 *Jicap ci* maker and carver

Jicap ci is made by *cisi-ipits* (*ci* maker expert) from a clan and is carved by *wow-ipits* (skillful sculptor). It means that although a lot of men are able to make a *ci*, only the chosen *cisi-ipits* can make the *jicap ci*. The tribal leaders will choose one or two of the *cisi-ipits* from a clan to lead the process of making the *jicap ci*. If the coordinator of the *cisi-ipits* is also *wow-ipits*, he can be the one to carve the *jicap ci*. However, a *wow-ipits* will be appointed to carve the *jicap ci* if the *cisi-ipits* is not a *wow-ipits*.

5.7.3 *Jicap ci* is involved in many rituals during its life span

It starts as a living tree until it decayed. A *Jicap ci* requires a lot of rituals starting from a very simple and personal level to the more complicated ones[9]. For example, before the *ci* tree is cut down, the men personally or communally do a simple ritual to communicate and ask for permission from the ancestral spirit who dwells in that tree. During the process of the *jicap ci* construction, the tribal leaders beat their drums (*em/tifa*) inside the

---

9   Honestly, none of my informants explained the details of a ritual. They just said, "Yes, there are many rituals in conjunction with the *ci*. However, we can only listen to these, not to tell to anybody else."

Figure 48. Amatus Ndatipits is explaining the position of the *jicap ci* when not in use.

jeu every night and day. Furthermore, the *jicap cis* are the first choice to be used in many other rituals and festive occasions in Asmat. The Asmat people will not hold a traditional ritual or feast without the *ci*. In other words, the decision to hold a traditional ritual is always based on the availability of the *ci* in a village.

5.7.4 *Jicap ci* owned by *ces omou*

Among the *jicap cis*, there is one or several *cis* that can be categorized as *ces ci*. *Ces* means war, and *ci* means canoe in Asmat language. So, *ces ci* means war canoe. The *ces ci* owner is a *cesmaipits*. These are the ones who are considered as *ces omou* (great men, great warriors). '*Cesmaipits*' comes from *cescu* (expert, skillful, great) and *jipits* (man). Hence, *cesmaipits* can be translated as **great man** or **big man**. In Kapauku of Papua New Guinea, the headman or the *big man* is distinguished from the rest of the members of his group by a set of criteria such as wealth, generosity, eloquence and verbal courage, physical fitness, bravery in war, and shamanism (Pospisil 1963:48). The same qualities are also required in Asmat society to be a *cesmaipits*. We can now see the relation between *jicap ci* and *ces omou*, particularly the *cesmaipits*. *Jicap ci* is not owned and used by ordinary people, even if all Asmat need a *ci*.

5.7.5 *Jicap ci* is kept very safe

As mentioned earlier, *jicap ci* is not for daily use. It is only used for very special occasions. It must be ready any time for emergency purposes. For example, it must be ready to defend when the enemy comes or when the *cesmaipits* proclaims to attack. War and headhunting are significant in Asmat history. *Ces ci* is for war and headhunting only. This is why the Asmat protect the *jicap cis* from any collision or taboo. They believe that any violation to the traditional regulations will affect the success in a war or headhunting. Violation will bring about harm and victims from within. When the *jicap ci* is not in use, it must be kept in a certain place, just like in a garage (see fig.48). Thus, the *jicap ci* will be dry, light, durable, and ready to use any time. The position of the *jicap ci* on land must be reversed unlike when it is in the water and must be covered with sago leaves. In addition, it has to be tied to a pole and must face the sunrise or the east. It is a symbol of relationship and unity with the spirit. If the tie is

Figure 49. A *wow-ipits* is carving the *ci cimen*. (Photograph courtesy of Fr. Vince Cole).

cut or removed, the spirit can go away. If the spirit goes away, the *jicap ci* has no more power and can bring about misfortune to the owner and his community. If a *jicap ci* is parked and tied in a riverbank, the prow must face the river in order to be used easily anytime.

5.8 Social dimension of *wuramon*

Technically, *wuramon* is made and carved inside a *jeu* to protect it from women or children who will try to observe it. The women's responsibility is only to provide food for the carvers. All carvers are related to one another, usually through bloodline, and are headed by a chief carver. When the carving is done, the men will bring the *wuramon* out and place it in front of the *Emak Cem*. The *wuramon* will then be brought back to the *jeu*, after the *Emak Cem* ritual has been complete. *Wuramon* is an integral part of the *Emak Cem* (male initiation ritual)[10].

Wuramon presents the balance system of the figures in the carving. The *wuramon* is divided into two symmetrical parts. All figures are carved in pairs, except *mbu* (turtle) and *okom* ("Z"-like figure) in the center. This reminds me of what Fleischhacker (1991:5) said, "Keeping the cosmos balanced is critical for survival and order in the Asmat society." *Wuramon* symbolizes not only the balance or the number of the figures in it, but also the balance of the universe, especially between the good and bad spirit. In other words, *wuramon* is not only possessed by the good spirits, but also by the bad spirits to remind young boys of what could happen in their lives. The main purpose of the *Emak Cem* ritual is to prepare a young boy to become a *ces omou* (great man), one who is responsible, brave, strong, sociable, and altruistic. If a boy has undergone the *Emak Cem* ritual, it means he has a great responsibility to help others, especially the needy and his relatives. As an integral part of *Emak Cem* ritual, *wuramon* teaches people to keep balance in their lives and to consider that either good or bad spirit can lead them in either ways. The young, initiated boys must keep in mind to cooperate with and to ask for protection from good spirits and not to surrender under the power of bad spirits. The *Emak Cem* ritual reminds people of the power of the community over an individual. An individual is socially shaped by his community.

5.9 *Ci* as an expression of art

The *ci* is one of the remarkable arts of the Asmat, aside from being an instrument of transportation and a representation of the ancestral spirit. Although every Asmat man

---

10   So far, I do not have data about female initiation in Asmat society.

is responsible in making a *ci*, only talented Asmat men are able to construct a *ci*. There is no guarantee that every single Asmat man is able to make a *ci* for himself and his family. Making and carving a *ci* need a wonderful skill and design from a gifted artist in order to please the users and observers.

The beauty of the *ci* not only satisfies the eyes of the living, but it also pleases the eyes of the spirits. With regards to the *Bis* pole (ancestor pole), Abraham Kuruwaib (1974:35) said, "Asmat carvings are expressions of beauty – intended by the artist to please the eyes of the ancestral observers and to solicit their protective presence." In this light, the *ci* can please every single eye observing it including the spirit because it comes from the expert's "touch." There is a need to mention here that every *wow-ipits* of the Asmat does not make a single sketch or pattern of their work before making it. They just carve and carve the object directly because they know what to do with it. They believe that the ancestral spirit is communicating with them during the time of carving (fig.49). They believe that the spirit is leading the mind and hands of the carver. In other words, the spirit is the one working through the hands of the living carver. Nevertheless, to produce a good *ci* or other art expressions, the cooperation of the living and the spirit is needed. The carving of the *ci* therefore is evidence of the united power of the intangible spirit and the tangible *wow-ipits* and *cisi-ipits*. In connection with this, Dirk A. M. Smidt said that carving is a form of communication between the living and the dead, between the community of human beings and the complex and pervasive world of the spirits (1999:ix).

5.10 The *ci*: symbol of masculinity

Indeed, I did not find in my interviews that owning a *ci* is one of the physical and psychological maturity symbols of Asmat men. I got the information that the *ci* is a symbol of the maturity of an Asmat man from a feedback seminar about the Asmat culture in Agats (see *Notulensi* 2012)[11]. During a discussion in that seminar, Fr. Virgil Petermeier, OSC, an American priest of the Order of the Holy Cross, addressed a question to the native Asmat who were there. The question was "*Apakah perahu yang dibuat oleh anak bungsu itu untuk mencari pasangan? Sebagai harta kawin?*" (Is the *ci* made by the youngest son used to look for a wife? Is it a bride-wealth?). Most of the Asmat participants agreed that the *ci* is a sign of the readiness of a man to marry. It is a sign of maturity of an Asmat man to have a wife. Nevertheless, the most obvious answer was given by Bartol Bocoropces, an educated Asmat and a local government staff member. In his explanation, Bartol said,

"*Saya minta izin dulu, bila ada orang yang lebih dahulu. Perahu bagi orang Asmat menjadi kunci. Perahu disebut sangat penting karena bisa menjadi lambang dari suatu keluarga. Perahu tidak menjadi jaminan sebagai harta, tapi tetap tersirat di dalamnya. Perahu sebagai jaminan hidup orang Asmat. Perahu menjadi segala-galanya. Laki-laki Asmat tidak semuanya dapat mengerjakan perahu. Perlu dilatih atau diajari oleh orang tuanya. Jika seseorang bisa buat rumah, perahu, dan dayung, maka anak itu sudah siap dan matang. Artinya kemudahan-kemudahan lain bisa diperolehnya*" (see *Notulensi* 2012:5). (Excuse me, if there is someone ahead of me[4]. The *ci* for the Asmat is key for

---

11   This feedback seminar was also part of my research method to obtain more data because I was the one who suggested the program to Mgr. Aloysius Murwito, OFM, the Bishop of Agats Diocese. Based on the Bishop's agreement and support, we arranged the schedule for the seminar.

life. The *ci* is very important because it can be a symbol for a family. The *ci* is not a guarantee of wealth, but it is always being part of it. The *ci* is a guarantee for Asmat life. It is for everything. Not all Asmat men are able to construct a *ci*. He needs training from his parents. It is a sign of a boy's maturity, whether he is able to make a house, a *ci* and an oar. It means he can get other things easily by having this ability).

Thus, the ability to make a *ci* is a sign of a young Asmat boy's maturity. He is not only physically mature, but also psychologically, socially, and spiritually prepared. I can say therefore that he is comprehensively mature because physically and personally, he proves that he can afford something for his present and future life. He also proves that he is a responsible man and has passed the childhood stage. Socially, he can relate to other people by using his *ci*. He can go to his own *dusun* and gather food for himself and his family. Spiritually, he is able to pay his obligation to his ancestors by making the *ci* and he will be able to build a hearth as a symbol of family life and the continuation of the life of his ancestors. His *ci* can also be used to go headhunting or to war to revenge a relative's death or just to look for the enemy's head to please his ancestors. Being able to make a *ci* is a personal achievement and a tangible object of a man to prove that he is an *Asmat nak* (the real man). It is therefore very reasonable to say that the *ci* is a symbol of maturity and masculinity in Asmat society. In other words, the *ci* is a symbol of independence.

Furthermore, according to Smidt, headhunting was part of a male's initiation in the past (1999:21). The young boys tried to prove their capacity and capability to be warriors for their society. However, a requirement in headhunting and other festive occasions is the availability of the *cis* (see fig.50). Without a *ci*, headhunting would not be arranged because the men would not be able to reach the destination nor to escape from their enemy's attack. The account of Smidt (1999:21) is a valuable report in dealing with male initiation and headhunting in Asmat.

Figure 50. Asmat men with their *cis* in a festive occasion in Atsj. (Photograph courtesy of Fr. Umar Sumardi, OSC).

"The importance of captured heads in traditional Asmat life is clearly demonstrated by the role they played in male initiation. It was impossible for boys to become men without taking a head. A man's vital strength is said to be particularly present in the skull, and the life force of another provided the energy necessary for a boy to make the jump to manhood. Initiation traditionally took place not long after the boy's first head-hunting raid. At one stage in the group ceremony, each of the boys held a recently severed skull in front of his crotch, and meditated on it. At this stage, the young man was given the head-hunted enemy's name, and his vital strength was assimilated into the group. To ensure the identification between initiate and victim was as close as possible, the boy meditated on the head for two or three days, and was also rubbed with the victim's blood and his burned hair. These acts were a tribute to the power of the enemy."

The headhunting practices can be understood as part of male initiation, not only as an opportunity to revenge their relative's death to keep balance (see Fleischhacker 1991:5). Sowada (1996:79), the former Bishop of Agats Asmat even said, "Headhunting and cannibalism gained acceptance within a homogenous Asmat culture as natural, integral parts of life, though they never become daily routine." In other words, headhunting is energy to live in Asmat, to make life secure and meaningful as defined by Leslie A. White (1959:8), "The purpose and function of culture are to make life secure and enduring for the human species."

5.11 The *ci*: a dominant symbol of gender identity

Obviously, I wanted to probe that the *ci* can be a significant way to understand gender among the Asmat. Through previous explanations and discussions, we see that the *ci* is the main instrument for Asmat mobility. But the most important thing is that the *ci* helps people to see the gender roles among the Asmat. It shows the division of labor between men and women. For example, men make the *ci*, while women take care of it; men are at *ci cimen*, women at *ci ep*; men's oar is longer and ornamented, while the women's oar is shorter and simple. Likewise, the *ci* shows the social stratification among the Asmat. In short, the *ci* becomes a tangible evidence of gender power relations among the Asmat.

In the light of Turner (1967:20), I would say that the *ci* and *po* (oar) are dominant symbols of gender power relations in Asmat society, just like "the milk tree" in Ndembu society. Turner distinguished symbols into two: dominant symbol and instrumental symbol. The dominant symbols, according to him, are the ethical and jural norms of society in close contact with strong emotional stimuli. Moreover, the dominant symbol possesses a high degree of constancy and consistency throughout the total symbol system. Meanwhile, the instrumental symbol may be regarded as means of attaining such goals (1967:30-32). In this way, the *ci* and oar in Asmat society strongly distinguish men and women. In other words, the *ci* and oar define how to be an Asmat man or woman in a community.

Finally, the *ci* is an instrument to see the division of labor, position, and social status between men and women in Asmat. However, it can be a symbol of unity and complementary work among the Asmat people. The *ci* can be a symbol of oneness and togetherness to reach the same destination. It is symbolized by a dugout *ci* which is paddled by both man and woman to reach the same direction.

6

Supernatural dimension of the *ci*

We have seen the uniqueness of the *ci* from the physical and social dimensions. Now, the supernatural dimension will intensify the idea that the *ci* is indeed unique. The supernatural dimension of the *ci* will show us that the *ci* relates the visible and the invisible worlds; the world of the living and the world of the spirits. The *ci* itself can become a dwelling place of the ancestor's spirits as Fleischhacker (1991:8) wrote, "Material objects can possess spirits and spirits power, making them useful in ritual and magic."

6.1 The *ci*: symbol of power

I think, 'power' is a significant word to understand the uniqueness of the *ci*. Power in this context simply means the ability to control, dominate, and use things such as the *dusun* (see Foucault 1980:102; Wartenberg 1990:5; Karlberg 2005:2). Because of its power, the *ci* can penetrate the deep and wide rivers, it is able to carry huge luggage, and escort people to their destinations. More than these, it bears a charming nuance that can frighten the enemy, thwart enemy attacks, and even provoke people to run after the enemy. The very first place to prove that someone has managed to kill the enemy is in a *ci*, not in the jungle or at the battlefield where the killing takes place. When the blood of the enemy flows into the *ci*, that moment shows that a warrior has succeeded in headhunting (see Amatus Ndatipits – *Fieldnote*, 22).

Furthermore, one of the differences between the *jicap ci* and *pakanam ci* is the *ci cimen*. The *ci cimen* of the *jicap ci* is carved in great detail with ancestor figures and headhunting symbols (Scneebaum 1985:157). I have mentioned in a previous chapter the *ci cemen* in relation to the sections of the *ci*. Briefly, the *ci cemen* can be an identification tool, both collectively and personally because it is the most obvious sign to cite the distinction among the *cis* from anywhere in the Asmat region. Every sub-ethnic group has its own style of carving the *ci cimen*, thus, it can also be used as an identification tool for a particular group.

The *ci cimen* is also a representation of the spirit of the ancestors who dwell in the *ci* (see Scneebaum 1988). According to Fleischhacker, "Male potency is very obvious in Asmat art. The *tsjemen* (penis) of the *mbis* (ancestor) pole is the most obvious example. Manliness, bravery, fearlessness, and the killing of an enemy also indicated potency" (1991:9). The *ci cimen* is similar to *bis cemen* in a horizontal position. They are both carved using open-wood carving style (see and compare fig.51 and 52). These are related and perform the same quality as symbol of power. For example, both carvings have *biskus* (human head figure), *was* (cuscus tail), and *fofoyir* (head of a hornbill). Moreover, in the

Figure 51. A typical carving of *ci cimen*.

lower portion of the *bis* the *ci* figure is carved. *Bis cemen* as well as *ci cimen* are basically fertility symbols as the source of life-enriching forces (see Kuruwaip 1974:50), in addition to a headhunting symbol. The Asmat frequently compare themselves to a tree: the feet are the roots, the torso is the trunk, the arms are the branches and the head is the fruit of the tree (Fleischhacker 1991:3). That is why the *fofoyir* (the head of a hornbill figure) is carved as symbol of cannibalism. In cannibalism the victim's brain is consumed by the war leader just like a hornbill eating the fruit of a tree (Fleischhacker 1991:7).

The *ci* carving is also a symbol of power. The Asmat believe that the spirit of their ancestor indeed dwells in a carved object such as *ci* and *bis* pole. It highlights the interpretation of Schneebaum (1999:5) who said, "Once the carving is named, the spirit and the body of the dead man reside in the carving until it has been released through the death of an enemy. The spirit of an ancestor lives again in the carved figure named after him." That is why it makes sense that a *ci* becomes lighter and faster, not only because of the human effort in rowing it, but also by the workings of the spirit in it. For example, if they carve a crocodile figure in the *ci cimen*, they believe that the crocodile spirit itself empowers the *ci*. In addition, the *ai cis* (new *cis*) in a village provoke the community to perform a festive activity such as holding a feast or going to warfare and headhunting or revenging the relative's death. Therefore, when a village holding a *ci pokmbu* (*ci* feast), other villages also prepare themselves to anticipate a sudden enemy's attack.

The Asmat believe that the *ci* carving and its decorations have power to frighten their enemies. It has the power to challenge, weaken, or drive away the enemies around the battlefield. The enemy's spirits can also be frightened by the *ci* carving. My informants said that the enemies run away once they see the *ci* decorations of their opponents (see *Fieldnote*, 69). Therefore, for the Asmat, the *ci* is a symbol of power, symbol of the conquerors, and a symbol of the *cesmaipits* (big man, great warrior). A good and strong *ci* has such a great influence in winning a battle.

6.2 Naming the *ci*

A family takes care of the *ci*, especially the *jicap ci* because before it was a tree from a *dusun*. According to Paulus Amanpen (*Fieldnote*, 47) and other informants, a *ci* tree is taken care by a family since it was a small tree. It is named after an ancestor who had been killed by the enemies in a battle. In a seminar in Agats, it was found out that:

Figure 52. A typical carving of a *bis* pole *cemen*.

> "*Di wilayah Pantai Kasuari, dulu mayat tidak dikubur tetapi diletakkan di atas para-para hingga membusuk. Kemudian tulang-tulangnya akan diambil untuk berbagai keperluan, misalnya tengkorak dijadikan bantal tidur sebagai symbol rasa sayang. Hal lain yang menarik adalah sebagian tulang yang tidak terpakai mereka bawa ke dusun/hutan dan diletakkan di bawah kayu perahu yang akan dijadikan sebagai perahu kelak. Darinya nama perahu itu kemudian menggunakan nama orang yang sudah meninggal tersebut*" (Keuskupan Agats. *Lokakarya Inkulturasi Liturgi*. 31 Maret – 06 April 2008, p.31). (In Pantai Kasuari region, in the past, the body of the dead was not buried, but they put him on a rack until it decays. Then, they took the bones to serve many purposes such as the skull used as a pillow serves as a symbol of love. An interesting thing to note is when they brought some of the useless bones to their *dusun*. They put these beneath the *ci* tree which would be used for *ci* in the future. Since then, the *ci* tree is named after the dead person).

It is clear therefore that the Asmat family prepares a good tree to become a *jicap ci* for their future. When the members of the family go to the *dusun* and see the *ci* tree, they usually perform a simple ritual or work as an expression of their love and affection for the tree like cleaning it and getting rid of wild plants and grasses. After this, they throw sago, fish, or shrimps towards it as if they were feeding it. This action is manifests their love and attention, not only for the *ci* tree but also for their ancestor whom they believe dwells in it. In return, the spirit of the ancestor takes care of them and sustains the fertility of the *dusun*.

An informant said, the *jicap ci* is mostly named after a male ancestor. Actually, choosing male name is symbolic because the male bears physical power and bravery. They do not choose female's names because they do not want the *ci* tree to have a hole in it, like a woman's vagina. If there is a hole inside the tree, it is not good to make a quality *ci*. For the Asmat, even the tree is sexualized and/or gendered.

Furthermore, the *Jicap ci* cannot be separated from many taboos. One of the taboos pertaining to the *jicap ci* is that women are excluded from using it, especially the new *ci* (*ai ci*). Women are not even allowed to enter it. The responsibility of women during the process of *ci making* is to provide food and other needs. They are strictly forbidden to enter the *jeu* area when the men are making the *jicap cis* in front of a *jeu*. The Asmat people believe that misfortune will come to the community especially to the clan, if a woman enters or uses the *jicap ci*. For example, the *jicap ci* will be heavier, can easily be broken, can lose in racing and headhunting. The *tesetor* (big man's wife) is the only woman who has the privilege to enter the *jicap ci* during war or headhunting times.

Another notion that is important to mention here is that it is a special sign when a big man and his wife go to a *dusun* using the *ces ci*. Everybody knows that the main purpose of the trip is to have sexual intercourse. Therefore, nobody will question where they are going. The community believes that they are going to have sacred intercourse for the benefit of the community. It can therefore be said that they are going to fulfill a sacred ritual for the sake of the community. They are going to have a sacred relationship with the spirits through sexual intercourse in the middle of a *dusun* to ask the spirits to sustain their lives and to continue providing fertility to their *dusuns* and rivers. It is a big favor and fortune for the community if the big man and his wife will do this ritual correctly; otherwise they will experience disasters, calamities, epidemics, or become victims of their enemies. In the past and even in present time, the Asmat have sexual intercourse in the middle of their *dusun*. This is based on the belief that women get pregnant from the spirit of the ancestor who dwells in the *dusun*. The action of the penis during intercourse shapes the embryo into a human form. Semen feeds the fetus in the womb (see Fleischhacker 1991:9).

From this context, we can interpret that the *ci* is very essential for the Asmat community. Without the *ci*, a big man and his wife will not be able to have sacred intercourse in the *dusun* for their own joy and for the benefit of the community. It is also a way to keep in touch with the ancestors. In other words, the *ci* ensures fertility not only for the big man and his wife, but also for the community. The *ci* facilitates a man and a woman to have sex in the *dusun* because the *dusun* is usually separated from the dwelling place by one or several rivers. The Asmat used to articulate this saying, "*Tanpa perahu, kampung jadi dingin, tidak ada api, tidak panas.*" (Without *ci*, the village becomes cold, there is no fire, no desire). New life comes through sex; however, sex will not happen if there is no fire, no desire, no penis. For the Asmat, the *ci* arouses their desire and warms their house and village, like a man stimulating the woman's passion to have sex. The *ci* takes them to their *dusun*, not only to look for food, but also to have sex. *Dusun* for the Asmat is a fountain of life where the spirits dwell.

The worlds of the living and of the dead are quite inseparable in Asmat. Fleischhacker (1991:4) said,

> "Carvings are embodiments of the ancestral spirits which control the universe. To keep the cosmos in order, the Asmat placated their ancestors through carvings, ritual feasts, warfare, the taking of heads and cannibalism. The carvings make evident the vital interdependence between tangible and the intangible."

Carvings, including the *ci* carvings, are representations of the spirits. Carvings show the relationship between the world of the living and the world of the spirit. Every time the Asmat see the carvings, it reminds them of someone whom they carved there, just like a Christian seeing Jesus when he/she looks closely at the cross. According to David Jimanipits, the main part of the *ci* carving exists in the *ci cimen*. However, the *wow-ipits* also carves all around the *ci* as a symbol of the spirit's protection on the entire *ci*.

6.3 A distinct *ci: wuramon*

The *ci* itself bears spiritual dimension. Aside from bearing a supernatural dimension of the ordinary *ci*, the Asmat have a very specific *ci* to articulate their intimacy with the spirits which they call *wuramon*. *Wuramon* is a distinct *ci* in the Asmat community. It is made of *ci nak* (special *ci* tree) and is used for rite of passage from boyhood to adulthood. It is carved out of a single piece of wood, and shaped like a dugout *ci* (Fleischhacker and Schneebaum 1976:95). The basic shape of *wuramon* is not very different from the ordinary *ci*. However, it has a specific characteristic that makes it distinctive. It is a bottomless *ci* and several figures are carved in it as symbols of good and bad spirits. These represent both ancestor figures and environmental spirits (Schneebaum 1989:63). Jim Daniels said, "Flowing water is a gateway to the next world, and the bottomlessness of the canoe frees these beings to focus in the way ahead" (in Freshman 2009:67; see also Schneebaum 1989:63).

Figure 53. Stefanus Jakfu (pointing to the figure) is explaining *wuramon* in the Yamas Parish priest house.

According to Stefanus Jakfu, (*Fieldnote*, 62; see also fig.53) a *wow-ipits* and tribal leader of Yeni village in Sawa district, *wuramon* is an integral part of *Emak Cem* ritual. *Emak Cem* is an initiation ritual for the young Asmat boy to become an adult man. The main purpose of the *Emak Cem* ritual is to prepare a young boy so he can become a **great man** – who is responsible, brave, strong, sociable, and altruistic. This is similar to the Keesing (1982:3) analysis in the context of Papua New Guinea as he reports, "They define the separation of men and women as a biological and religious as well as social imperative; and they transform gentle boys into warriors capable of killing rage, stealthy murder, and bravery." If a boy has undergone the *Emak Cem* ritual, it means he has a great responsibility to help others, especially the needy and his relatives. He leaves behind all the weaknesses and fears of childhood and moves into the adult responsibility with new power bestowed upon him by his ancestors. As an overview of the *Emak Cem* ritual, Tobias Schneebaum (1998:62) wrote,

"Initiates were confined for months in specially built houses. They were not fed and were not allowed fires and could leave the house only under cover of darkness. When all ritual acts had been performed, the soul ship was carried by the men to the initiates' house and moved partially through the doorway. The men then groaned and moved the ship rapidly in a back and forth motion; the groans imitated a woman's giving birth and symbolized the new birth of the initiates as adults. The soul ship was then placed in front of the house and the new adults crawled out of their prison over the ship. They were also required to sit on the carved turtle in the center of the *wuramon*, while the elders carved scarification marks onto their legs with an animal tooth."

Figure 54. The carving of *Emak Cem*, carved by Stefanus Jakfu.

Therefore, *wuramon* is not an independent carving; it is an integral part of the *Emak Cem*. It should not be separated from the entire process of the *Emak Cem* ritual. Unfortunately, many outsiders consider *wuramon* as a single being. Moreover, most of the Asmat people introduce *wuramon* as only a kind of Asmat carving. This can be understood because *wuramon* itself is already a wonderful thing as a single carving. As an object of art, it is easy to perceive independently because *wuramon* by itself is rich with symbols and meanings. This phenomenon can be observed directly in the festival of the Asmat culture, in which the Asmat people display *wuramon* in their stands without other materials of *Emak Cem* (see fig.54).

In this study, I focused my discussion on *wuramon* only because it relates to the *ci* in general. For instance, the basic shape of *wuramon* is similar to the ordinary *ci*. In addition, *Emak Cem* ritual is very complicated, therefore, it needs further and specific studies. I discussed *wuramon* only because, my topic is about the *ci*, and on the other hand, I do not have enough data about the complete process of the *Emak Cem* ritual.

Emak Cem ritual can be found only in sub-ethnic group of Joerat region which is comprised of several villages. These villages belong to Joerat: Yamasj-Yeni, Yufri-Yaun, As-Atat, Ao-Kapi, Nakai (Biakai 1981). According to Yakobus Serambi, Adam Do, and Kornelis Erem (*Fieldnote*, 92) of Sawa-Er, the *Emak Cem* ritual is also celebrated in the sub-ethnic of *Kenok* region in the past, however, this ritual brought about many victims. There were many people who died during the ritual celebration in a village. The people of Kenok therefore do not want to celebrate the *Emak Cem* ritual anymore. They believed that *Emak Cem* ritual is not suitable for them.

Furthermore, while *wuramon* is celebrated and developed in the same sub-ethnic group of Joerat, every village has its own characteristics. For example, the position of all figures inside the Yamas-Yeni's *wuramon* face the same direction, while the *ci cimen*, and the *mbu* (turtle) face downward (see fig.55). Meanwhile, the figures in Yufri's *wuramon* face the opposite direction. The center of all figures, both in Yufri and Yamas-Yeni, is *mbu*. However, the *mbu* in Yufri's *wuramon* faces upward[12] (see fig.56). In Yufri's *wuramon*, the figures before *mbu* as the *wuramon* center, face the *ci cimen*, while the figures after *mbu*

---

12 According to Amatus Ndatipits, the *mbu* facing upward symbolizes the availability to have sexual intercourse. In other words, it is a symbol of fertility.

Figure 55. Yamas' *wuramon*. The *mbu* (turtle) faces downward and in one direction with the other figures.

Figure 56. Yufri's *wuramon*. The *mbu* (turtle) faces upward and in opposite direction with the other figures.

face the opposite direction, the *ci ep*. Thus, *wuramon* can be an identification tool for a specific group in Joerat region, aside from being the *ci* in general.

According to Jakfu, *wuramon* comes from the words: "*wur*" which means thunder and "*amon*", meaning calling. So, *wuramon* literally means thunder calling. Nevertheless, the Asmat perceive it as the spirit canoe and other writers translate it as soul ship.

In a *wuramon*, we can find different figures such as *eco* (the human figure), *dat* (satan), *amerak* (man's head bird), *mbu* (turtle), *okom* ("Z"-like figure), *jinicowut* (woman in sitting position), and *irimbi* (black king cockatoo beak). *Eco, dat, Amerak, jinicowut,* and *irimbi* are carved in pairs and placed symmetrically before and after *okom* and *mbu*. Every figure has a meaning. For example, *okom* symbolizes the water spirit, while *mbu* symbolizes fertility (Schneebaum 1989:63). The basic meaning of these figures is that the boy who is being initiated will face a lot of good and bad spirits during his lifetime, as it is figured out in *wuramon*. He must be able to deal with all of them wisely in order to have a harmonious life.

It is necessary to know that there is only one *wuramon* for every *Emak Cem* ritual. It can be made by several men of a clan, but it is led by an expert who serves as coordinator. According to Jakfu, the *wuramon* made of *ci nak* (*ci* tree), the ordinary *ci* material. However, the *ci nak* for *wuramon* does not need to grow specifically as *jicap ci* or *jo-ti* material. The *wuramon* is usually named after the dead father of the chief carver at the end of the carving process (Fleischhacker and Schneebaum 1976:99).

Additionally, it is very interesting to note and to analyze *wuramon* as the bottomless *ci*. Schneebaum (1989:63) says, "The bottom of the canoe is open, presumably so that the

Figure 57. *Wuramon*

human-like figures representing the ancestors will be able to escape into the waters of *safan*, the land of the dead." Flowing water is a gateway to the next world, and the bottomless *ci* will enable the ancestor spirits to reach the *safan* (Huber 2009: 67). However, according to David Jimanipits (*Fieldnote*, 34), the bottomless *ci* symbolizes the unknown world because human beings do not know the end of this world. The future is unpredictable. In other words, the bottomless *ci* is a symbol of the hidden world, the world of the spirits. It is also a symbol of human limitations and weaknesses. Human beings know nothing about the next world; and the Asmat symbolize 'know nothing' through their carvings, especially in *wuramon*, by empty space, that is, the bottomless *ci*. Both arguments are reasonable, – - the *etic* perspective of Schneebaum and the *emic* perspective of Jimanipits. However, I am in favor of the *emic* perspective because it is true that people in any society know nothing about the spirit world. In that sense, the Asmat symbolize it beautifully through the bottomless *ci* (see fig.57).

7

Economic dimension of the *ci*

The *ci* is very fundamental in the lives of the Asmat. It helps them to fulfill their daily needs. The Asmat articulate how the *ci* cannot be separated from their life. In this chapter, I elaborate some Asmat expressions about the position of the *ci* as a primary need of the family and the community.

7.1 *Ci opak, jis opak* (no *ci*, no firewood)

Traditionally, the Asmat cook their food using firewood gathered from the *dusun*. It is easy to gather firewood if their house is built next to a *dusun* because they just walk to get it. Unfortunately, many Asmat build their houses not in the middle of a *dusun*, but in a village. This means many of them stay far from their *dusun* which is not accessible by foot because the Asmat area is surrounded by rivers. Consequently, they need the *ci* to be able to reach their *dusun* and to gather their needs, including firewood (fig.58). Therefore, the "*Ci opak, jis opak*" statement is indeed relevant to the Asmat.

The Asmat prefer to use a metaphorical word or a symbolic behavior to communicate their needs or emotions. For instance (see Chapter 5), if a neighbor named Helen, for example wants to borrow a *ci* from Maria, Maria then would not say directly that the *ci* cannot be borrowed at the moment. Rather, she would say (while looking at the fireplace), "Oh, there is no firewood at the hearth. Moreover, last night this little girl cried loudly because there was no fish in her sago." These words will be well understood by Helen that the *ci* cannot be borrowed at the moment because the owner will use it. Similarly, the

Figure 58. Two Asmat men are bringing firewood in their *ci*.

Figure 59. Hearth and paddles in the Catholic Church of Sawa-Erma Parish.

Asmat use metaphorical words "*Ci opak, jis opak*" to express their dependency on the *ci*. The *ci* is highly valuable to fulfil their daily needs.

Furthermore, by saying "*jis opak*", the Asmat actually wanted to say that they have no food; there is nothing to cook; nothing to eat. Remember, firewood is very important for cooking in Asmat. Without firewood, they will not be able to cook. Nothing to cook means, nothing to eat. In other words, "*jis opak*" implies hunger to the Asmat. As a result, sooner or later, they would die or "*habis*" (literally meaning, finished). Therefore, the *ci* is very essential to keep the Asmat alive because they can look for firewood to be able to cook their food and then eat joyfully. The fig.59 shows symbolically the relationship between hearth and the *ci*-paddle.

In this part of the chapter, by simply quoting what my informants have said, I tried to demonstrate how the Asmat people express their dependency and intimacy with the *ci*. Even if the informants expressed their ideas differently, all expressions have the same meaning, that is, the *ci* is very vital to the everyday life of the Asmat.

When I met Bernardus Ayurkap (*Fieldnote*, 39), chieftain of Yasiw village of Atsj district, he was very happy and he seriously answered my questions. The following sentences are part of his answers.

"*Kalau tidak punya perahu, akan sangat tergantung pada orang lain. Tidak memiliki perahu juga bisa dimengerti sebagai keluarga pemalas. Kalau tidak punya perahu, kita merasa sangat kecewa karena tidak bisa mencari makan. Perahu menjamin hidup keluarga, bahkan menjadi penyambung kehidupan sehari-hari karena bisa menyeberang sungai-sungai yang luas dan dalam.*" (Without a *ci*, a family will be very dependent on others. Not owning a *ci* implies a lazy family. If they do not own a *ci*, they feel very sad because they will not be able to look for food. The *ci* guarantees the family needs; it connects their daily life because it transports them to cross big and deep rivers).

For Ayurkap, it is impossible to cross rivers to look for food without the *ci*. The rivers, are rich with seafoods, but they are dangerous because of the deep water and the wild animals such as crocodiles that can kill people. It is therefore understandable that the *ci* becomes *"penyambung kehidupan"* or the life connector of people.

Another saying was articulated by Primus Ostji (*Fieldnote*, 41) a senior teacher and one of the tribal leaders of Atsj. According to him,

> *"Perahu dan dayung merupakan focus hidup orang Asmat atau jantung hidup orang Asmat. Perahu merupakan jembatan untuk mencapai penghidupan; sarana paling utama dalam memenuhi kebutuhan hidup keluarga. Perahu memungkinkan orang untuk bergerak: melanjutkan kehidupan yang diturunkan turun-temurun dari leluhur. Perahu juga merupakan alat dasar untuk penghidupan."* (The *ci* and oar are the focus or core of Asmat life. The *ci* is a bridge to reach livelihood; it is a main instrument to fulfil the needs of a family. It is a guarantee for mobility and continuing the ancestors' lives. The *ci* is a basic tool for life).

In my opinion, one of the important elements that needs to be highlighted from Ostji's statement is "continuing the ancestors lives." Why is this important? Because the present generation comes from previous generations, that is, their ancestors. If the present generation of the Asmat abandon the *ci*, it means they have no more respect for their ancestors who used and introduced the *ci* for future generations. They do not want to continue the ancestors' lives and spirits that had been passed down to them. In other words, they have no more fear of ancestral spirits. If this happens, the community life of the Asmat will be in disharmony because the spirits are also part of the community. If the ancestral spirits go away with anger, the living people will be in danger. All Asmat are aware of the consequence of neglecting the *ci*. Therefore, it is very important to preserve the *ci* in order to keep the community always in harmony.

Tadeus (*Fieldnote*, 45), about 70 years old, (because he himself does not know his own age), a tribal chief of Yasiw-Atsj, in a very simple expression said, *"Kalau tidak ada perahu dan dayung, tidak ada kayu bakar, tidak ada makan. Kalau ada perahu, hidup kita baik."* (If there is no *ci* and paddle, there would no firewood, no food. If there is a *ci*, our lives will be good). From his words, I figured out the sub-title of this chapter, *"Ci opak, jis opak."* Although Tadeus spoke in a very simple *bahasa* Indonesia, he can formulate his ideas effectively. It was a big favor to meet and interview him because in my opinion, he is one of the tribal leaders who is wise and a gifted man. His statement was validated by a carver group of Yasiw-Atsj (*Fieldnote*, 49) when they said,

> *"Perahu, dayung, dan alat pangkur sagu merupakan kekayaan utama orang Asmat. Perahu merupakan kunci hidup orang Asmat. Kalau tidak ada perahu, kayu bakar tidak akan tersedia apalagi sagu dan kebutuhan lain."* (*Ci*, oar, and sago pounder are Asmat treasures. The *ci* is a key for Asmat life. Without *ci*, there is no firewood, no sago, and no other needs).

A different idea from the group is that "the *ci* is a key for Asmat life." The group used the word 'key'; perhaps they got the idea of a key to a speedboat machine. A key is needed to turn on the speedboat. If there is no key, the speedboat will not function. So, the group used the perspective of a "key" to see their lives that without a *ci* is similar to a speedboat without its key. It means the Asmat life will function well if the people own *cis*.

Aside from the statement *"ci opak, jis opak"*, I also tried to underline the Tadeus saying *"Kalau ada perahu, hidup kita baik."* (If there is a *ci*, our lives will be good). For me, this statement not only tells us about food or physical needs, but more importantly, about our well-being. It is about the feeling of being happy physically, psychologically, and spiritually. In contrast, without *ci*, Asmat life will be terrible. This is similar to what Paulus Amanpen said, *"Yang tidak punya perahu, kasihan sama sekali: perahu kaki tangan yang bisa mengantar ke tujuan."* (Those who own no *ci* are pitiful: the *ci* is like hands and legs to reach one's goal).

Daniel Ayas (*Fieldnote*, 55), one of the Asmat *wow-ipits* and *cisi-ipits* from Atsj, was a little bit emotional when he stated, *"Tidak ada perahu, sama dengan tidak ada makanan, dan tidak makan sama dengan mati."* (No *ci* means, no food and without food means, death). As a *wow-ipits* and *cisi-ipits*, Ayas knew well that food is very basic for his life. Without food, he will have no energy to create such remarkable woodcarvings. The *ci* is very essential in looking for food, both in the water and in the forest. That is why, in conjunction with Ayas, Yuvensius Yapndi (*Fieldnote*, 6) argued that,

> *"Kalau tidak ada perahu kebutuhan rumah akan kosong. Kalau tidak kenal perahu dan dayung, berarti 'mata hidup' sebagai orang Asmat hilang. Untuk cari makan jadi susah. Tidak bisa cari makan secara cepat."* (If there is no *ci*, the house will be empty. If the Asmat abandon the *ci* and the paddle, it means the source of Asmat life is extinct. Looking for food becomes difficult. We cannot instantly look for food).

Yapndi used a new term in his explanation - - *"mata hidup."* Literally, *'mata'* means eye, and *'hidup'* means life. However, in this context, the meaning of *"mata hidup"* is the source of life. At the same time, we can also imagine how difficult it is to be a blind person. So, if there is no *ci*, life will be very difficult just like a blind person facing his or her life. If you own a *ci*, you can see (your eyes can see), and you can fulfill your own needs as well as the needs of others.

Nicolaus Ndepi (*Fieldnote*, 11), a former member of the local Asmat legislature, emphasized a different thing. Most probably because of his former position in public service, Ndepi was able to look closely at his individual responsibility in the society. He said, *"Seseorang yang tidak punya perahu menandakan orang tidak bertanggungjawab sehingga menjadi tergantung, dan jadi tidak bebas."* (A person without a *ci* symbolizes an irresponsible person, so he becomes a dependent person, and has no freedom). It is true that a person or a family without *ci* is dependent on others. They have no idea how to go farther or how to go to their *dusun* to gather firewood or to pound sago. In connection to this topic, I remember the Yoel Manggaprahu's (*Fieldnote*, 31) story about living in a village. According to his story,

> *"Di kampung-kampung sudah banyak orang yang tidak memiliki perahu. Lebih banyak juga yang sudah tidak tahu membuat perahu. Akibatnya mereka hanya ikut-ikut orang lain untuk cari makan. Atau meminjam perahu orang lain. Sebagai contoh, saya*

membeli perahu dari mereka, lalu mereka sendiri yang datang pinjam silih berganti setiap hari." (There are many people who own no *ci* in villages. There are a lot of men who do not know how to make a *ci*. Consequently, they just follow other people to look for food or borrow other's *ci*. For example, I bought a *ci* from them, but then they come to me everyday to borrow the *ci)*.

It is funny and ironic, not only for me but also for Manggaprahu because the villagers sold the *ci* to him, but then they are the main users of the *ci*. Indeed, it is ironic because they received the money but then they were the people who used the *ci*, so they got double profits. Meanwhile, Manggaprahu, as the owner, got the title only – - that the *ci* is his property. Yoel Manggaprahu is not a native Asmat, that is why he was so surprised with the fact that the Asmat, the natives, own no *ci*. His ancestor came from another part of Papua and moved to Asmat decades ago. He is a protestant pastor and now he is a local legislator. As a legislator, he knows very well the *ci's* availability in every Asmat village because he visits those villages frequently. Although he is not a native Asmat, he feels sad to observe the present reality that many Asmat villagers do not preserve the *ci* as a means of their livelihood.

It is very interesting to note that only one of my informants connected the *ci* to sin. She was Seravia Tojamter (*Fieldnote*, 60) from Sawa village. She confidently told me,

"Tidak punya perahu sama dengan berdosa karena Tuhan Allah sudah menciptakan dan menyediakan kayu untuk dijadikan perahu, tetapi tidak membuatnya." (No *ci* is considered to having committed a sin because the Lord God has created and provided wood abundantly for making *ci*, but why you do not make it).

Tojamter is one of the talented and artistic Asmat women who designs mats and bags. In the Asmat view, she is one of the *cescu cepes* (great or talented women – see Konrad (ed.) 2002:87). According to Fr. Vince Cole, the parish priest of Sawa, Seravia is a great and honorable woman because she knows a lot of things about her traditions and without fear says so to others, even before men. That is why Fr. Vince Cole strongly recommended that I interview Seravia. I found her very charming, friendly, intelligent, and with a good sense of humor. She was very serious when she talked about the *ci*. The *ci* for her is not only a personal and social responsibility to society, but also to the Lord God, our Creator. The *ci* harmonizes the relationship among members of a community, as well as the relationship between human beings and God.

Last but not the least, in my FGD with Bartolomeus and Donatus Tamot, I found that their ideas cover almost all key words that have been discussed earlier. For example, to emphasize the importance of the *ci* in Asmat life, they used words such as 'key', 'dead', and 'hearth'. Precisely they said,

"Keluarga yang tidak punya perahu dan dayung sama dengan mati: tidak ada kesan hidup di dalam rumah tangga karena ke mana-mana mencari makanan dengan perantaraan perahu. Maka, perahu merupakan kunci kehidupan Asmat. Tidak punya perahu sama dengan tidak punya tungku." (A family who owns no *ci* and oar is equivalent to dead: there is no sign of life because going somewhere to look for food not without the *ci*. Therefore, the *ci* is a key for Asmat life. Owning no *ci* is considered as owning no hearth).

From these statements, we can see that although each person has not used the same words or sentences to express his or her vital relationship with the *ci*, they all agreed with one thing: the *ci* is very essential and cannot be alienated from the daily life of the Asmat. The *ci* is an integral part of Asmat's mobility.

7.2 *Ci* for men, *jouse* for women

More than just being a son of a mother, the *ci* is considered as male. This consideration perhaps comes from the comparison between men and the *ci*. Both men and the *ci* share a similar capability and function, particularly in terms of physical power. The Asmat people believe in men's power to protect, help, facilitate, and transport his fellow men and goods from one place to another. The *ci*, on the other hand, has the power to bring and transport people and goods from one place to another. The *ci* transports people to cross rivers and enter jungles. It is a guarantee for Asmat mobility. The Asmat say, "*Kalau ada perahu, rumah jadi panas.*" (If there is a *ci*, our house becomes hot or if there is a *ci*, our hearth has light). It means, the *ci* makes them alive and happy because there is something to eat. I guess, eating is a very happy moment for the Asmat. The statement is based from my experiences and observations when I was a parish priest of Agats diocese in Asmat. For instance, when we had a meeting in a parish or a village and people know that the committee had provided food or drinks for the participants, this made the people come. However, if they know that there is no food, no drink, and no cigarette provided for the meeting, only a few would come. Again, eating makes the Asmat happy and enthusiastic. Therefore, it makes sense that the burning hearth is a symbol of life, a symbol of existence, and a symbol of happiness. With respect to the *ci*, the *ci* keeps the hearth burning and family life happy. The fig.60 demonstrates how the Asmat use their *ci* for fishing.

I was very surprised when I first conducted interviews. I heard the saying: "*Ci opak, cemen opak.*" It means a man who does not own a *ci* is considered impotent. It literally means, no canoe (*ci*), no penis (*cemen*). Amatus Ndatipits and Bartol Bokoropces are both educated Asmat, and acknowledged the saying as a general belief in the Asmat society. The *ci* is very important for the Asmat, just like the penis for a man. A man without a penis, is not a complete man because he is not able to fulfill his duty as male. In other words, a penis is a symbol of being a male. The penis identifies a male when he is born. It is biologically given, that a human being is considered as male because of his penis. So, if a man has no penis, how could people define him because he is not a woman either. Having a penis is a basic to being a man. Therefore, it is very embarrassing if an Asmat man has no penis or is impotent because he cannot attract a female.

Aside from "*Ci opak, cemen opak,*" there is also a similar saying that states: "*Ci opak, jouse opak.*" *Jouse* means hearth or fireplace. So, literally it means, "No *ci*, no hearth." This can be interpreted as if you own no *ci*, you would not able to provide either transportation or food for yourself and your family. Without *ci*, your hearth is cold because there is no fire to cook something. If your hearth is cold, it also means you have no energy because you have nothing to eat. So, "*Ci opak, jouse opak*" implies a lot of meanings. It leads people to the inner core of Asmat life.

For the Asmat, a hearth is very vital, aside from the *ci* itself. Hearth is a symbol of family life. If the hearth of a family house is smoking, it means they are still alive. Likewise, the hearth in a *jeu* symbolizes the existence of a clan (see fig.61). If a person or a family has no hearth in a *jeu*, it means they are no longer part of that *jeu*; they are considered outsiders or strangers.

Figure 60. A man with his young boy are fishing using casting net on the *ci*. (Photograph courtesy of Fr. Eduar Daeli, OSC).

Figure 61. *Jouse* (hearths) inside a *jeu*. The Asmat use the *jouse* for cooking and also to warm their drums when they are fitting the sound. Likewise, they can use the rack above the fireplace to place their valuable belongings such as drum, spear, bow and arrow, shield, paddle, and carving. (Photograph courtesy of Fr. Eduar Daeli, OSC).

Fire on the hearth symbolizes spirit, life, and power. Thus, the Asmat always keep the fire alive or keep the hearth lighted in order to keep the spirit alive. Normally, one way to keep the hearth burning is to cook something on it, such as sago, fish, or other kinds of food (see fig.62). If you have no more fire in your hearth, it implies that you have no more spirit to live.

A man who owns no *ci* is similar to a man who has no penis or a family who owns no hearth. The *ci*, penis, and hearth are all important things in Asmat society. The *ci* is a symbol of mobility and power. The hearth is a symbol of life of a family, while penis is a symbol of fertility and power. A penis has the ability to penetrate a woman's vagina, which means a new creation, new generation, or new life comes on earth. The penis engenders life through its power to ejaculate sperm into a woman's body. A man who has no penis or is impotent, loses the opportunity to create new life or to continue his generation, through sexual intercourse.

The Asmat perceive the *ci* in the same manner as it is as essential as a penis for a man. The *ci* can across rivers and enter jungles, just like *cemen* (penis) can enter *cen* (vagina). The penis arouses and stimulates the vagina to undergo such a joyful experience. The penis brings hope, fertility, and happiness to create a new life. In a similar way, the *ci* brings about happiness to a family and society to produce more food and other needs. Therefore, the *ci* is indeed identical to masculinity. This description is accentuated by Amatus Ndatipits (*Fieldnote*, 22) as he says,

> "*Kalau seorang laki-laki tidak punya perahu dapat dianggap sebagai 'cowut' (perempuan) yang hanya menerima saja. Dia tidak bisa memanasi, tidak bisa menembusi vagina. Kalau tidak ada penis, suasana jadi dingin, tidak menarik. Demikian pula, bila tidak punya perahu suasana keluarga jadi 'jif' (dingin) karena tungku tidak menyala. Namun, kalau ada perahu suasana keluarga menjadi 'amop' (panas), seperi laki-laki yang agresif penuh nafsu memanasi perempuan.*" (A man who owns no *ci* is considered as *cowut* (female) who can only receive. He is not able to arouse the desire and is incapable of penetrating the vagina. If there is no penis, no desire, and the situation of life is cold and uninteresting. Likewise, if there is no *ci*, the situation in a family becomes *jif* (cold) because the hearth has no fire. But, if there is a *ci*, the situation of a family becomes *amop* (hot), just like a man who aggressively stimulates the woman's desire).

When I asked this question, "What would be the woman's symbol, if the *ci* is the man's symbol?" Erick Sarkol, a curator of Agats Museum in Asmat, explained that the hearth could be accepted as a woman's symbol. Hearth belongs to women because most of their activities are related to it. For example, it is the women's responsibility to gather firewood and to cook food. So, it is reasonable if *jouse* (hearth) symbolizes women in Asmat society.

Based on a sacred ritual, one of my informants[13] in a secret way explained:

> "*Pater, ini adalah rahasia, tapi saya mau kasi tahu karena pater orang suci. Pesta semalaman di jeu baru itu sebenarnya adalah perayaan persetubuhan suci antara roh dan bumi. Hal ini disimbolkan oleh* **erampok** *yang ditancapkan di atas wayir (tungku*

---

13   Intentionally, I did not put the informant's name because this thing is part of the Asmat's secret. The informants verbally allowed me to write this story in my dissertation. He hoped this story can be archived for future generations, when there are no more storytellers.

Figure 62. Asmat children are playing a cooking game.

api utama) di jeu. Hanya laki-laki dewasa yang boleh ikut acara tersebut." (Father, this is our secret, but I will let you know because you are a holy man. The whole night ritual feast for a new *jeu* is a celebration of holy intercourse between the spirit and the earth. It is symbolized by sticking the *erampok* (a sacred tree) to the *wayir* (main hearth) of a *jeu*. Only adult men can participate in that ritual).

The *erampok* is a representation of the spirit, while the hearth is a representation of the earth. Earth for the Asmat is considered as mother, a woman. So, it is clear enough from this story, that the hearth symbolizes women. Hearth is the receiving subject of the *erampok* coming, as a woman's vagina for a man's penis. Moreover, the main material of the hearth itself is soil which is gathered from the earth, the symbol of a mother.

In addition, *Bis* pole[14] (ancestor figures – see fig.63) ritual, after a series of rituals in a *jeu*, the *bino* (lower pointed end of the *Bispole*) is implanted into the ground in a major ceremony in the middle of sago grove (Kuruwaib 1974:78). According to Kuruwaib, there are five meanings associated with the *bis*, i.e.: (1) Symbol of ancestral presence; (2) Reminder of revenge-obligation, (3) Physical and spiritual health; (4) Fertility, and (5) Beauty (1974:38-40). In conjunction with the male and female symbols, I want to emphasize the meaning of fertility in relation to the *bis*. The very obvious symbol of fertility of the *bis* is a representation of the phallus, *bis cemen*, and the vagina, *bis cen* and frequently the depiction

---

14 Gunter Konrad in his article, "On the Phallic Symbol and Display in the Asmat" in *An Asmat Sketch Book No. 6*, reported: "The pole expresses a mythological image; it is simultaneously a monument to and record of the past. The *mbis* pole actualizes the spiritual and cultural elements of the *Mbis* people signifying the presence of the forefathers and confirming a conviction and determination for revenge. The *Mbis* is a remembrance of those once influential men (1978:90; see also fig.63).

Figure 63. *Bis* poles in the Agats Museum.

of a turtle (Kuruwaib 1974:39). Moreover, to assure the fertility of the sago trees, the *bis* is transported and implanted to the ground. The implantation itself is a symbol of sexual intercourse between the spirit and the land, so the fertile land bears fruits for the benefit of the community. In the same manner, the penis penetrates a vagina for procreation.

7.3 Power over *dusun*

The *ci* is a symbol of man's power, especially power over his *dusun*. According to my informants, the first *dusun* (forest) division system was based on the river water ways.

It means, the rivers were the borders of the *dusuns*. An example is the Catholic mission's compound around the Atsj parish center. The piece of land was donated decades ago by the ancestors of Atsj to the Catholic mission through the former parish priest of St. Paulus Atsj. It is very interesting to me because the boundaries of the donated land follow the two river basins: from the Pit and Ndatimits river estuaries until where the rivers come and flow into the middle of the jungle. The boundaries are still valid until today, though some villages use the area for farming. Therefore, to identify and ultimately control his *dusun*, *sine qua non*, one must own a *ci*. Without the *ci*, he will not be able to reach the boundaries of his *dusun*.

The disadvantage of owning no *ci* is that a *dusun* cannot be maintained and it could easily be accessible to outsiders. The *dusun* is believed to be a mother or a wife who could bear and nurture new life. Such is the *dusun* that grows sago, the staple food of the Asmat; it grows trees which are very useful for them to live, and provides countless varieties of animals that can be taken as food. The *dusun* is not only an empty land, but it has everything in it, including rivers, trees, sago, and animals. Thus, the *dusun* is very important for the Asmat. The *dusun* is the ancestral domain of the Asmat.

When someone does not own a *ci*, it means he has no power to control, maintain, and preserve the source of his life. It is similar to one who could not protect his wife from the enemy's attack. If a man lets everybody else enter his *dusun* freely, it is similar to allowing his wife to be raped by other men. Therefore, owning a *ci* is not only a symbol of power, but also a symbol of responsibility and protection of both his wife and his possessions, including a *dusun*. Another meaning of responsibility to the wife is that a husband will be able to support his wife by giving her a *ci*, so that she could go anywhere to meet the needs of her family. Thus, it is very natural that Paulus Amanpen (*Fieldnote*, 47) said that every single wife would be very happy to hear that her husband had cut down a tree for making a *ci*. It is good news for her because she would be able to find food and meet all the needs of the family without waiting for other's help by borrowing their *ci*. If a household owns no *ci*, the wife would go to borrow a *ci* from their neighbor, or just follow others to find food for her family. As such, she is separated from the control of her husband. If a wife leaves her husband, in a sense it could be interpreted to mean that the husband loses his power to control his wife. So, to maintain power, a man should provide a *ci* for him and his family.

7.4 Do not call him *bitni*

According to Seravia Tojamter, a man who does not have a *ci* can be called *bitni* (knows nothing to work). Therefore, fighting or quarreling in a household can take place if they have no a *ci* because the abscence of a *ci* symbolizes a husband who is not able to do anything. Providing the *ci* is one of the man's responsibilities. So, it is reasonable for a wife to ask her husband for a *ci*.

It is possible that other people can humiliate a family who do not own a *ci* because they cannot live on their own. If a man is called *bitni*, it means he is considered impotent, a man who does not have initiative or a man who knows nothing but to eat. Thus, his status as a real man is nil. He is similar to someone who does not have a penis (*cemen opak*) because he is not capable of performing his duties as a male, that of piercing the vagina. Of course, an Asmat man is not willing to be called *bitni* or *cemen opak* because it is very insulting. Self-esteem for an Asmat man is very important, that is why he has to prove and defend it. Therefore, in order not to be called a *bitni* or a *cemen opak*, an Asmat man must own a *ci* as a proof that he is a real man (*Asmat Nak*), a person who knows how to work. It does not matter if a husband is not a *cisi-ipits* (talented *ci* maker), he can ask help or hire someone else to make a *ci* on his behalf. Owning a *ci* is a symbol of initiative, responsibility, and power.

7.5 One family in one *ci*

In a feedback seminar about the Asmat culture recently held in Agats, a participant asked: "In a war *ci*, who can get in, anyone or just the immediate family? The question was answered directly by Bartol Bokoropces. He said, "In conjunction with war, a clan or a close family stays in the same *ci*. However, there are specific customary provisions. Later on, the *cesmaipits* (see fig.64) in that *ci* will examine the readiness of the people who want to go to war. If a man is not ready, then he cannot go to war. His readiness is also related to his relationship with his spouse because one of the taboos during the war season is having sex with any woman, including his wife. If everything is okay, so everybody in that *ci* can participate" (*Notulensi*, 2012:4). This explanation can be interpreted as family unity in a *ci*. The *ci* apparently unites the family members, both the living and dead. The representation of the deceased family member appears the form of the carvings in the *ci*. The spirits of the ancestors from the same family are believed to support their families who are fighting in a battlefield. In addition, the shape of the *ci* itself symbolizes oneness of the people in it. The *ci* unites them to go to the same destination by paddling it together, and nobody among them would paddle to the opposite direction.

Figure 64. Paddling the *ci* together. Standing at the middle with ornamented paddle is *cesmaipits* or tribal leader. (Photograph courtesy of Fr. Eduar Daeli, OSC).

Each clan has its own *cesmaipits*. A *cesmaipits* has limited authority over his own clan or close family. He has no authority over other clans or *cis*. Above all, a stranger should not be allowed to get into the *ci* if nobody knows him or his intentions. He could either be a good or bad person for the clan. So, the Asmat would not allow anybody to enter their *ci* if they do not know him personally. The *ci* therefore becomes a symbol of unity and strength to a clan or family.

In an interview with David Jimanipits (see fig.6) conducted beside the new *ci* that he was making behind his house in Ewer, I asked him, "Why is a *jicap ci* carved at the *ci cimen* and all around the *ci*?" With a smile and confidence he answered, "*Ukiran perahu merupakan symbol kehadiran roh-roh nenek moyang. Jadi, jika sekeliling perahu diukir, itu berarti roh-roh menjaga dan menguatkan perahu tersebut secara menyeluruh*" (*Fieldnote*, 34) – (The carving in the *ci* is a symbol of the presence of ancestral spirits. If the *ci* is carved entirely, it means the spirits protect and strengthen the whole *ci*). I was amazed by his answer because what I know is that Asmat carvings represent the ancestor's spirits. I did not think that the carvings around the *ci* represent the integrity and protection of the ancestors for the whole *ci* and the people in it. This means that the power of the ancestral spirits dwell entirely in the *ci*. If they carve only a certain part, the spirit's power may be limited to stay only in that specific part of the *ci*. However, if they carve completely all around the *ci*, it means the protection of the spirit over the *ci* is infinite. The strength and the power of the spirits encompass the entire *ci*. A challenging question is thereby posed: What is the role of the ancestral spirits if the *ci* is already extinct?

7.6 The *Ci*: a key for Asmat economy and festive activity

According to Pius Woyakai (*Fieldnote*, 49), prior to any party or feast, the *cis* should be made available first. As I have mentioned earlier, if there are no *cis* and no paddles, a ritual feast should not be arranged. The *ci* and the paddles are very essential because these are guarantees that all needs for the ritual feast to be celebrated will be provided. Basically, the *ci* is a primary need that will provide the secondary needs.

The *cis* in the past are also a measure on the readiness to go on war or headhunting. It is a big honor to win the war or to take many heads if the *cis* are excellent. Conversely, if the *cis* are of low quality, they are heavy, and can easily be damaged. This can be a good chance for the enemy to win the war or to take as many victims because the people in the *cis* will not be able to escape in case of emergency. Thus, the *cis* are prerequisite for any festive occasion and are a symbol of readiness to arrange warfare or headhunting. It means that if a clan or a family wants to win a war or raid, they must prepare their *cis* seriously, otherwise they will succumb to the enemy.

Furthermore, some of my informants expressed their attachment with the *ci*. On this part of my study, I want to highlight some ideas that can show the economic dimension of the *ci*. For me, it is easier to state the disadvantages of not owning a *ci*, rather than the advantages of owning a *ci* because the Asmat can do anything using the *ci*. This is why I preferred to examine the economic implications of not owning a *ci*.

First, the *ci* is a basic need for the Asmat. As already mentioned, the *ci* is part of the Asmat *habitus*, so owning no *ci* brings about difficulties in their lives. Metaphorically, the Asmat articulate this through the saying *ci opak, jis opak*. If a family does not own a *ci*, it would be very difficult for them to go fishing, hunting, and gathering. The *ci* facilitates their meeting their needs. In other words, without a *ci*, a family will go hungry. If they are hungry they will have no energy to work or to produce something for their own lives and for the community. Therefore, economically, they might become a dependent family or society because they cannot afford to produce such products even for domestic use only.

In addition, the *ci* is a means of transportation. The *ci* helps people to go anywhere and to transport goods from one place to another. That is why a family will spend a lot of money for transportation if they do not own a *ci*. In other words, one of the advantages of owing a *ci* is to save energy and money. The *ci* itself is useful in making money. For example, before the establishment of a wharf in Atsj and Agats, people used the *ci* as a means of transporation to reach the ship which is at the middle of the river. At that time, the owners of *cis* earned much money transporting people and goods to and from the ship. Furthermore, the *ci* can be bartered with other goods or services, although this rarely happened.

Second, the *ci* makes clearer the division of labor between men and women. The *ci* makers are men, while the firewood gatherers are women. This means the availability of the *ci* is men's responsibility. If there is no *ci*, the women will not be able to gather firewood and other needs. Thus, the *ci* clearly shows the difference between men and women's responsibilities, but at the same time stresses the complementary work of both men and women. On the one hand, a woman can fulfill her responsibilities such as gathering firewood and fishing because of the availability of the *ci* which is made by a man. On the other hand, a man is able to make a *ci* because of the energy that comes from food and drink provided by the woman. Hence, the *ci* motivates everybody in the family to fulfill their responsibilities for the sake of all the members of the family. The *ci* creates a productive person who can become a producer of things rather than a consumer. The members of a family will be totally dependent on others if they do not own a *ci*, including the search for food.

Third, not owning a *ci* brings results to the non-maintainance of the *dusun*. A *dusun* is the ancestral domain of the Asmat. *Dusun* provides many things for the Asmat such as sago (their staple food), a countless variety of animals that can be taken as food, wood for many purposes, and the river contains seafood. Economically, the Asmat take everything from the *dusun* to sustain their lives, including the *ci* tree. However, the Asmat can reach the *dusun* only through the *ci* because the area is surrounded by rivers. In other words, one of the disadvantages of not owning a *ci* is that a *dusun* cannot be maintained and could easily be accessible to outsiders. Outsiders could easily benefit from a *dusun* that is not maintained by its owner. For example, an outsider can take the sago, wood, and everything in the *dusun* to use personally or to sell. As a result, the owner of the *dusun* will lose his power and benefit from his *dusun*.

Owning a *ci* will help people to minimize their expenses and avoid starvation. I could therefore say that an Asmat family would continuously live in harmony if they own a *ci* and paddles even if they have no money. However, they will face difficulties in their lives if they have no *ci*, even if they have much money.

Last, not owning *ci* triggers conflicts for an Asmat family or a community. For example, a wife can blame her husband continuously or even leave him because he cannot provide a *ci* for their family. Paulus Amanpen (*Fieldnote*, 47) said this truly happened, "*Setiap istri sangat senang ketika mendengar bahwa suaminya telah menebang pohon untuk dibuat perahu.*" (Every wife would be very happy to hear that her husband had cut down a tree to make a *ci*). This is good news for her because she would be able to find food for them and meet all the needs of the family without asking other people's help by borrowing their *ci*. If a household does not own a *ci*, the wife would go to the neighbor to borrow their *ci*, she would just follow others to find food for her family. Borrowing a *ci* continuously could lead to quarrels, not only in the household but also with the neighbor. Therefore, this is an economic issue that may result to a social conflict in a community.

Moreover, a husband who cannot provide a *ci* for his family can be called *bitni* (know nothing to work). A wife can leave a *bitni* husband and look for another man who can provide her with a *ci*. Therefore, making or providing a *ci* is an important condition to determine the readiness of a man to marry a woman, even if it is not considered as bride-wealth. In short, owning a *ci* will prevent conflicts among family members and among people in a community. If they own a *ci*, they can focus on their work and gain more benefits.

8

Continuity and discontinuity in Asmat Society

Reflecting on the *ci* issue that has now changed in many aspects, I tried to examine the tendencies that probably will or will not happen in the Asmat society. The findings of this study were generally based from firsthand data and from my personal observations during my previous stay in Asmat. My observations were also concretized by the opinions and experiences of my informants. Despite the fact that the focus of this study is gender power relations, I also endeavored to portray the other aspects in the social life of the Asmat.

8.1 Social change

To determine social change among the Asmat, one should look back and trace the footsteps of the Dutch, the missionaries, the Indonesian government, travelers, and traders. Encountering new people with different cultures has brought about significant changes among the Asmat. In my opinion, it is important to note that the first most significant agents of social change among the Asmat are the Christian missionaries (see Suter 1982:12), both Catholics and Protestants, followed by the Indonesian government and then traders. Fr. Gerard A. Zegwaard, a Dutch missionary of the Sacred Heart (MSC), who founded the first permanent settlement in Asmat in 1953 said, "I was the first white man to take up residence among them and there was no representative of the Dutch Colonial Administration to enforce the ordinances against headhunting that were carried out elsewhere" (1959:1020). So without hesitation, I can say that the Catholic missionaries as well as the Protestants were primarily the pioneers in changing Asmat, although prior to the missionaries' settlement, the Dutch had been here for some expeditions and explorations. The local government of Indonesia followed the missionaries' steps and then did their own programs. At present, the Indonesian government, through the local government's programs, is the strongest medium in building "new Asmat", especially since Asmat became an autonomous regency (*kabupaten*) of Papua in 2002.

Social change in Asmat is not totally caused by external factors, but also by internal factors. The internal factor refers to the adaptability of the Asmat to absorb a new culture or modernity. This is accelerated by the weaknesses of the local people, especially the tribal leaders who controlled and selected the new culture. The tribal leaders themselves were comfortable with and enjoyed the modern lifestyle. Such internal factors provided a good way for the modern way of living to flourish easily and dominate the local and traditional culture. Consequently, the local people who were uncertain about their daily lives, either stayed with the traditional values or followed the modern way of life. I found that the local people hesitate to preserve their own traditions and values because they perceive these as old, boring, tiring, and a waste of time. On the other hand, the majority of the Asmat have no capability yet to compete with non-Asmat in many aspects of modern living.

Honestly, I can say that social change has brought about advantages, development, and transformation in Asmat. For example, headhunting practices have now ceased because of the missionaries' teaching and the Indonesian government's enforcement of laws. Moreover, many Asmat can obtain higher education and have good work in various sectors. Furthermore, the Diocese of Agats built an Asmat Museum of Culture and Progress in Agats in 1973 as a way to honor the local artists, to preserve the woodcarving tradition, and to make Asmat known worldwide. Unfortunately, social change has also brought about disadvantages in the everyday life of the Asmat. For example, the *ci* as a material culture is critical and is about to be replaced by modern tools, and the Asmat become a less independent society.

8.2 Water transportation is still needed

In the first period (2002-2008) of my stay in Asmat, I heard several times directly from Yuvensius Biakai who was elected as regent in 2004 about his dreams and plans to construct Asmat as a *"kota kendaraan"* ("vehicles city"). He dreamed that one day Asmat would be like other cities that are full of cars, motorcycles, and other vehicles. This is quite evident now when I returned to Asmat. I was so surprised because in Agats city, I found a lot of electric motorcycles as well as bicycles. It was indeed a surprise to me because people could not find those things in Agats City four years ago when I left. This is triggered by the construction of cemented roads in the center of Agats City. Yuvensius' dream is not only limited to Agats city proper, but it also reaches other areas in Asmat to build a link between cities and villages. This dream has already started and will continue to be realized even when Yuvensius Biakai is no longer in position as regent.

Apparently, it is not only Yuvensius as regent who wants Asmat to be a "vehicle city", but also the local community. In many conversations with the Asmat, I found that they also long to see Asmat like any other area which has advanced in many aspects of life. For example, when there was a meeting with the local parliament members in Atsj district in 2005, a *kepala desa* (village head) (equivalent to a barangay captain), expressed his desire by saying, "This city (Atsj) should be a vehicle city! Let Agats be the capital city of Asmat, but this area should be the benchmark for the entire Asmat. Atsj should be a vehicle city" (Daeli 2005:1). The desire of the village chief is quite reasonable because until that day the community built roads called *"jembatan"* (bridges) both in cities and in villages using ironwood. Because the consumption of ironwood is unlimited while the supply is very limited, in few years the ironwood will vanish. Moreover, there has been no effort to cultivate ironwood because the people feel that there are still many of such trees in the forests so they see no need to plant new ones. However, they should realize that the consumption and growth of ironwood is pretty much different. Thus, there is no other way but to import materials from other areas in order to build at least the roads, both in the city and in the villages. Thus, the community need not walk in the muddy grounds anymore because Asmat itself does not possess stones, sand, cement, and iron to be used as the basic materials for road construction. Actually, this is the village chief's dream.

Although there are efforts to construct Asmat to be a "vehicle city", water transportation is still needed. The community and the local government cannot escape from the Asmat's *habitus* which is located geographically in the lowlands and in the middle of a huge swampy area. Moreover, numerous rivers separate or isolate one place from another. Therefore, even if there are roads constructed with concrete, cement, or asphalt, this will happen only in the center of the capital city and in the center of districts. It means the *ci* and other water vehicles are still important to reach out to many other areas, especially to people who have to go to the forest and to the river to look for their daily needs.

Recently, in a feedback seminar about the Asmat culture in Agats held on April 30, 2012, I addressed these questions during group discussions. The questions asked were: Do you think that the *ci* will become extinct? If yes, what would be its impact on Asmat life? A summary of the group discussions is as follows: The *ci* will not be extinct (or will not die) as long as the Asmat people themselves maintain their identity as *Asmat Nak* (people of the tree). Another group said the *pakanam ci* (family or daily used *ci*) can be extinct because it tends to be replaced by modern transportation, but the *jicap ci* (feast or war *ci*) will remain because it is useful for traditional feasts. To answer the second question, the groups said that social relationships in society will be characterized by business and profit orientation which will be followed by moral degradation such as theft (*Notulensi*, 2012:6).

There is a strong possibility that the *ci* which has been the source of the Asmat life will be replaced by machinery boats, such as speedboats and longboats. There is also a greater need for speedboats and longboats. This is proven by the existence of a boat factory in Atsj that manufactures machinery boats which probably would be followed by another developer in other places in Asmat. Machinery boats will then increase in number while the *cis* will be extinct or be minimized in number. As a consequence, the demand for fuel oil as well as spare parts for the boats will increase. Likewise, the need for money will also increase in order to buy both boat and fuel oil. In connection with this, new problems will arise. How will the Asmat people earn money? Those who have jobs, whether in government or in the private sectors, may not find difficulties to earn money because they have salaries. Unfortunately, many people have no regular income; for them money would be a major problem. Again, money is a basic need for the modern Asmat. One way to make money is by selling land or other natural products such as wood, fish, and shrimps. Perhaps, other people would do so through illegal means (by stealing) as mentioned in the group discussions held during the feedback seminar.

8.3 *Pes* (ironwood) and *ci nak* (*ci* tree) are in danger

Until now the use or necessity of wood especially ironwood is extremely unlimited. Ironwood is used in almost all physical development needs because it is strong and durable. For example, ironwood is used as the main material in building houses and all other buildings. Ironwood is also used to build *"jembatan"* (roads) in villages and cities which are miles away. Actually, ironwood is one local commodity that is income generating. Unfortunately, it may bring or cause ecological disasters and the extinction of ironwood in a matter of a few years. The people in Asmat use the ironwood without control and without limits because of the great demand and because nobody controls its use.

Ironwood comes in various forms and sizes and can be used as poles, beams, and boards. The average diameter of ironwood for poles is 15-25 cm. Meanwhile, a bigger diameter is needed to produce various sizes of wooden beams and boards which are

Figure 65. A new school building. All wood materials used here are ironwood.

approximately 50 cm and above in size (see fig.65). Because of this, ironwoods in various sizes certainly will vanish. The extinction will occur sooner than expected.

As of now, the concentration of the physical development is in Agat City and in the central districts of Asmat. Such physical development will be more widespread in the near future and the demand for ironwood will likewise increase significantly. Therefore, if there is no effort to regulate the use of ironwood and other natural resources, both from the local community and from the government, then it will not be surprising that within 10 years, the growth and production of ironwood would be in a critical level and will be extinct soon afterwards.

The focus of people to use timber in various physical development needs is still ironwood which is the best wood as compared with other kinds of red wood that have lower quality. With the deficiency in ironwood and red wood, it is possible that people may use the *ci* tree as a new kind of commodity to produce wooden boards. I could very confidently say now that the *ci* tree will be used for other purposes. Before long, the material to be used in making a *ci* will be of poor quality because the *ci* tree will have been used for other needs. As a result, the Asmat *ci* is in danger, although the need for a canoe still remains.

My prediction about the existence of the *ci* tree is the same as that of Yoel Manggaprahu, a member of the local Asmat parliament and also Sr. Korina Ngoe, OSU, the director of YPPK Yan Smith Agats. Manggaprahu said,

"*Material pembangunan di Asmat adalah kayu. Namun, suatu saat nanti kayu perahu pun menjadi sasaran dan sarana komoditi. Sekarang ini, memang pada umumnya masih menggunakan kayu besi. Namun, tidak akan lama lagi, kayu besi akan habis karena pemakaian yang tiada batas*" (Fieldnote, 31). (The main material of every single building in Asmat is wood. One day the *ci* tree will be a target and be used as a commodity. As of now, people generally use ironwood. However, it will not be long, ironwood will run out because of unlimited usage).

There is a tendency among the Asmat people not to be concerned about the *ci* and they are more excited with longboats or speedboats which are faster and modern. According to Sr. Korina, the Asmat people now tend not to use the *ci* even if their travel distance is relatively near. The reason is that longboats are already available. Likewise, the people often say that paddling the *ci* is difficult, slow, tiring, and boring. Sr. Korina added that the function of the *ci* is reduced to as a means of transportation. According to her, the function of longboats which were distributed by the local government to several groups of fishermen has now changed. Initially, they were given to the fishermen to be able to get more fish and to market these easily. Unfortunately, the longboat is now being used as regular means of transportation like the *ci* (*Fieldnote*, 20).

Despite modernization, there are still some people who long for the *ci* especially the elderly. One day Paskalis Osakat, a *wow-ipits* from Yasiw village of Atsj district, shared his experience with me. He told me,

> "*Pater, saya pernah ke Agats naik longboat dari Atsj. Saya merasa capek dan pusing karena hanya duduk saja, berbeda dengan naik perahu di mana kita harus mendayung sehingga badan tetap segar. Waktu itu saya sangat sedih, bahkan menangis ketika dalam perjalanan saya melihat saudaraku orang Asmat mendayung perahu. Saya sangat sedih. Saya seolah-olah ingin meloncat dari longboat yang saya tumpangi dan naik ke perahu dayung tersebut.*" ("Father, I have ridden a longboat from Atsj to Agats. I felt very tired and dizzy because I was just sitting down as opposed to riding the *ci* in which we paddle it so that our body remains fresh. I was very sad, and even cried when I saw my fellow Asmat paddling the *ci* on their way back to their village. I was very sad, as if I wanted to get out of the longboat that I was riding to jump into that *ci*.").

That was the feeling of an Asmat who has lived with the *ci* for many years. It is quite different for the young generation who dream of motor boats. Paskalis Osakat explained further that the *ci* is better and healthier as compared with the longboat. "When we ride the *ci*, our body stays fresh and will be able to immediately and directly run after wild animals. Whereas riding in a speedboat or longboat, our body aches, stiffens, and needs time to adjust to the situation in the mainland" (see also Erick Sarkol).

In short, both ironwood and *ci* tree are threatened as well as other natural resources. The ironwood in particular because of unlimited use, and the *ci* tree will be used for many other purposes. Water transportation is still needed in Asmat, even if it is not the traditional boat or the *ci* which is being used now. The new kind of boat and other water transportation vehicles probably will be made by non-Asmat or will be imported from other places. When that time comes, the glory of the *ci* will just be a memory. Preserving the *ci* and other natural resources means preserving the earth from natural disasters (see Oliver-Smith and Hoffman 1999; Milton 2002).

8.4 The changed meaning and function of ritual

In an informal interview with Fr. Charles Loyak, OSC, a Crosier who has been working in Asmat 27 years ago, I got a confirmation that the *ci* is a kind of "*jembatan*" (bridge) to relate or facilitate the orderly use of many things. "*Jembatan*", according to him, is a medium to access one place to another. In Asmat context, if there is no *jembatan* which is generally made of wood, then the people would walk in the muddy ground. Therefore,

Figure 66. Opening ceremony of a new *jeu* construction in Atsj, Feb. 2012. A tribal chief (with dog teeth and double-curved shell nose ornaments) is performing an opening ritual as witnessed by Camat (district head) of Atsj, the Police, Local parliament member, and the Indonesia military.

jembatan is very important to facilitate the travel of people in meeting their needs easily without stepping in the mud. With the same perception, the *ci* also facilitates and connects people with one another and with the things they need. If the traditional *ci* does not exist anymore, there will be many things that will fall apart. And with the *ci* extinction, the relationship of people and other things will probably be disconnected.

One of the traditional elements that undergoes changes is ritual. If the *ci* is gradually being replaced by modern transportation, many rituals will also be gone or will no longer be practiced. For example, the *ci* tree will no longer be grown and there will be no more rites in giving the *ci* a name of an ancestor. Many taboos will lose their significance. Brotherhood and intimacy with nature and the spirits of ancestors will be banished because there is no medium to relate them to each other. The ritual is a medium to invite, unite, and celebrate life in the community as well as to relate the living world to the transcendental world (see fig.66).

If we observe closely, nowadays one of the motivations in holding a ritual in Asmat is to look for donations from the local government, local parliament, and from other parties, which people believe would give them funding either in the form of cash or goods. Is it wrong to receive donations? I do not want to say much about this new issue because everybody has their own interpretation about the matter. However, my concern is to look at the paradigm shift of holding a ritual feast. Motivation to look for donation is very different from Abraham Kuruwaip's explanation in his article entitled, "The Asmat Bis Pole: Its Background and Meaning." Kuruwaip figured out five points of the meaning of *Bis* pole and its impact to society: (1) Symbol of ancestral presence; (2) Reminder of revenge obligation; (3) Physical and spiritual health; (4) fertility; and (5) Beauty and remembrance (1974:33). Based on Kuruwaip's explanation, I did not find any hidden agenda in looking for benefits from other parties such as from the local government, church, and various parties, except from the ancestral spirits. Nevertheless, we have to realize that the present generation is not the same as the previous ones. The traditional ritual may be perceived differently in accordance with progress and development over time.

Recalling an experience in 2007, I was very surprised when I met several tribal leaders from a village. They came to our parish priest's house with one intention. One of them said, "*Pater, kita punya patung bis itu banyak sekali. Mungkin pater mau ambil ka?*" (Father, we have many *bis* poles. Are you willing to have some?). They were asking and offering me to buy the *bis* poles which they recently ritualized. I answered them with anger, "*Apakah kamu tega menjual nenek moyangmu?*" (Do you dare to sell your ancestors?) They were speechless to hear my comment. At that time, when they had no words, I expressed my emotion. I said, "I am very sad to hear that you are willing to sell your ritual objects which you have named after your ancestors. Are you not afraid of your ancestral spirits? I know you were celebrating the *bis* poles ritual for many long months, to commemorate and honor your ancestors. At the final rite, you gave the *bis* poles the names of your ancestors. I know that the spirits of the ancestors remain in those *bis* poles once they are named. Once again, do you dare to sell your ancestors? Even if you do so, I won't be able to take care of your ancestors." Honestly, I was very sad and angry to see people who abandoned their rituals and even their ancestors because of money. I think, if the *bis* poles which they were offering me had not been ritualized, maybe I would have had a different response, and I would probably have helped them look for customers. I think, their actions were not fit to the *bis* pole ritual celebration. Ideally, the *bis* is transported to the sago areas after the ritual feast and implanted there to assure fertility of the sago trees (Kuruwaip 1974:40). What would happen if the people were to sell their ancestors? I am worried about the waves of modernization in Asmat society because these can change the people even to the extent of their spiritual level.

8.5 Carving: not because of inspiration, but because of order

With regards to the *bis* pole ritual as mentioned earlier, the *bis* is not only part of a ritual, but also tangibly it is an expression of high art. Kuruwaip stressed that the Asmat carvings, including *bis* pole, are expressions of beauty to obtain happiness. *Bis* pole and other Asmat carvings are works of the hands of gifted persons (*wow-ipits*) who are inspired by the ancestral spirits. The carvings are the visible representations of the ancestors in the world of the living (Fleischhacker 1991:4). It means, the *wow-ipits* is not working alone. Though a certain way, he is communicating and working together with the spirit while carving an art object.

I am astounded to witness that many Asmat carvers today work not because of the inspiration of the ancestral spirits or because of personal expression, but because of the buyer's order. Their carvings are not based on the personal drive to actualize himself, but because of the lure of money. This is my observation as an outsider and not as a carver. Perhaps another response would come out if I were a *wow-ipits*. I think, sooner or later, the role of ancestral spirits will be viewed as out-dated because people would have proven that even without the influence of the spirit, they could carve and stay alive (Daeli 2011:11-12). This assumption is supported by the testimony of Fr. Virgil Petermeier who has been working in Asmat for more than 30 years. He said, "I remember that a long time ago, the Asmat bag (*noken*) was woven by men only. However, now women can also work on it. It is interesting because it was a taboo in the past for women to weave a bag, but now it has become regular work." The same opinion was expressed by Jennifer Hile when she said, "The Asmat people of Papua New Guinea believe in the magical powers of the *gaharu* tree. They burn its resin to connect with their ancestors and to cast spells. Outsiders, meanwhile, value *gaharu* as the source of a costly incense. But now, commercial interests want to log and mine the very forests where these trees grow" (Hile, 2010). If that is the case, then great changes are taking place in Asmat. Change is not just the outer appearance, but also the worldview of the Asmat about their existence as an independent self. For example, something that was considered as taboo or sacred in the past is now just a common thing. Moreover, in the past to arrange a ritual feast, people always used the *jicap ci* (feast *ci*) because each boat has a name which is empowered by the ancestral spirits. However, now longboats and speedboats have become part of customary rituals, although they were not celebrated through the traditional ritual and have not been named after the ancestors. This happens because now, according to Most Rev. Aloysius Murwito, Bishop of the diocese of Agats, people only look at the efficiency of the *ci* and do not see another meaning beyond the *ci* existence (*Fieldnote*, 2).

8.6 Money-oriented mentality

As a leader of the local Church, Bishop Aloysius is closely observing his people. One of his concerns about the dynamics in the Asmat society is "money-oriented mentality" – everything is measured by money. According to him, nowadays in Asmat, there is nothing that is given for free. Voluntary work is also difficult to find because everyone must be paid. The native Asmat views the non-Asmat to have more money. If the Asmat goes to a store, no matter how much money he has, it will all be spent at once. As an example, still according to Bishop Aloysius, when we built a church for the Catholics in a certain village, instead of contributing something to help, the people would ask to be paid for their participation, although the church is built for them. The bishop compared this fact with other local churches in other places where people volunteered to help. This is also noteworthy to compare the process of building a new *jeu* where all villagers participated without being paid. The bishop saw this as a discontinuity. Ideally, every member of the local church participates voluntarily to build their own church because it is for the benefit of all just like the *jeu*. In fact, the Asmat people consider the *jeu* as village property, while the church belongs to the bishop, priest, and other pastoral ministries. In short, the Asmat would say church-building belongs to the mission. "The missionaries come to help us, to make our lives better." It makes sense therefore that the people expect that the missionaries would build the church themselves for the local people. For the local people, it is improper if the mission or bishop and his priest ask for money or goods from the members of the local church as form of personal participation in building the church. In my opinion, there is a way of thinking among the Asmat: "*Misionaris datang untuk membantu kita, kenapa sekarang justru dia yang meminta-minta apa yang kita punya*" (The missionaries came to help us, why are they now asking for our belongings?).

While observing the new *jeu* construction in Atsj (see fig.67), I asked Alfons Sinokos, a local government staff member, what he thinks about the traditional celebration like new *jeu* feast? His answer was,

"Di dalam pesta adat banyak nilai penting dalam hidup muncul, seperti kerjasama dan saling memberi. Hal ini tidak bisa dibayar dengan uang. Sayangnya, masyarakat Asmat semakin dikomandoi oleh uang. Semakin diberi uang semakin tidak mandiri" (*Fieldnote*, 38). (There are many valuable things in life in the traditional ritual such as togetherness and reciprocity. These values cannot be paid by money. Unfortunately, the Asmat people have been influenced by money. The more they get money, the more they become less independent).

As a native Asmat, Sinokos felt pity for his people because of their money-oriented behavior. However, for him, money is not everything. Money cannot make the Asmat an independent society.

In many pastoral activities, I also witnessed the influence of money in their lives. For example, at the end of a three-day seminar for the local church leaders, some participants asked, "*Pater, kita su tiga hari di sini. Apakah ada 'uang duduk' untuk kami bisa bawa?*" – (Father, we have been here for three days. Do we have an incentive that we could bring home?). As a parish priest, I felt sad upon hearing this question. After three days, my fellow priests and I were very busy preparing everything for the seminar including food and drinks for the participants. Moreover, we were the speakers of the seminar which meant that we deserved to be paid. However, we received nothing. In this situation, some participants of the seminar were even asking for incentives. Again, this is a symptom of money-orientation.

Whether they are aware or not, the traditional values that cannot be paid by money, as mentioned by Sinokos, have now been changed by modern considerations where everything is measured by money. Being money-oriented is affecting many Asmat in many ways.

Figure 67. Interview with Alfons Sinokos while observing the new *jeu* construction in Atsj.

8.7 *Asmat nak* – the real people

Asmat nak means the real people or the men of tree. Based on this perspective, the Asmat always try to be the best in every aspect of life as stated by Yuvensius Biakai (see Chapter 3), "The Asmat possess a competitive trait and high self-esteem. Every individual or ethnic group when they perform something, believe that they are the best. The Asmat dream to be the best in everything." In the past, the measurement and proof of being a great man is success in battle and taking the enemy's head. Because of his great performance in warfare and headhunting, an Asmat man is called *cesmaipits* (big man, great warrior). The enemies are afraid to face the *cesmaipits*. Moreover, the *cesmaipits* status cannot be transferred to others, even if a new one comes. The *cesmaipits* will always be honored and die as one *ces-omou* (great man).

The spirit of an *Asmat nak* still remains in every Asmat. But then, what would be the proof for the Asmat if there are no more warfare and headhunting? I believe, this question can be answered through the following experiences. First, an Asmat will be very happy if he can reach a certain position or obtain a special role in an organization such as being village chief, chairman of parish council, chairman of sports committee, etc. Later, instead of saying his name when he meets someone, this man will introduce himself by using his title or status. For example, instead of saying, 'Hi, I am Tremendus', he would rather say, 'Hi, I am the village chief of A" or 'I am former staff of district head.' I think this is a way of showing power and achievement.

Second, one of the parish priests in Agats diocese shared his experience which happened in his parish. Here is the summary of his story, "It was very difficult for me to renew the parish board and replace the chairman of the parish council even though he has been in position for more than fifteen years. I really wanted to have a new chairman because of some considerations. Let us say the name of the chairman of the council is Tremendus. When I let him know my plan to renew the board, he felt extremely rejected and was angry. He did not want to be replaced by anyone else. He did not think that his position would be taken over by others. He thought being the chairman is forever. The point is he refused to be replaced. Fortunately, at that time I found a good inspiration. I said to him, Tremendus, may I ask you a question? "Yes, Father," he answered. How many years have you chaired the parish council? And then he said, "More than 20 years, Father." Wow! That is amazing! You did a lot for our church. However, do you think that the chairman is lower than a counselor? "No. I don't." So, I think you must go to a higher position rather than just being a chairman. You can be a counselor which is higher than being a chairman. "Oh, really, Father? If that is the case, okay get anybody else to be a chairman. I want to be a counselor of the parish council." This story highlights the Asmat's need for a position to prove that they have power.

Third, several years ago in our parish, there was a volunteer women's group to clean the church building every Saturday morning. One day, I met them in the church. I saw there was a part of the church that had not been cleaned yet. I asked one of them to clean it, but she refused. She said, *"Pater, tidak bisa. Itu ibu Cantik pu bagian. Saya bisa kasi bersih, tapi ibu Cantik nanti akan marah saya."* (Father, I cannot do it. It is not my part, but ma'am Cantik. Actually, I can clean it, but ma'am Cantik will be angry with me). Even in doing good, there are regulations. They cannot easily take over the responsibility of others, even though the one in charge is absent.

Fourth, just by chance I met a man from a village who usually portrays the role of Jesus in the drama of Christ's Passion. He told me spontaneously, *"Pater, pada Jumat Agung yang akan datang saya akan pulang ke kampung. Kita akan buat drama seperti biasa. Yang jadi Yesus, saya ini sudah. Yang lain-lain tidak bisa. Kalau saya, saya su tahu semua.*" (Father, I will go back home to my village this coming Good Friday. We will perform a drama as usual. I will act as Jesus. Yes, I am the only one who could act as Jesus. Other people know nothing in acting like Jesus. Unlike me, I know everything). This man thinks he is irreplaceable.

These stories are examples of how the Asmat stay in power, position, and self-esteem. In Asmat, it is very difficult to replace the names in committees or boards of an organization because the one who is in a certain position would keep it as long as possible. For example, when one registers as a member of a youth organization, it is valid until he dies, despite age limitation. In my opinion, the spirit to keep the position until one dies not only comes from cultural setting, but it is also supported by the position of the Catholic Church officers. For instance, the bishop is bishop forever as well as the priests. The Asmat people will be very surprised if there is a replacement of the board members of an organization. Replacement and regeneration can take place in Asmat to follow modern laws, but it will be very difficult or even hurting for some Asmat.

8.8 New style of hunting and gathering

The Asmat until today are still a hunting and gathering society. Nature has abundantly provided many things for them. If they need something, they just go to the forest or river to gather or hunt for materials or food. They need not plant because Nature has provided trees, plants, and animals for them. This is the traditional way of living in Asmat.

However, at present a new style of hunting and gathering gradually exists. Instead of going to the forest or river to meet their needs, some Asmat go to the local government offices or other agencies which they believe can answer their needs. Usually, they make a proposal of their needs then submit it to the concerned office. They will stay patiently in front of the office until their proposal is answered, just like what they do in a fishing in the river. It is very common to see people in front of offices in Agats such as the office of the regent, district head, and local parliament. They are all there to wait for the response to their proposal. I think this activity is a kind of hunting and gathering practice in modern era.

The Asmat are very close to nature and depend on it. Their lives are very dynamic just like the low and high tide movements. For example, in a moment they can be very playful and energetic to do something as if they are in the high tide moment when a lot of things can be done easily. On the other hand, they act as if their "battery" is fading. They are in low spirits to do something as if they are in the low tide situation when the *ci* cannot be paddled because the river lacks water. Nevertheless, together with acculturation and modernity, the attachment of the Asmat to nature as their main source of life is not as strong at present as it was some decades ago. Their new dependency mostly goes to the Church mission, local government, and other agencies.

8.9 The changed concept of gender

The previous chapter shows the division of labor between men and women in the Asmat society. The *ci* is one of the keys to understand the concept of gender among the Asmat because, both symbolically and practically, the *ci* shows the differences between men and women. For instance, the man is at *ci cimen*, while the woman is at *ci ep*. Man is responsible in making the *ci*, while the woman has to fill it. The division of labor cannot be exchanged, even though the men and the women are able to do the labor. The gender roles are regulated and given by the ancestors. Labor exchange between men and women can be considered as a violation that can bring about danger and death in the community. Thus, I think the Asmat treat the customary law as sacred, although it is formed culturally, including the concept of gender. Everybody tries not to violate any customary law if they wish a happy and long life.

However, the native perspective about the customary law has now changed. In the past, women were always busy with food production, both in private houses and in the public spheres where the men celebrated a ritual. There were many prohibitions for women's involvement in traditional rituals, including entering a *jeu*. The Asmat believe that a *jeu* is sacred, therefore women are forbidden to enter it any time because they can make it "dirty" by their menstrual blood. The menstrual blood is considered as "dirty" and dangerous for the community, especially for men and their tools.

Taboos and other prohibitions for women have now changed also. Most probably, the educational programs, whether formal or informal, have engendered changes in many aspects of Asmat lives, including the changes of the concept of gender among the Asmat. Nowadays, there are many Asmat women who have graduated from the higher education programs. Asmat women are not willing to be controlled forever by men. There is a spirit of resistance in them to fight for their rights. In other words, there is an emancipation of spirit to obtain equality in their lives, as shown by Florentina Bifae, "*Kembali ke kampung sama dengan kembali ke tabiat. Hanya bisa mengikuti keputusan laki-laki. Adat tidak memberi kesempatan kepada perempuan untuk terlibat mengambil keputusan.*" (Back to the village means back to the old *habitus*, we only follow the men's decision. The customary law does not give opportunity for women to be involved in the decision making). This expression is a sign of resistance to male domination. In different words, Karola Biakai says, "*Adat sangat tidak mendukung perkembangan perempuan dalam segala bidang di Asmat, bahkan perempuan menjadi warga kelas dua dan terjajah oleh karena ego laki-laki.*" (The customary law does not support Asmat women to develop in many aspects. More women become second-class citizens in society because of men's ego). Karola considered herself as a defender and rebel to fight for women's rights. She hopes that the life of women tomorrow will be better than today. Through a metaphor she said, "*Kebiasaan yang tidak baik dalam masyarakat harus dibersihkan; perempuan keluar dari jajahan laki-laki: Awan hitam harus dibersihkan jadi hawa putih.*" (We have to reject every bad custom in society; women must be free from men's colonization. The dark cloud should become white).

In short, the concept of gender among the Asmat is changing. Many people are now aware of the equality of men and women. This awareness is not only experienced by women but also by men. Aside from women's awareness and resistance, many educated Asmat men also see the importance of equality. According to Fr. Charles Loyak, OSC, the changes of the concept of gender are both natural and intentional. Natural, means the changes come from the awareness of local people without external influence; whereas intentionally it means changes come from human intervention. An example according to Fr. Charles' experience,

"*Saya masih ingat ketika menjadi pastor Paroki Agats periode pertama (kira-kira akhir tahun 90-an) yang membawahi juga pembinaan di Asrama Putera/Puteri, beberapa kali kami memakai kesempatan kalo ada tokoh perempuan Papua, terdidik (tamu Keuskupan atau Pemerintah), kami mengundang ke Asrama untuk bicara, supaya putera/i Asmat melihat dan mendengar sendiri, bahwa perempuan Papua bisa hebat juga, bukan hanya bisa bakar sagu dan ikan saja."* (I still remember when I was a parish priest of Agats in the late 1990s. The parish had male and female dormitories. Several times we used the situation when an educated Papua woman comes to Agats as a special guest of the diocese or the local government. We invited her to speak about Papuan women's rights before the young Asmat in the dormitories. We wanted to show that Papua women are also great; they are not only great in preparing food).

In that way, Fr. Charles and his team implanted gender equality awareness among the young Asmat. Nowadays, the results of that lesson can be seen through the transition of Asmat's lives. For example, women were not allowed to enter a *jeu* any time in the past. However, today women enter a *jeu* relatively easy because the tribal leaders are not as strict as before. This means the customary law is relatively flexible, especially for educated and working Asmat women. Thus, gender equality awareness is not only for the women and young generation, but also for the elderly.

8.10 Urbanization: *dusun* and village unmaintained

As the capital city of Asmat, Agats is a main destination for both local people from various villages and non-Asmat from everywhere in Indonesia. Large-scale urbanization is taking place in Agats. Agats is like a small and sweet candy for hundreds of ants. The people come from everywhere for various purposes. Among those who are working and studying, there are also many people who stay in Agats waiting for the response to their proposal or are just as parasites in the city.

The effect of this urbanization is, on one hand, Agats city becomes over populated that creates many other social problems such as a significant increase in need for food, money, transportation, and jobs. On the other hand, the original villages of outsiders become quiet. Consequently, the traditional house (*jeu*) is being abandoned and the traditional rituals are neglected because both the elders and the young villagers leave the village. The *dusuns* are also neglected because the owners do not take care of them. This reality opens the possibility for others (outsiders) to enter the *dusun* and get much "produce" from that *dusun* such as wood and sago. Later on, this issue triggers conflicts in that village because normally the owner of the *dusun* does not allow anybody to enter his *dusun* because entering a *dusun* without permission is equivalent to raping the wife of the *dusun's* owner.

Apparently, urbanization brings about negative effects to the traditional rituals and feasts. There will not be a ritual celebration if a village is almost empty because nobody will be invited to arrange it. On the contrary, it is impossible for the Asmat to celebrate a ritual in another place. For example, the people of Atsj will find it impossible to hold a traditional ritual in Agats because any ritual is connected to the *dusun*, *ci*, tribal leaders, tribal singers, and *jeu*. The Asmat cannot build a *jeu* in another village because it is related to their history and their ancestors (see Pius Woyakai – *Fieldnote*, 49).

Hence, urbanization in Asmat influences both the urbanized areas and the not urbanized places. Interestingly, the elders and the young generation blame each other because of the negative effects of urbanization. The elders say that the young generation does not pay attention or they are no longer concerned about their traditions while the young generation says that the elders left the *jeu* and went to urbanized areas.

8.11 Marginalization of the Asmat in many aspects

I was very surprised when I revisited the village of Syuru, which is only about one kilometer away from Agats City. The situation of the village is very different as compared to my last visit four years ago. In 2008, I saw that the Syuru villagers were biologically Asmat. There were some non-Asmat residents, but they did not stay at the core of the village only near the Syuru-Agats boundary. When I returned to that village at the beginning of 2012, I was very surprised because I found a lot of stores and houses in Syuru belonging to the non-Asmat. Because of the stores and new houses of the non-Asmat, the native Asmat houses looked very different. They appeared old and dilapidated. It was no wonder when a tribal leader of another Asmat village exclaimed during a meeting of the church and tribal leaders: *"Dalam waktu 10 tahun ke depan Syuru tidak memiliki kampung lagi. Ini akibat haus uang sehingga membiarkan pendatang masuk sebebasnya pada teritorialnya."* (In about 10 years, Syuru will no longer have a village. This is the result when people now are money-oriented, when they freely let foreigners enter their territory). Consequently, native villagers will be driven away from their ancestral domain.

According to Sr. Korina Ngoe, OSU, the Asmat want to be equal with other people possessing many material goods and in having jobs. Unfortunately, they do not have the capacity to compete, whether in terms of skills or economic status. These facts add to the Asmat's marginalization, including being marginalized from their ancestral domain. The Syuru village case is a good example of Asmat marginalization. Another is Mbai village in Cemnes which is located on the opposite side of Syuru. It has been occupied by non-biological Asmat. My forecast is that other villages will undergo the same thing if they do not learn from the Syuru case. The process of marginalization of Asmat will be more aggravated in many aspects if the native Asmat do not exert efforts to protect their ancestral domains.

In summary, I would say that the discussion above articulates the continuity and discontinuity in Asmat society. I do not have the right or authority to judge which part of their social life and culture should be preserved or eliminated. My purpose here is to show the phenomena and the movements that are now taking place in Asmat. Hopefully, the native Asmat themselves and other people who are concerned about Asmat culture will take appropriate actions to face both continuity and discontinuity in Asmat.

9

Reflection and conclusion

To conclude this work, I want to emphasis some ideas that have been discussed in the previous chapters. My own reflections as a researcher and as a Roman Catholic priest in the field, embolden me to share such valuable information about the advantages and disadvantages of doing fieldwork in this place that I am familiar with. Some recommendations will follow at the end of this chapter.

9.1 Personal reflections as priest and as researcher in the field

Going back to Asmat with a specific objective made the visit quite different from my previous assignment. I went back to Asmat not only as a priest, but also as an anthropology student, a researcher. My previous assignment to Asmat in 2002 to January 2008 had no connection with my formal anthropological studies. At that time, I went to Asmat as a domestic missionary assigned by the Provincial (Superior) of the Order of the Holy Cross of the Indonesia Province in Bandung. Meanwhile, my second visit in January to May 2012 was part of my anthropological studies. I went there for fieldwork to study Asmat culture, particularly the relationship between the *ci* and gender. I went back to Asmat, with "new eyes", the eyes of a researcher.

I think, it is important to include my reflections as part of this book because I was able to examine my own feelings, both as a priest and a field researcher. I cannot make a clear cut difference of the roles, between being a priest and a researcher in this particular field. There are some ethical values within the roles that needed to be observed. This reflection helped me to examine my personal presence in the middle of the Asmat, both as a priest and as a researcher. Hopefully, this reflection will give insights to other researchers. I found that being a priest and a researcher had advantages and disadvantages, even if it is done in a field that is already familiar.

9.1.1 Advantages

There were only a few people who knew that my return to Asmat was to do fieldwork or research. Many people thought that my coming back was to do pastoral ministry among the Asmat again, especially those whom I served before when I was a parish priest. I think this is an advantage because I already knew the people and the place where I would do research. Likewise, the people also knew me. I was able to determine this through the enthusiasm of the people to talk with me. There was an expression from the people that I cannot forget when I revisited Atsj, my former parish. They said, *"Kita punya pater datang!"* (Our father has come!).

Honestly, this statement consoled, motivated, and strengthened me to do my fieldwork among the Asmat because I was acknowledged as part of them. I felt I am not an outsider among them. Indeed, it is a great advantage when we know each other as brothers and sisters.

Despite the fact that people knew my specific purpose in revisiting Asmat, their friendship remained the same. They were happy to talk with me and so was I. Moreover, they were willing to help me in doing my fieldwork. They looked at my fieldwork as a positive attempt to study and to preserve their material culture. According to them, this study will be very useful for their children and grandchildren in the future. They were aware that the local people pay too little attention to their own culture.

Another advantage is that I could save time because I knew the informants whom I had to interview. Knowing one another made the informants more willing or open in answering the research questions. Moreover, they knew me as a priest, a missionary who usually struggles for their rights. The Asmat honor, protect, and listen to a priest more than the police or the local government officials. They believe that my coming back was for them, regardless of what work I did. The mentality that *"misionaris datang untuk kita"* ("the missionaries come for us") still remains. They believed that I would not use the information for my own benefit, but for the benefit of all Asmat and other people in the world. This idea motivated the informants to speak freely and honestly.

I understand that the Asmat will not share their myths, stories, and information with anybody. Even if they do, in particular cases when they have no choice, they will tell any story that comes to their minds. Based on my recent fieldwork among the Asmat, usually soon after KII (Key Informant Interview) or FGD (Focus Group Discussion), one or a few informants would come to me and tell me more information to confirm or to correct previous information that had been given during the interviews or FGDs. For example, during the first interview, an informant did not feel free to articulate his/her ideas because of the presence of other people. Likewise, there were some informants who said, *"Pater, beberapa informasi yang saya ceritakan ini sebenarnya tidak boleh disampaikan kepada orang lain. Tapi, pater kan orang kudus. Jadi, pater perlu tahu. Kita tidak boleh tipu pater!"* (Father, some information that I told you actually cannot be shared with anybody. But since you are a holy man, you deserve to know it. I cannot tell you a lie!"). This means it is very possible that they tell lies to a researcher whom they do not know. They just have to say something to please the one they are talking to, even if the information they give is not true. I felt that it is my privilege to listen to their true stories because I am a researcher-priest. They believe that telling a lie is a sin, especially when they tell it to a priest.

As part of my reflections, I included the reflection of Fr. Virgil Petermeier, OSC. He reflected on the advantages of living as a priest in Asmat. He wrote in his email:

"I think the Asmat feel disappointed when the non-Asmat do not understand their speaking style. However, based on my experience, the Asmat are very patient in seeing the "foolishness" of the non-Asmat when they violate customary laws. They even refuse to tell about it. For example, stepping on a *ci* with muddy feet is a violation to the *ci*. Another example, asking a person who is going to fish, "Hi, are you going to fish?" is considered a violation too and will fail the fisherman in catching fish because the spirit of the fish already knew the purpose of the fisherman. These violations or other similar cases, based on my experiences have not created conflicts. Is this because I am a priest, or because I am an American, or...?"

Through his reflection, Fr. Virgil tried to say that the Asmat people are very open and friendly to non-Asmat. I agree with him. My experience as a former parish priest among the Asmat who are predominantly Catholics, helped me to do my fieldwork relatively easy. I felt free and more confident to raise a question or to even take pictures. This experience was very different when compared to my other experiences in doing research among the highland people of Papua in 2009 and 2010. At that time, I felt uncomfortable because I was not familiar with the people and the environment.

Another advantage of being a researcher-priest aside from the friendship and closeness of the local people is the religious community in the fieldwork site. The advantage was not only about the availability of shelter and other physical facilities, but also about their psychological support. For example, they were always available when I needed them to share my difficulties and stress with them. Frankly, at times I found myself hopeless and in a bad mood when in the field. It was during such situation when the community's support was very useful and helpful.

9.1.2 Disadvantages

In my opinion, the first disadvantage in doing fieldwork in a familiar place is the feeling of over-confidence. I really experienced this feeling when I was in the field. Fortunately, I came to realize that I have to focus on my topic and act as if I knew nothing. When the over-confident feeling appeared, my curiosity became dull because there was a tendency to be satisfied with all my previous knowledge. I think that I knew enough, so I did not do more research about a specific topic. I assumed that this feeling was also experienced by other researchers who preferred to do research in other places rather than in their own places. This over-confident feeling is very dangerous and becomes a disadvantage to any researcher because it kills the curiosity to know more. A researcher should have a high curiosity level to lead him to a new and deeper understanding of the topic of his research.

Second, when we do fieldwork in our own place or in a place that we are familiar with, sometimes the informants will not give us adequate answers because they presume we already know the answers. Probably they think it is funny if we ask a simple question that most people already know the answer to. It is quite different if the interviewer is a newcomer who knows nothing about the local people that he is interviewing. The informants will understand a very simple question being asked by a new researcher but not by one whom they presumed knows a lot.

For example, some of my informants laughed when I asked them who are stronger, men or women? For them, this question is no longer relevant because it is pretty obvious that men are stronger than women. They presumed that I knew that men are much stronger than women by considering the fact that Asmat men bring ironwood from one place to another, which cannot be done by women. Nevertheless, when other informants probed deeper into the question such as Daniel Ayas and Seravia Tojamter. Tojamter's answer was different in responding the question: Who are stronger, men or women? She did not only say, a man is stronger than a woman, but she provided a new alternative answer. Daniel Ayas and Tojamter expressed the same answer to the above question: a man is stronger in his part of the labor, as well as a woman in her part. They said this because in Asmat, there is a clear-cut division of labor between men and women. Men are stronger than women in performing their responsibilities such as making *ci*, building a house, and going to war. Women are stronger as well when providing food for the family and in taking care of children. This new alternative answer opened my mind to something that I had not thought of. It says to me that do not make an absolute interpretation upon a certain thing because it might not totally true. Therefore, this is one of the disadvantages when we assume we already know the point. I think, combining this way of thinking with over-confident feeling will make the fieldwork fail.

The third is the ethical issue. Although I have mentioned the feeling of overconfidence, I sometimes felt a dilemma while in the field. For instance, I wanted to investigate something more and probe deeper, but I knew my informant would keep the answer to himself. There was a strong desire in me to scrutinize the issue by asking more questions. However, I did not want to open the issue that my informant is keeping away from me. I did not want my informant to have a guilty feeling because of answering my probing questions. In other words, I did not want to write or publish something that my informants secretly shared. Perhaps, it is easy for a newcomer to ask the informants any question because he does not know that some questions might put the informant in danger.

9.2 Conclusion

The *ci* is very essential in Asmat life. It is an integral part of their life. However, through this study, I am not implying that the Asmat return to their old way of life when there were no other choices, except the *ci* to transport people and goods from one place to another. My purpose is to show and to emphasize that the Asmat have a lot of valuable things that need to be considered as local treasures. The *ci* is my focal point to show how remarkable Asmat culture is particularly in relation to gender. Indeed, the *ci* is a significant key to understanding gender among the Asmat. The *ci* assists people to observe directly the division of labor between men and women. It shows the distinctions between men and women, both practically and symbolically. For example, a man stands upright at *ci cimen*, while a woman sits down at *ci ep*. Furthermore, changes in the *ci* bring about changes in society, including the concept of gender. Through this study, I was able to prove or to answer the general objective of this study that the *ci* and gender among the Asmat of Papua are really inter-related. The *ci* is a significant clue to understanding gender among the Asmat. Moreover, this study shows that gender is not only limited to people and their behavior, but also to material culture. Therefore, material culture is also gendered.

This study highlights the local wisdom of the Asmat through the *ci*. Hopefully, some people will appreciate this work and take practical steps to keep the material culture and the local wisdom alive. Reflecting on the *ci* life and the advent of modernization shows that the traditional way of life as well as the local wisdom of the Asmat are in danger.

Indeed, I do realize that I am not able to convince the local people that to own a *ci* is very fundamental for the Asmat, for I do not own a *ci* myself. Even the officials and the educated Asmat are not able to force their fellow Asmat to use and preserve the *ci* as a traditional heritage because instead of using and owning a *ci*, they possess a speedboat or other modern means of transportation. The Asmat do not like to be taught by anyone else without a real example. They need a proof or evidence of a teaching before they practice it. This means a theoretical lesson must be followed by practical actions, otherwise, people go home with nothing, even after a series of seminars. For example, the Asmat believe that rice planting is very good to practice after some high school teachers made a successful

Figure 68. The *ci* is nipped between the machinery boats.

rice field around the school area in Atsj. Prior to the high school teachers' work, some Asmat had attended a lot of training in agriculture held by the Department of Agriculture of Asmat, but nobody practiced it because they had no proof or evidence that they could see before their very eyes. The tutors themselves had no rice field, so the people did not believe in them. This mentality is one of the challenges in implementing such programs in Asmat, either from the local government or from private agencies.

Reflecting on the officials and educated Asmat who possess a lot of modern facilities and tools such as speedboats, many young Asmat dream to obtain the same thing. I think, dreams like these accelerate the extinction of the material culture such as the *ci*. For the Asmat, modern tools are interesting and promising, while the traditional way of life is less interesting and out of date, although it bears a lot of traditional values.

Related to this is the concept of gender among the Asmat which is now undergoing changes. The younger generation realizes that the decision makers are not always the men and the elderly in society because in some cases, the youngsters and the women are more powerful.

Until today, the *ci* still exists in Asmat. It is not yet totally lost. However, as can be seen in fig.68, the *ci* is nipped between the modern and motor boats. I could say then that the existence of the *ci* is critical and tends to be replaced by motor boats. This is caused by both internal and external factors. The internal factor comes from the weaknesses of the tribal leaders. They are not able to maintain their traditional power through cultural activities such as rituals and feasts. The tribal leaders themselves enjoy the modern style. I found that the local people hesitate to preserve their own traditions and values because they perceive it as old, boring, tiring, and a waste of time. The external change factor is the influx of people from everywhere who go to Asmat carrying with them their own cultures and backgrounds. The advent of modern water transportation such as speedboats, longboats, and ships also affect the dwindling existence of the *ci*. Moreover, local government programs are not yet helpful enough to maintain local production. In short, the *ci*'s being nipped between the modern and motor boats symbolizes the life of the Asmat which is being nipped by modernity and new ways of life.

Furthermore, I will point out some ideas that accentuate the necessity of the *ci* in the Asmat way of living. If the Asmat family or clan does not own a *ci*, then the following statements would come true:

- The more they do not own a *ci*, the more they become dependent.

- *Ci opak, jis opak*" – (no *ci*, no firewood). This means, even the very simple thing for cooking activities such as firewood cannot be provided without a *ci*. If they do not have firewood, so they cannot cook something to eat. That is why there is another saying, "*Ci opak, jouse opak*" – (no *ci*, no hearth). If there is no *ci*, then there would be no hearth. As a result, people will have no food, and they will die.

- "*Ci opak, cemen opak*" – (no *ci*, no penis). The *ci* is symbol of power because it can cross deep and wide rivers and enter jungles as well. If a man owns no *ci*, he is considered impotent. He has no ability to cross the river and infiltrate a jungle just like an impotent man who has no power to penetrate a woman's vagina. As a result, a man's dignity is low because making a *ci* is man's responsibility. He can also be called *bitni* (know nothing) if a man cannot provide a *ci* for his family. In other words, a man or a family will be powerless if they do not own a *ci*.

- *Dusun* will not be maintained and threatened. If a family does not own a *ci*, their *dusun* is in danger because they have no power to maintain and control it. If this is the case, other people will probably have access to the *dusun* and get everything in it such as sago and wood. This can trigger conflicts in the society if the owner of the *dusun* comes to realize that his *dusun* is being exploited by strangers.

- Nicolaus Ndepi said that the dignity of the Asmat is not in static carving, but in the *ci* (*fieldnote*, 11). Therefore, if the Asmat themselves abandon the *ci*, most probably they will be uprooted from their own culture and will be strangers in their ancestral domain.

- The social life of a family and neighborhood can be broken. A wife may leave her husband because he cannot provide a *ci* for his family. The *ci* is the main vehicle for a wife to fulfill the needs of her family. There is a possibility for a wife to look for someone else who can provide her a *ci*.

- Physically, if there is no *ci*, there will be many things that will remain apart from each other.

- Socially, the relationship among families and relatives will not be as strong as before unlike when the *ci* is their medium for gathering their needs from the forest and in helping one another.

- Spiritually, their relationship with the ancestral spirits will be disconnected or will no longer be the focus of their attention because many rituals will not be celebrated anymore.

- Crimes will increase because many people will have nothing to sustain their lives. Stealing will be an alternative way to stay alive. Moreover, some people may try to prove that they are still *Asmat nak* (the real people) in the midst of modernization and in the absence of warfare, crimes such as fighting, rape, robbery or thefts will become prevalent.

The *ci* is nipped between modernization and motor boats that endanger it and will cause its extinction. Together with this, the Asmat will not only lose their myths and rituals, but also their folk stories, folk songs, and other oral traditions. Many cultural elements are related to the *ci*, either directly or indirectly. If the *ci* as an example material culture is replaced by modern transportation, many other cultural elements will also be lost. Actually, the Asmat keep their myths, stories, art, and rituals in their lives. But how can they keep such traditions if there are no media to use as channels? The usual way to pass on traditions from one generation to the next is through rituals or feasts. Thus, the alternative ways used by the Asmat nowadays affect many other elements in society such as their myths, rituals, oral traditions, and the concept of gender. In addition, the elderly will not have the opportunity to teach the new generation about the richness of their culture if there are no more rituals and other traditional celebrations. At the same time, the intimacy and respect for the ancestral spirits will fade away. For example, when they buy a new speedboat, they no longer name it after an ancestor; there is no accompanying ritual and no social debt that should be paid.

Lastly, based on my analysis of the *ci*, I found that the concept of gender among the Asmat is basically grounded on three elements: warfare, sexuality, and social status. First, warfare situates women as the ones who need to be protected while men are treated as warriors. That is why the position of men must be at the *ci cimen* (in front) of the *ci* and stand upright in order to be able to anticipate any sudden attack, and at the same time protect the women behind him. Moreover, most of the carvings in the *ci cimen* symbolize warfare and headhunting such as the hornbill beak. Second, as with sexuality, the Asmat put women as recipients. In this context, they have an excellent saying, "*Ci opak, cemen opak*"- (no *ci*, no penis), and there is no equivalent saying "*Ci opak, cen opak*" – (no *ci*, no vagina). The *ci* also implies that the hearth becomes hot because of cooking, just like a man who stimulates a woman's sexual desires. The *ci* is a symbol of power, especially a man's power, including power to penetrate a woman's body. Third, pertaining to social status, Asmat men consider themselves higher and stronger than women. This notion can be seen through prohibition that women cannot participate directly in the process of making a *ci*. Women are not allowed to enter or to use such a *ci*. The paddles of men and women are also different which only shows that men are stronger and better than women. Most of all, these three elements – - warfare, sexuality, and social status are interrelated. Indeed, they highlight patriarchy in Asmat society.

The Asmat area is a pregnant swamp of natural resources because ritually and supernaturally, there is a spiritual and perpetual intercourse between the ancestral spirit and the land as symbolized by the implantation of *bis* pole to the ground in a *dusun*. Moreover, the *ci* as a male symbol bears power to cross rivers and enter the jungles, just like a *cemen* (penis) that penetrates a vagina for procreation. This is the very reason why the *ci* brings hope, life, and happiness to the Asmat community, just like a penis bringing about fertility and new life to a family. A pregnant swamp of natural resources will continue if the Asmat preserve their *ci*.

9.3 For future research

This study is a valuable contribution to anthropological studies, especially on studies about the *ci*, gender, and social change among the Asmat of Papua. Previous studies about the Asmat are mostly about Asmat art (Konrad 1978, 1996; Schneebaum 1985, 1988, 1989) and their notorious behavior regarding warfare, headhunting, and cannibalism (Zegwaard 1953, 1959; Sowada 1996). This study bridges the gap in the anthropological theory about the Asmat people and their *ci*. Nevertheless, I do realize that this study is not free from weaknesses. Therefore, I would like to recommend some studies that can be used for future research in the Asmat area.

First, the Asmat elders, especially the tribal leaders, have the authority to persuade, recommend, organize, and to decide the best things for their community. Moreover, the Asmat have LMAA (*Lembaga Masyarakat Adat Asmat*) or Tribal Council of Asmat. This can be used as a channel of aspirations for the local people. Future researchers can focus on leadership among the Asmat in order to investigate how tribal leaders respond to modernization and the preservation of their culture. For instance, the future researcher can question the tribal leader's concept of the *ci* and modern transportation. Do they want to preserve the *ci* as a traditional and local way of life that bears a lot of values? Do they have strategies to preserve or at least to formulate regulations in entering and using the *dusuns* and their contents. In my opinion, the role of tribal leaders among the Asmat is still very important. This means strong leaders will benefit the Asmat community; otherwise it will become powerless and dependent on other communities.

Second, social change among the Asmat has come through acculturation in many ways. Aside from church missions, the Indonesian government has brought about changes in Asmat. The local government of Asmat has many programs to 'build' Asmat in the perspective of modernization. For example, the government supports many fishermen groups by giving them longboats (motor boats) without first instilling into their minds the positive and negative effects of that support. For future research, it will be interesting to see how modernization benefits the Asmat and how devastates it. Does the local government help the Asmat to develop themselves in various aspects of life? Moreover, how does the local Asmat parliament in consultation with tribal leaders, create such laws to control, regulate, and maintain the use of forest products like ironwood and the *ci* trees, including the prices for such products.

Third, perhaps in the future, there will be many non-Asmat researchers who will do studies about Asmat and its people. That would be very good and praiseworthy. However, it will be much more adequate and comprehensive if the native and educated Asmat do the research themselves about the richness of their own land and their culture. Local researchers are in a better position to deeply examine their local beliefs, rituals, and traditions that are not known by non-Asmat. I realized that I cannot or should not investigate some topics about Asmat life that are reserved for the local people only because I am not a native Asmat. I know that the non-Asmat researcher will not have the opportunity to listen to every story or to be involved in such rituals. Not every story can be spoken or be told to anybody because some stories are considered sacred and secret. Local researchers will have better opportunities and access than the non-Asmat to collect as much data that they need from the elders and the people because they are part of the community. Moreover, knowing the local language is one advantage of the local researcher. Indeed, I will motivate local researchers to tell and write about their people and culture.

Fourth, I recommend that this topic about the *ci* be studied further. For example, is not owning or non-ownership of a *ci* an expression of resistance to the traditional values? This question will be valuable in assessing the adaptability of the Asmat to modernization.

It will be a useless attempt to motivate the Asmat to preserve their *ci* if they themselves refuse to do it because they desire a modern way of life that probably would make them a happier community.

Fifth, still related to gender power relations, women in Asmat are getting better and better in terms of education, job, and organization. Many Asmat women are now aware of their dignity and they should not be colonized by men. It is a good research topic to study further how Asmat women change their own lives as well as their community. On the other hand, it is also interesting how Asmat men look at women's achievements in society? Would they perceive this as an advantage for the community or a kind of resistance?

Lastly, based on my research in Asmat, I found that methodologically, it was more effective to use Key Informant Interviews (KII) than Focus Group Discussions (FGD) in doing ethnography. Theoretically, FGD is very useful to validate data among informants. Unfortunately, this did not happen in Asmat. The Asmat would not correct or argue with each other in public. Another reason why FGD is not recommended in doing fieldwork in Asmat is that one of the informants can become a speaker on behalf of all. Moreover, if there is a special topic to talk about like a story, they will not tell it freely before other informants because there are many versions of a story in Asmat, such that other people will doubt the veracity of the story. Therefore, I recommend to future ethnographers to use KII so that they can focus on their topic and save their time. Aside from KII, Participant Observation is also highly recommended.

Glossary of terms

A=Asmat; I=Indonesian; L=Latin
"C" pronounced as "ch" as in chew.

Ai ci (A)	New canoe.
Aipmu (A)	Moiety.
Akat Cepes (A)	Asmat Women Organization. Literally means beautiful girl.
Amer (A)	Snake.
Amerak (A)	Man's head bird figure.
Amon (A)	To call.
Asesinokos (A)	Centipede.
Asmat (A)	lit. real men. It refers to either people or area.
Asmat Nak (A)	The real people.
Asmat-ow (A)	The people of the land or people of the tree.
Bevak (A)	Bivouac, hut.
Biawak (I)	Lizard.
Bipane (A)	Double-curved shell nose ornament.
Biskus (A)	Humans's head figure.
Bitni (A)	Someone who do not know how to work.
Bupati (I)	Regent.
Cem (A)	House.
Cenepir (A)	Pelican head.
Cepes (A)	Women.
Cepes di em (A)	Women's feast in a new *jeu*.
Ces (A)	War.
Ces Ci (A)	War canoe.
Ces Omou (A)	Great people (plural).
Cescu (A)	Talented, great.
Cesmacepes (A)	Great woman.
Cesmaipits (A)	Big man, great warrior (single).
Ci [tʃiː] (A)	*Perahu* (I) – the Asmat canoe. It is an Asmat word to call their dugout canoe. It is made of a long single wood. I use the word "*ci*" to indicate the Asmat canoe, and not to any canoe in the world.

Ci ak (A)	Canoe curve (keel) – outer.
Ci aman (A)	Canoe curve (keel)- interior.
Ci cimen (A)	Prowhead.
Ci ep (A)	Canoe tail.
Ci nak (A)	kayu kuning (I); *Nonau Cleaspp* (L) – canoe tree.
Ci Nak (A)	kayu perahu (I) – canoe tree.
Ci pim (A)	Edge that resembles a lip.
Ci Pokmbu/mbu (A)	Special canoe feast.
Ci tereyef /cipine (A)	Canoe ears hole.
Ci wowuts (A)	Keel.
Ci yan (A)	Canoe ears.
Cimbai (A)	Legs of canoe.
Cimbak (A)	Back of canoe.
Cimen-afir (A)	First part of the canoe curve.
Cinamakat (A)	Keel, middle part of a canoe.
Cindem (A)	Keel, middle part of a canoe.
Cisi-ipits (A)	Talented canoe maker.
Citere (A)	Canoe decoration made of rattan leaves.
Cowut	Woman.
Depi (A)	White.
Dusun (I); bokot (A)	Ancestral domain. Forest that is occupied by clans or families. Compare to *wasan* (A) which is meant jungle. *Wasan* is occupied by nobody. Everybody is free to enter the *wasan*, but not the *bokot*. *Dusun* is an Indonesia word, which is meant village far from urban area, however, in the Asmat context, it is understood by both Asmat and non-Asmat as ancestral domain. That is why I prefer to use the word "*dusun*" than "*bokot*."
Eco (A)	Human figure in a *wuramon*.
Em (A); tifa (I)	Drum.
Emak cem (A)	Bone house. An initiation ritual in Joerat area.
Ep afir (A)	Last part of the canoe curve.
Esakam (A)	Red.
Eu djim (A)	Crocodile ribs.
Facep (A)	Cuscus tail ending.
Fofoyir (A)	Hornbill head.
Gaharu (I)	*Aquilaria malaccensis* – kind of sandal wood; sweet-smelling wood.
Gender	The difference between males and females which is socially constructed, changeable over time, and that have wide variations within and between cultures (cf. Barfield 1997:217).
Habis (I)	Finish. In this context, it means died or extinct.
Hutan (I)	Forest, jungle.
Ipar (I)	Brother-in-law.
Irimbi/ufirmbi (A)	Black king cockatoo beak.
Ja Asamanam Apcamar (A)	*Berjalan dalam keseimbangan* (I) – walk in a perfect balance.
Jembatan (I)	lit. bridge; road which is made of ironwood in Asmat.
Jeu/je/jew/yew (A)	Men's longhouse; localized patri-oriented descent group.
Jewer (A)	*Gempol* (I); *Nauclea spp.*(L) – canoe tree.
Jicap ci/ jia ci (A)	Feast or ritual canoe. It is similar to *ces ci*.

Jinicowut (A)	Woman in sitting position of a *wuramon*.
Jipits (A)	Male.
Jiran (A)	*Ketapang* (I); *Terminalia Canicu* (L) – canoe tree.
Jo ti (A)	Clan's canoe.
Jouse (A)	Hearth/fireplace.
Juwur (A)	*Mersawa* (I); *Anispotera spp.*(L) – canoe tree.
Kabupaten (I)	Regency; administrative area in Indonesia.
Karu (A)	Taboo.
Kepala perang (I)	Big man; war-lord (see *Cesmaipits*).
Kepala suku (I)	Tribal chief.
Key	A thing that makes you able to understand or achieve something (Sally Wehmeier 2005:844).
Machinery Boat	Every boat with machine such as speedboat and longboat.
Mbianam (A)	Stone axe.
Mbu (A)	Turtle.
Meti (A)	Recede, low tide.
Ndat (A)	Satan.
Ndet (A)	Soul.
Okom (A)	"Z" -like figure of *wuramon*.
Pakanam ci / Pomer ci / Pokmber ti (A)	Family canoe for daily used.
Pakman ci (A)	= *Jicap ci*: feast or ritual canoe.
Papish (A)	Ritual-ceremonial wife-swapping in situations of socio-political or cosmological danger.
Peri (A)	Neck of a canoe.
Pes (A)	Ironwood.
Pinwo (A)	Carving around *cindem*.
Po/pu (A)	*Dayung* (I) – paddle, oar
Pokmbu/pokmbi(A)	Feast.
Safan (A)	World of spirits; heaven.
Soaramak (A)	*Katakao* (I) – canoe tree.
Tarep (A)	Flying-fox foot.
Tesetor (A)	Big man's wife.
Tinaw (A)	*Pala merah* (I) – canoe tree.
Tow (A)	*Pala putih* (I); *Myristica argentea warb.* (L) – canoe tree.
Ulat sagu (I)	Sago grubs.
Wakanmbe (A)	Special motive behind *ufirmbi*.
Was/focep (A)	Cuscus tail.
Wayir (A)	Central of a *jeu*; the main hearth in a *jeu*
Wenet (A)	Praying mantis.
Woro (A)	Frog.
Wow-ipits (A)	Sculptor, carver.
Wur (A)	Thunder.
Wuramon (A)	Spirit canoe.

Bibliography

Ap, Arnold C. and Johsz Mansoben. 1974. "Building of an Asmat Perahu". In *Asmat Papers Part II: Research Report No 6,* edited by Malcolm T. Walker, Ph.D. Jayapura: University of Cenderawasih.

Appadurai, Arjun (ed.). 1986. *The Social Life of Things: Commodities in Cultural Perspective.* Cambridge: Cambridge University Press.

Armstrong, Karen. 1993. *A History of God.* New York: Ballantine Books.

Baal, J. Van, K. W. Galis and R. M. Koentjaraningrat. 1984. *West Irian: A Bibliography.* Cinnaminson-USA: Foris Bublications.

Baal. Dr. J. van. 1966. *Dema: Description and Analysis of Marind-Anim Culture* (South New Guinea). Amsterdam: The Ministry of the Interior and the Royal Tropical Institute.

Bappeda dan Badan Pusat Statistik Kabupaten Asmat. 2011. *Asmat in Figures.* Agats: BPS Kabupaten Asmat.

Barfield, Thomas (ed.). 1997. *The Dictionary of Anthropology.* USA: Blackwell Publishers Inc.

Bariarcianur, Frino and Ahmat Yunus. 2011. *Papua: An Expedition to Remember.* Jakarta: PT. Gramedia.

Barnard, Alan. 2000. *History and Theory in Anthropology.* United Kingdom: Cambridge University Press.

Barthes, Roland. 1972. *Mythologies.* New York: Hill and Wang.

Biakai, Yufensius Alfonsius. *Pengertian Inisiasi Suku Asmat sebagai bahan pertimbangan Integrasi ke dalam Inisiasi Kristen.* Jayapura, November 1981.

Boas, Franz. 1955. *Primitive Art.* New York: Dover Publications, Inc.

Bowie, Fiona. 2006. *The Anthropology of Religion: An Introduction.* 2nd ed. UK: Blackwell Publishing.

Child, Alice B. and Irvin L. Child. 1993. *Religion and Magic in the Life of Traditional Peoples.* New Jersey: Prentice Hall, Englewood Cliffs.

Cochrane, Glynn. 1970. *Big Men and Cargo Cults.* London: Oxford University Press.

Douglas, Mary. 1966. *Purity and Danger: An Analysis of Concepts of Pollution and Taboo.* New York: Frederick A. Praeger, Publishers.

Eilberg-Schwartz, Howard. "The Father, the Phallus, and the Seminal Word: Dilemmas of Patrilineality in Ancient Judaism." In *Gender, Kinship, Power: A Comparative and Interdisciplinary History,* edited by Mary Jo Maynes, Ann Waltner, Birgitte Soland, and Ulrike Strasser. New York: Routledge. 1996:27-41.

Eller, Jack David. 2009. *Cultural Anthropology: Global Forces, Local Lives*. New York: Routledge.

Elliot, Faith Robertson. 1996. *Gender, Family and Society*. London: MacMillan Press LTD.

Eriksen, Thomas Hylland. 1995. *Small Places, Large Issues: An Introduction to Social and Cultural Anthropology*. Second Edition. London: Pluto Press.

Eva, Gamarnikow (ed.). 1985. *Gender, Class and Work*. England: Gower Publishing Company Limited.

Evan-Pritchard, E. E. 1968. *The Nuer: A Description of the Modes of Livelihood and Political Institutions of A Nilotic People*. London: Oxford University Press.

Firth, Raymond. 1963. *Elements of Social Organization*. Boston: Beacon Press.

Firth, Raymond. 1967. *Tikopia Ritual and Belief*. United States: Beacon Press.

Fleischhacker, Marcus B. OSC. 1991. *Making the Invisible Visible: Asmat Art and Spirituality*. Minneapolis: The Crosier Fathers and Brothers Province, Inc.

Fleischhacker, John and Tobias Scheebaum. 1978. "The Wuramon Initiation Feast of Jamasj." In *An Asmat Sketch Book*. No.6: 94-99.

Foucault, Michael. 1980. *Power/Knowledge*. Brighton, UK: Harvester.

Frazer, Sir James George, F.R.S., F.B.A. 1951. *The Golden Bough: A Study in Magic and Religion*. New York: The MacMillan Company.

Freshman, Phil (ed.). 2009. *Time and Tide: The Changing Art of Asmat of New Guinea*. Minneapolis: Minneapolis Institute of Arts.

Geertz, Clifford. 1973. *The Interpretation of Cultures*. New York: Basic Books.

Geetha, V. 2002. *Gender*. Calcuta: STREE.

Gennep, Arnold van. 1960. *The Rites of Passage*. Chicago: The University of Chicago Press.

Gerbrands, Adrian A. (ed.). *The Asmat of New Guinea: The Journal of Michael Clark Rockefeller*. New York: The Museum of Primitive Art.

Giay, Benny & Yafet Kambai. 2003. *Yosepha Alomang: Pergulatan Seorang Perempuan Papua Melawan Penindasan*. Jayapura: ELSHAM.

Godelier, Maurice. 1992. *The making of Great Man: Male Domination and Power among the New Guinea Baruya*. Cambridge: Cambridge University Press.

Gregor, Thomas. 1985. *Anxious Pleasures: The Sexual Lives of an Amazonian People*. Chicago and London: The University of Chicago Press.

Hays, Terence E. "No Tobacco, No Hallelujah": Missions and the Early History of Tobacco in Eastern Papua. In *Pacific Studies*, Vol. 14, No. 4 – December 1991:91-112

Heady, Patrick. "Barter." 2005. In *A Handbook of Economic Anthropology*, edited by James G. Carrier. Northampton, MA, USA: Edward Elgar Publishing, Inc.

Herskovits, Melvile F. 1960. *Economic Anthropology: A Study in Comparative Economics*. New York: Alfred A. Knopf.

Hontheim, Astrid de. 2010. "Healing Despite Christianity; Struggles Between Missionary and Traditional Conceptions of Medicine." In *Religion Dynamics in The Pacific*, Cahiers du Credo, Francoise Douaire-Marsaudon (dir.), Marceille: Pacific Credo Publications.129-142.

Hoogerbrugge, Jac. 2011. *Asmat: Arts, Crafts and People*. Leiden, C. Zwartenkot Art Books.

Hoskins, Janet. 1998. *Biographical Objects: How Things Tell the Stories of People's Lives*. New York and London: Routledge.

Isaac, Barry L. 2005. "Karl Polanyi". In *A Handbook of Economic Anthropology*, edited by James G. Carrier. Northampton, MA, USA: Edward Elgar Publishing, Inc.

Karlberg, Michael. "The Power of Discourse and the Discourse of Power: Pursuing Peace through Discourse Intervention. In *International Journal of Peace Studies,* Volume 10, Number 1, Spring/Summer 2005.

Keesing, Roger M. 1982. "Introduction". In *Rituals of Manhood: Male Initiation in Papua New Guinea,* edited by Gilbert H. Herdt. Berkeley, Los Angeles: University of California Press.

Konrad, Gunter and Ursula Konrad (eds.). 1996. *Asmat: Myth and Ritual the Inspiration of Art.* Venezia: Erizzo Editrice.

Konrad, Gunter, Ursula Konrad, and Tobias Schneebaum. 1981. *Asmat: Life with the Ancestors.* Germany: Glashutten/Ts.

Konrad, Gunter. 1978. "On the Phallic Symbol and Display in The Asmat". In *An Asmat Sketch Book.* No.6:86-93.

Konrad, Ursula, Alphonse Sowada, and Gunter Konrad (eds). 2002. *Asmat: Mencerap Kehidupan dalam Seni.* Monchengladbach-Jerman: B. Kuhlen Verlag.

Kunst. *Asmat.* December 1976-May 1977 Rijksmuseum voor Volkenkunde, Afd. Breda.

Kuruwaip, Abraham. "The Asmat Bis Pole: Its Background and Meaning." In *Irian: Bulletin of Irian Jaya Development.* Jayapura: University of Cenderawasih. June, 1974 Vol.III, No.2:32-71.

Lindsey, Linda L. 1990. *Gender Roles: A Sociological Perspective.* New Jersey: Prentice Hall.

Lips, Hilary M. 2005. *Sex and Gender: An Introduction.* 5th edition. New York: McGraw-Hill.

Louw, Bro. Joseph de (translator.). "De Missie Geschiedenis Asmat Missie." In *An Asmat Sketch Book.* Tome II, 1970-1978:119-179, edited by Fr. Frank Trenkenshuh, O.S.C.

Lundskow, George. 2008. *The Sociology of Religion: A Substantive and Transdisciplinary Approach.* Los Angeles: Pine Forge Press.

Lutkehaus, Nancy C. and Paul B. Roscoe (eds.). 1995. *Gender Rituals: Female Initiation in Melanesia.* New York and London: Routledge.

Malinowski, Bronislaw. 1922. *Argonauts of the Western Pacific.* London. George Routledge & Sons, LTD.

Malinowski, Bronislaw. 1945. *The Dynamic of Culture Change: An Inquiry into Race Relations in Africa.* New Haven and London: Yale University Press.

Malinowski, Bronislaw. 1954. *Magic, Science and Religion.* New York: Doubleday Anchor Books.

Mangahas, Maria F. "Fishing and Performing Fair Shares." *AGHAMTAO.* Volume 10, 2001.

Marcus, George E. and Fisher, Michael M.J. 1986. *Anthropology as Cultural Critique: An Experimental Moment in the Human Sciences.* Chicago and London: The University of Chicago Press.

Mauss, Marcel. 1967. *The Gift: Forms and Functions of Exchange in Archaic Societies.* New York: W.W. Norton & Company.

Mbait, Jeremias and Br. Martin Mc Quire, O.S.C. "Dayung Asmat" (An Asmat Oar). In *IRIAN: Bulletin of West Irian Development.* Vol. 1, No. 2. Jayapura: University of Cenderawasih: 78-82.

McGee, R. Jon and Richard L. Warms. 2000. *Anthropological Theory: An Introduction – Second Edition.* California: Mayfield Publishing Company.

Milton, Kay. 2002. *Loving Nature: Towards an Ecology of Emotion.* London and New York: Routldge.

Mraz, Fr. Louis OSC. 1976. "Mbai of Atsj". In *An Asmat Sketch Book*. No.6:84-85.

Muller, Kal. 1990. *Irian Jaya: West New Guinea*. Singapore: Periplus Editions, Inc.

Muller, Kal. 2009. *Highlands of Papua*. Indonesia: DW Books.

Muller, Kal. 2011. *Pesisir Selatan Papua*. Indonesia: DW Books.

Muller, Karl and Yunus Omabak. 2008. *Amungme: Traditional and Change in the Highlands of Papua*. Jakarta: PT. Freeport Indonesia.

Neles Tebay. 2009. *Dialog Jakarta-Papua: Sebuah Perspektif Papua*. Jayapura: Office for Justice and Peace – Diocese of Jayapura.

Newman, Philip L. 1965. *Knowing the Gururumba*. New York: Holt, Rinehart and Winston.

Oliver-Smith, Anthony and Susanna M. Hoffman (eds.). 1999. *The Angry Earth*. New York: Routledge.

Ortner, Sherry B. 1996. *Making Gender: The Politics and Erotics of Culture*. Boston: Beacon Press.

Oxford Advanced Learner's Dictionary. 7th edition. Oxford, New York: Oxford University Press, 2005.

Pandian, Jacob. 1991. *Culture, Religion, and the Sacred*. New Jersey: Prentice-Hall, Inc.

Pickell, David. 2002. *Between the Tides: A Fascinating Journey Among the Kamoro of New Guinea*. Singapore: Periplus.

Pitka, Frank. "25 Years of Crosiers in Asmat." In *Asmat Drums: Special Issue*. 1958 – December 15 – 1983.

Portmann, Adolf, Ernst Benz, Christopher Rowe, et al. 1977. *Color Symbol*. Dallas: Spring Publications, Inc.

Pospisil, Leopold. 1963. *The Kapauku Papuans of West New Guinea*. New York: Holt, Rinehart and Winston.

Pouwer, Jan. 2010. *Gender, Ritual and Social Formation in West Papua*. Leiden: KITLV Press.

PT Freeport Indonesia. 2008. *Core Values*. Jakarta: PT. Freeport Indonesia.

Rappaport, Roy A. 1968. *Pigs for the Ancestors: Ritual in the Ecology of a New Guinea People*. New Haven and London: Yale University Press.

Rappaport, Roy A. 1979. *Ecology, Meaning, and Religion*. California: North Atlantic Books.

Rutherford, Danilyn. "The Bible Meets the Idol: Writing and Conversion in Biak, Irian Jaya, Indonesia. In Cannell, Fenella (ed.). 2006. *The Anthropology of Christianity*. London: Duke University Press.

Said, Edward W. 1979. *Orientalism*. New York: Random House, Inc.

Saulnier, Tony. 1961. *Headhunters of Papua*. New York: Crown Publishers Inc.

Schieffelin, Edward L. 1976. *The Sorrow of the Lonely and the Burning of the Dancers*. New York: St. Martin's Press.

Schneebaum, Tobias. 1985. *Asmat Images: From the Collection of the Asmat Museum of Culture and Progress*. Minnesota: Asmat Museum of Culture and Progress.

Schneebaum, Tobias. 1988. *Where the Spirits Dwell: An Odyssey in the New Guinea Jungle*. New York: Grove Press.

Schneebaum, Tobias. 1989. "Change in Asmat Art." In *People of the River – People of the Three*: *Change and Continuity in Sepik and Asmat Art*, Minnesota Museum of Art in Cooperation (Organizer) with Crosier Asmat Museum. Minnesota: Saint Paul.

Schneebaum, Tobias. "Spirits and Spirituality." In National Arts Club. *Asmat Benefit Auction*. New York. May 11, 1990.

Sorensen, Marie Louise Stig. 2000. *Gender Archaeology*. Cambridge: Polity Press.
Sowada, Alphonse A. 1996. "Fundamental Concepts of Asmat Religion and Philosophy." In *Asmat: Myth and Ritual the Inspiration of Art,* edited by Gunter Konrad and Ursula Konrad. Venezia: Erizzo Editrice.
Strathern, Andrew. 1993. "Dress, Decoration, and Art in New Guinea." In *Man as Art New Guinea,* edited by Malcolm Kirk (photographer). San Francisco: Chronicle Books.
Strathern, Marilyn. 1988. *The Gender of the Gift*. Berkeley, Los Angeles: University of California Press.
Strauss, Claude Levi. 1966. *The Savage Mind*. New York: Oxford University Press.
Suter, Dr. Keith. 1982. *East Timor and West Irian*. London: Minority Rights Group Ltd.
Tapol Bulletin. 1983. *West Papua: The Obliteration of a People*. London: Tapol.
Tebay, Neles. 2009. *Dialog Jakarta – Papua: Sebuah Perspektif Papua*. Jayapura: SKP Jayapura.
The Asmat Progress and Development Foundation. *The Dynamic of Irian*.
The Roman Missal. 1985. *The Sacramentary*. New York: Catholic Book Publishing Corp.
Todd, Alexandra Dundas and Sue Fisher (eds.). 1988. *Gender and Discourse: The Power of Talk*. New Jersey: Ablex Publishing Corporation.
Trenkenshuh, Fr. Frank O.S.C. 1970. *Profile: A People, A Mission, A Bishop*. Asmat: The Diocese of Agats.
Tsing, Anna Lowenhaupt. 1993. *In the Realm of the Diamond Queen: Marginality in An Out-of-the-Way Place*. New Jersey: Princeton University Press.
Turner, Victor. 1958. *The Origins of Culture*. New York: Harper & Row, Publishers.
Turner, Victor. 1967. *The Forest of Symbols: Aspects of Ndembu Ritual*. Ithaca and London: Cornell University Press.
Turner, Victor. 1969. *The Ritual Process*. Chicago: Aldine Publishing Company.
Tylor, Edward Burnett. 1974. *Primitive Culture: Researches into the Development of Mythology, Philosophy, Religion, Art, and Custom*. New York: Gordon Press.
Tylor, Paul M. *Irian Jaya: The Land and Its People*. in Konrad, Gunter and Ursula Konrad (eds.). 1996. *Asmat: Myth and Ritual the Inspiration of Art*. Venezia: Erizzo Editrice.
Walker, Malcolm T. "The Future of the Asmat." In *IRIAN: Bulletin of West Irian Development*. Feb.,1973 Vol. II, No. 1. Jayapura: University of Cenderawasih. 97-101.
Wartenberg, Thomas E. 1990. *The Forms of Power: From Domination to Transformation*. Philadelphia: Temple University Press.
Wassing, Rene. 1999. "History: Colony, Mission and Nation." In *Asmat Art: Woodcarvings of Southwest New Guinea*, edited by Dirk Smidt. Leiden: Periplus. 27-31.
Webster's Third New International Dictionary. Springfield, Massachusetts: Merriam-Webster, 1976.
White, Leslie A. 1959. *The Evolution of Culture: The Development of Civilization to the Fall of Rome*. New York: McGraw-Hill Book Company, Inc.
Whiteman, Darrell. "Melanesia: Its People and Cultures." In *Point*, Series No. 5, 1984 – An Introduction to Melanesian Cultures: 85-104.
Wilson, Monica. 1954. "Nyakyusa Ritual and Symbolism." *American Anthropologist*, vol.56, no.2:228-241.
Yassin, Ress. 1987. "The History of Irian Jaya." In *Irian Jaya: The Land of Challenges and Promises,* edited by Izaac Hindom. Jayapura: PT. Alpha Zenith.

Young, Michael W. and Julia Clark. 2001. *An Anthropologist in Papua.* Honolulu: University of Hawai'i Press.
Zack, Naomi, Laurie Shrage and Crispin Sartwell (eds). 2004. *Race. Class, Gender, and Sexuality: The Big Questions.* Oxford: Blackwell publishing Ltd.
Zegwaard, Gerard A. 1959. "Headhunting Practices of the Asmat of Netherlands New Guinea." In *American Anthropologist,* 61(6): 1020-1041.
Zegwaard, Gerard A. 1978. "Data on the Asmat People" in *An Asmat Sketch Book,* edited by Fr. Frank A. Trenkenshuh, O.S.C. Agats: Asmat Museum of Culture and Progress. 15-25.
Zubrinich, Kerry M. 1999. "Asmat Cosmology and the Practice of Canibalism." In *The Anthropology of Canibalism,* edited by Laurence Goldman. USA: Greenwood Publishing Group, Inc.

Unpublished Articles/Papers

Cole, Vince (Collector and translator). *Asmat Myths: From the Villages Sa and Er.* Asmat. 2012.
Cook, Carolyn D. *Influx Management Case Study of PT Freeport Indonesia in Papua, Indonesia.* June 2008.
Daeli, Onesius Otenieli. *Kayu Besi.* Agats. 2005.
Daeli, Onesius Otenieli. *The Asmat of Papua: From Traditional "Genuine" to Modern Ambiguity.* Quezon City. 2011. Paper delivered at 20th IFSSO General Conference, held on 18-20 of November 2011 at Lyceum of the Philippines University, Batangas City, Philippines.
Daeli, Onesius Otenieli. *Fieldnote: Summaries of Interviews and Direct Observations in Asmat Papua.* 2012.
Keuskupan Agats. "*Lokakarya Inkulturasi Liturgi.*" Agats, 31 Maret – 06 April 2008.
Keuskupan Agats. "*Notulensi Lokakarya Inkulturasi Keuskupan Agats – Asmat.*" Agats, 18-21 April 1995.
Keuskupan Agats. 2001. "Musyawarah Pastoral II Keuskupan Agats." Agats, 22-29 April 2001.
Keuskupan Agats. 2007. "Musyawarah Pastoral III Keuskupan Agats." Agats, 25-30 September 2007.
Ndepi, Nicolaus. 2012. *Asmat Bukan Patung Kayu, Melainkan Pengukir Terbaik bagi Kaimana, Mapi, dan Boven Digul.* Agats.
Petermeier, Virgil OSC. 2012. *Sejarah Singkat Reksa Pastoral Keuskupan Agats.*
Pirap, Salomon. In "*Notulensi Studi Budaya.*" Agats, 30 April 2012.

Websites

Elardo, Justin A. *Marx, Marxists, and Economic Anthropology.* Available online at: http://rrp.sagepub.com/content/39/3/416. Accessed on Oct. 11, 2010.
Hile, Jennifer. Curse of Gaharu. Available online at http://www.ecologyasia.com/news-archives/2003/nov-03/thestar_20031111_1.htm, Accessed on Oct. 13, 2010.
Kayu Gaharu, Sang Dewa Pohon dari Papua. Available online at http://www.kamusmalesbanget.com/forum/Kayu-Gaharu-Sang-Pohon-Dewa-dari-Papua. Accessed on Oct. 11, 2010.
McMonagle, Natalie Adron and Julie Risser. Deconstructing Eden: Asmat Identity Rediscovered. Available online at http://www.stthomas.edu/arthistory/asmat/files/Deconstructing_Eden_Brochure.pdf. Accessed on Sept.7, 2012.

About the author

Onesius Otenieli Daeli is an ordained Roman Catholic priest and a member of the Order of the Holy Cross (Ordo Sanctae Crucis), born in Nias, North Sumatera, Indonesia. He spent more than five years (2002 – 2008) among the Asmat people. He was participating in many aspects of the Asmat life, including rituals, traditional feasts, rural economy, and politics. He published a book of religion in Asmat in 2006 entitled Ketika Salib Diarak (Lifting up on the Cross) (Sangkris Press, Bandung-Indonesia). He wrote some articles, personal experiences, and short stories about Asmat and its culture. In January 2012 to May 2012 conducted a fieldwork among di Asmat for the sake of his study in Cultural Anthropology. He graduated his Ph.D in Anthropology in the University of the Philippines – Diliman, Quezon City, Metro Manila, Philippines (2013). He studied Philosophy and Theology in Parahyangan Catholic University, Bandung, Indonesia. He lives in Bandung with some major responsibilities such as Lecturer in Parahyangan Catholic University (Unpar), Bandung, Indonesia; Rector of Scholastics Program of The Order of the Holy Cross (OSC), Sang Kristus Province, Indonesia (2014-2018); and Chaplin of the Catholic University Students Church of the Diocese of Bandung, Indonesia

Endorsement

By Nick Stanley

Emeritus Professor, Faculty of Arts, Design and Media, Birmingham City University

Honorary Research Fellow, Department of Africa, Oceania and the Americas, British Museum, London.

This work is the result of the author's six years spent living in Asmat and another five months of intensive research in the field exploring the significance of the *ci* (the canoe) in Asmat life. There are detailed reports from knowledgeable informants about the construction, the decoration, the various uses of the *ci* and its symbolic and cultural significance. There are excellent illustrations taken by the author and others.

The choice of the *ci* as the focus of study is excellent because, as the author shows, the canoe is the key to all aspects of Asmat life. The *ci* represents a form of communication between the living and the dead. Being able to make a *ci* is also a sign of a man's maturity which publicly displays his coming-of-age. Daeli's central argument is that the *ci* can be considered one of the best sites for the analysis of gender relationships. Men protect all from the front of the canoe and stand to row, women sitting at the rear steer the boat - a symbol of the complementarity of the sexes. The *ci* also epitomises the complexity of social relationships not only between men and women but equally it is a major dimension of distinction between those who own and those who have to borrow canoes in order to obtain food from the rivers or jungle.

The book looks at a number of aspects of the canoe including the physical description (prow, body and tail) and types (regular transport and war or ceremonial canoes and soul ships); carving as the expression of personal experience of the carver and the owner and the depiction of specific spirit symbols (snake; hornbill head; flying fox feet; praying mantis). The work concludes with a commentary on recent changes involving speedboats and longboats which are supplanting the *ci* in daily life.

This book offers an excellent and detailed account. Through an understanding of the social role of the *ci*, readers will gain an genuine insight into the world of the Asmat people and their way of life.